THE HUMAN FACTOR
IN DEVELOPING
AFRICA

THE HUMAN FACTOR
IN DEVELOPING
AFRICA

Senyo B-S. K. Adjibolosoo

PRAEGER

Westport, Connecticut
London

Library of Congress Cataloging-in-Publication Data

Adjibolosoo, Senyo B-S. K.
  The human factor in developing Africa / Senyo B-S. K. Adjibolosoo.
      p.   cm.
  Includes bibliographical references and index.
  ISBN 0–275–95059–X (alk. paper)
      1. Africa, Sub-Saharan—Economic policy.   2. Human capital—
  Africa, Sub-Saharan.   I. Title.
  HC800.A55255   1995
  338.967—dc20   94–42565

British Library Cataloguing in Publication Data is available.

Library of Congress Catalog Card Number: 94–42565
ISBN: 0–275–95059–X

First published in 1995

Praeger Publishers, 88 Post Road West, Westport, CT 06881
An imprint of Greenwood Publishing Group, Inc.

Printed in the United States of America

The paper used in this book complies with the
Permanent Paper Standard issued by the National
Information Standards Organization (Z39.48–1984).

10 9 8 7 6 5 4 3 2 1

scratch me where i itch
me where i itch
where i itch
i itch
itch
where i itch
me where i itch
scratch me where i itch
don't tickle my soles
the itches soundly roost
in my mind, emotions and will
the fire-balls glide like jet fighters
in my soul
as my visions itch
and my dreams tickle me
in their march across my thought-fields
they sing tall-titilating songs
and dirges all around me
they arm my dreams with wings
and they are ready to fly
let my kinsmen tell the world
let them tell the world
to scratch me where i itch

Senyo Adjibolosoo

This book is dedicated to my sweetheart, Sabina. It would not have been written without her unflinching sacrifices, support and encouragement.

Contents

Illustrations

Preface

This book aims to provide sub-Saharan African countries with alternative explanations for, and solutions to, their problems of economic underdevelopment. It discusses why economic development policies and programs have failed in sub-Saharan African countries and provides relevant answers to their economic underdevelopment malaise.

The basic premise of this book is that the human factor (HF) is the main integrating core, the engine of growth, the handmaiden of progress, the foundational foothold and the king-pin of the economic development or underdevelopment of nations. As such, conventional economic development theories must integrate the human factor if they are to be applicable to sub-Saharan African countries. The contents of this book will challenge every orthodox economic development theorist and will move all development planners, policy makers and international economic development experts and consultants either to revise or abandon their currently held views about how to achieve economic development and cultural change in sub-Saharan African countries.

As a principles book that is solely concerned with the role of the human factor and its engineering for economic development and cultural change, this book is the first of its kind. It pioneers an alternative approach to economic development thinking, policy making and program development. The book is not aimed at the development of empirical proofs for orthodox economic development theories. It is about the realities of economic underdevelopment and how to achieve economic progress in sub-Saharan African countries.

I have written this book because the current tradition of pure empiricism in modern economic analysis has bred economists who see darkly through their contaminated empirical microscopes and/or telescopes and therefore fail to perceive that there is more to economic analysis than mere applications of fanciful high-powered quantitative techniques to verify the validity of orthodox economic theories. Data that have been severely beaten to confess under quantitative duress what economists desire to hear and have published most often lie after too many discomforting massages. Such confessions are often time very misleading because they are either too simplistic or abstract or nonsensical. Leading economists have, therefore, for many decades failed both to successfully explain and suggest effective solutions to the problems of economic underdevelopment in sub-Saharan African countries.

I am convinced that this book will be of interest to many scholars of economic development theory, leaders of developing countries and international and non-governmental organizations. Professors, students and researchers of economic development will find the book a useful teaching, learning and research tool. The book opens a new horizon for further research. Academicians and social scientists of all persuasions will also find this book challenging, intriguing and rewarding to read. Above all, its contents are directly relevant to every society--be it developed or developing.

Acknowledgments

The birthing pains of this book have been mostly borne by my wife, Sabina. She is more qualified to be the author of this book than I am. But as divine providence will have it, I leaned heavily on her to write every single chapter of this book. Her sacrifices and support have made this book a reality. To her I say, *merci beaucoup*. Thus, the lion's share of my gratitude goes to her. To our children Selassie and Selorm, I say that I deeply appreciate their willingness to allow me to be away from them frequently to collect relevant materials for the book. We will one day make up for all the lost time and tell many more African stories.

I am also deeply indebted to my colleagues, who have reviewed several of the chapters or sections of individual chapters and provided me with invaluable insights and suggestions that have led to the enhancement of this book. Notable among these are Dr. Benjamin Ofori-Amoah, Dr. Francis Adu-Febiri, Dr. Fidelis Ezeala-Harrison, Dr. John Anonby, Dr. Deane Downey, Dr. Harold J. Harder, Mr. Mahamudu Bawumia, Mr. Moses Acquaah, Mr. Salomon Agbenya, Dr. Donald M. Page, Dr. Harold W. Faw, Dr. Douglas H. Shantz, Mr. Orville Lyttle, Mr. Glenn Isaac, Mr. Curtis Cunningham, Mr. Eddy Yuen, Miss Kelly Ip and many others who contributed in many other significant ways toward the writing of this book. I also thank my colleagues in the Faculty of Business and Economics, Trinity Western University and Mrs. Karen Kelly and Mrs. Brenda Sawatzky, the faculty secretaries, who have contributed in many different ways to my writing of this book. I am grateful to the participants at the various international conferences and seminars where some of the ideas presented in this book were first presented publicly while they were being developed. Above all, I am extremely grateful to the International Institute for Human Factor Development (IIHFD) Society for providing me with the opportunity and the resources required for writing this book. To these individuals, I say that no one will attribute any errors to them. The responsibility for any errors is mine.

Finally, I extend my sincere thanks to my acquisitions editor, Ms. Marcy Weiner, my production editor, Ms. Karen E. Davis, and to the Greenwood Publishing Group for their invaluable assistance and cooperation in making this dream a reality.

Part I

THE HUMAN FACTOR AND THE AFRICAN ECONOMIC DEVELOPMENT PROGRAM

1

Introduction: Goals of Economic Development

One of the greatest desires of any people is to use its resources in the manner that provides the highest welfare for its members. To achieve this goal, for many years economic development theorists have been developing a body of knowledge on which to draw as a guide to the economic development process. Soon after independence, many sub-Saharan African countries (ACs) scrambled to use these theories as the basis and justification for economic development planning and policy. Although policies based on these economic theories have been effective in the developed countries (DCs), the story is different in sub-Saharan Africa. In view of this observation, the main objective of this chapter is to explore and discuss the goals of the political economy of economic development in general and highlight what it should be in sub-Saharan Africa. This chapter reviews and presents the goals of economic development from antiquity to the present.

THE CONCEPT AND OBJECT OF ECONOMIC DEVELOPMENT

The basic necessities of life--food, clothing shelter and belongingness--have been and will always be humanity's primary concerns.[1] Regardless of what we do and crave for, these four desires lie at the heart of all human endeavors. All business and economic activities are geared toward increasing human wealth, which is, in turn, necessary but not sufficient for human happiness--the good life. Very little is known and written about economic development in classical antiquity. However, this does not mean that these people did not care about economic development. Gleanings from historical records reveal that their concerns were mostly about wealth creation and how to improve the lot of their citizens. The Greeks, Romans and Jews; people of the ancient kingdoms of Egypt, Persia and sub-Saharan Africa; and many other European nations put programs in place to encourage wealth creation and the production of food to feed the populations. In difficult times, leaders in the past tried their best to mediate between the wealthier and the laboring classes. For example, there arose revolts against the aristocratic class by the lower classes in the mid-seventh century B.C. in Corinth. Similarly, there were revolts in Athens, where the famous leader Solon was able to mediate successfully between the classes involved. Solon brought in several programs to help settle the disagreements between the landowners and the laborers. He abolished debt bondage to alleviate the growing burdens experienced by the underprivileged poor working class (Anderson, 1974, pp. 29-44).

These reforms and many others did not last long because they did not actually address the nagging problems of the lower classes. When the Solonic reforms failed, Peisistratus seized power and became the tyrannical ruler. Anderson (1974, p. 32) noted that Peisistratus promoted building programs that created employment opportunites for urban people and controlled a flourishing marine traffic in the Piraeus. He made financial help available to the peasantry in Athens. All these developments ensured the continuing survival of small- and medium-size farmers.

Thus, from the classical Greek perspective, economic development was aimed at the reformation of existing institutions, the various modes of production and the social relationships among the classes with divergent interests. Similar changes also occurred in Sparta in the seventh century B.C. In this case, programs were put in place to achieve land reforms. Although total equality was not achieved in the Spartan society, most reform programs were aimed at the achievement of this goal.

Again, the use of the Greek word *oikonomia* seems to suggest that to the classical Greeks, economic development constituted effective and efficient estate management by a steward to achieve the best benefits for all whose livelihood depended on that particular estate (Goyder, 1951, Chapter 1). Economic development to the Greeks, therefore, did not only mean proper estate management, but also adequate maintenance of the estate so that it could continue to provide for its owners and their dependents in perpetuity. It was efficient household management. Embedded in all these was the Greek belief that it was necessary to build a true society in which no one would be severely isolated. Finley (1973) discussed the ancient economy and its development.

Unlike the Greek empire, the Roman empire was bent on external expansionism. To achieve this goal, a general social infrastructure was laid down through the use of slave labor. Roads, buildings, canals, aqueducts, drains and many other structures were constructed using slave labor. Within the empire itself, very little was done to improve the welfare of the slaves. The Roman citizens, however, were provided with many opportunities to improve their own welfare. Like the Greeks, the Romans created several programs designed to achieve land reforms, although some of these did not achieve their intended goals. Large estates--*latifundia*--were encouraged and developed. International trade was one of the main pillars of the Roman economic development program. Much was done to attain national self-sufficiency and the creation of marketable surpluses. Both commercial and agricultural activities were encouraged.

Both the Greek and Roman empires were consumed with passions for political, economic and cultural development in their epochs. To achieve these goals, each settlement had a feudal lord whose duty it was to see that people's interests were protected and that law and order was maintained in the village. Both the Greeks and the Romans adored pleasure as part and parcel of their national heritage. Above all, the Greeks sought wisdom on a continuing basis.

The Jewish story regarding economic development and progress is also fascinating. In ancient Israel, the basic concern revolved around the improvement of social welfare and the maintenance of law, justice and the social order. A strongly religious society, the Jewish people believed that every development in their society must first honor their God, *Yahweh*. In most cases, Jewish development programs were aimed at the plight of the poor, orphans, widows and many other underprivileged people in their society. The Jewish people, then as now, believed that their God, *Yahweh*, had shown them what was good and what *Yahweh* required of them: to do justly and to love mercy and to walk humbly with *Yahweh*.[2] Therefore, in general terms, the Jewish economic development program was directed at the protection and maintenance of human welfare, justice, fairness and the social order. Obedience to God and duty to humanity were mandatory for every Jew--although deviant behavior persisted.

To the British mercantilists of the Middle Ages, "economic policy was intended to create [a] national economy which could be directed to enrich the nation as a whole. . . . Medieval economics was obsessed with questions of distribution and of maximizing the goods available for consumption: mercantilist economics redirected attention to the encouragement of production and exportation" (de Vries, 1976, p. 237). The English Navigational Acts reveal clearly that mercantilism strongly favored exports and restricted imports. The main objective was to acquire gold and other precious metals to enrich and strengthen the British Crown. With this as the major object of the economic development program, tariff laws, industrial controls, trade restrictions, varying forms of duties and many other methods were used to acquire the necessary wealth for the Crown and the merchant classes. Mercantilism was an economic development program whose basic motive was to build the British nation-state and to unify the economies of its kingdoms. Mercantilism was not concerned with unemployment and the untold hardships its policies brought to the poor people in general. An added dimension to the mercantilist economic development program is the continuous attainment of a favorable balance of payments position with the rest of the world. In view of this, import substitution was highly encouraged. The mercantilist view of economic development and its associated policies and programs were, therefore, aimed at growth in national wealth. Cameron (1993, pp. 20-77) contains a detailed presentation on the economic development in ancient times and Medieval Europe.

The French physiocratic view of economic development implies knowing the natural laws and harnessing and using them to offer the best to humanity. The physiocrats discussed how the removal of excessive government regulations could lead to increased productivity of the agricultural class. Their theory is a response to excessive controls in the French economy due to mercantilist policies and programs. The physiocrats argued for and discussed how a society's wealth is generated. To them, individual freedom, the right to acquire property and above all the right to enjoy the fruits of one's labor are integral parts of a progressive society.

Today, economic development in developed nations focuses on what Adam Smith called increasing labor productivity and capital accumulation. He discussed extensively how these things serve as the basis for the growing wealth of nations and economic development. Letiche (1960, p. 84) pointed out that both Adam Smith and David Ricardo stressed the role "of knowledge, effective government, protection of private property, social infrastructure, improved agriculture, entrepreneurship, labor specialization, technological innovations, accumulation of capital, and free trade in economic development."

Both Saint-Simon (1760-1825) and Auguste Comte (1798-1857) viewed development as evolutionary and progressive changes in society--usually achieved through the development of the human intellect. To them, the process of development requires extensive scientific thinking and analysis (Barnett, 1989). Spencer (1820-1903) drew a parallelism between a biological organism and society and suggested that societal development can be likened to that of the biological organism (Spencer, 1967, pp. 3-5).

Durkheim (1858-1917) wrote a great deal about the process of development. According to the Durkheimian view of development, society begins with a mechanical organizational solidarity and is arranged and operated in a simplistic manner. These tribal societies grow, expand and become more complex and social relationships become intricately intertwined. These complexities lead to the creation and use of division of labor, which in turn breeds specialization-- moving society toward a more developed and advanced stage. At the more developed stage of society, individual intimate loyalties and devotion may be lost. However, "the bonds holding individuals to the commonweal and to one another are of a higher calibre, and more effective. This new state of solidarity is reached as individualism becomes elaborated and understood as a new moral centre of industrial society" (Fisher, 1993, p. 61). To Durkheim, this process is zig-zagged in the sense that it exhibits both postive (good) and negative (bad or anomic) features and/or characteristics. Thus, in the Durkheimian development models, the role of government in coordinating the whole process of change becomes crucial.

Tonnies (1885-1936) viewed development as relating to the changes that take place in the moral fiber and ethical foundations of every society--as they relate to interpersonal relationships. The evolutionary process, in his view, is gradual and uneven. The mixing and continuous interactions among individuals have the power to effect changes in society. This process of change occurs at a snail's pace, and although it may exhibit an upward trend over a long period of time, it is in many ways stable.

Economic development has been perceived by many other scholars in various ways. Some have viewed the economic development process as the means whereby the poor are helped to become richer. Berger (1974, pp. 11, 18) noted that economic development can be seen as a growing evidence of "hope for better things to come. The problem here is not in the making of policy or the plausibility of theories, but in coping, from day to day, with suffering and dilemmas caused by often bewilderingly rapid change in the social environment [hunger, disease, early death, declining values, etc.]. . . . Development is not just a goal of rational actions in the economic, political, and social spheres. It is also, and very deeply, the focus of redemptive hopes and expectations." Economic development is, therefore, seen as a process of creating hope and the attainment of positive changes in society.

Whereas to modernization theorists economic development is modernization, dependency theorists always see economic development as the ability of the exploited nations to free themselves from the chains of capitalist imperialism. Moore (1964) defined modernization as "a total transformation of a traditional or pre-modern society into the types of technology and associated social organization that characterizes the advanced, economically prosperous and relatively politically stable nations of the Western World." Galbraith (1964, p. 4) labeled it as symbolic modernization. He pointed out that "this is designed to give the developing country the aspect, though not necessarily the substance, of development." It is characterized by structure building. Human welfare is not its primary objective. Similarly, Barnett (1989, p. 26) also discussed the main features of modernization theory (for a collection of papers on the modernization perspective in African development, see Ghosh, 1984).

Black (1966) viewed modernization as a process that brings about continuing alterations or changes in the social institutions of societies due to technological progress. Its main objective is to aid humanity, not necessarily to depend on nature for existence, but rather to furnish it with relevant tools with which to be lord and master over its habitat. Gutek (1993, pp. 66-67) observed that "educators who are proponents of modernization through development often see themselves as building nations out of developing societies. For these educational nation builders, the process of development involves an inevitable and necessary tension between the poles of modernity and tradition. While the tension brings with it cultural dislocation and discomfort, the anticipated consequences would be to move custom-bound traditional societies toward modernity." By this reasoning, progress in society must bring about positive changes in the intellectual, political, economic and social dimensions of human activities (Gutek, 1993, pp. 67-71).

Mabogunje (1989, p. 38) noted, however, that "the emphasis in development as modernization is thus on how to inculcate wealth-oriented behavior and values in individuals. This, in a sense, represents a shift from a commodity to a human approach. It involves principally how to make the population of a country understand and accept the new rules of the economic growth game."[3]

These views of development have been captured by Rostow (1960) in his stage theory of economic development. The Rostowian characterization of economic development is classified into five arbitrarily demarcated stages, namely (1) the traditional society, (2) the preconditions for take-off, (3) the take-off, (4) the drive to maturity, and (5) the high mass consumption. This Rostowian characterization of economic development seems to suggest that economic development is a piecemeal step process. As soon as the conditions of one stage are fulfilled, that stage vanishes and gives way to the next one, and then to the next better one, until all subsequent stages are advanced through and until the highest stage of economic development--high mass consumption--is attained. This is a process whereby societies are transformed from primitive agricultural to modern industrial societies. Thus, "Rostow sees economic growth and development as a product of capitalist economic and social practices" (Fisher, 1993, p. 59). As noted by Hunt (1989, p. 62), in the views of Lewis (1954) and Rostow (1960), "economic development entails the transformation of a traditional, stagnant, subsistence-oriented economy into a dynamic, capitalist economy based on wage labor, capable of self-sustained growth and of providing, in the long term, rising real wages."

The Marxian view of economic development maintains that the interactions between the means of production, social forces and/or relations and the ownership of the means of production set forces of change into motion, and their continuous interactions and effects on each other move society from the rubble and remains of a self-destroying capitalist system into a socialist society and then finally into the highest stage of development--Communism.

Approaching the problem from the socialist perspective, Seers (1972) argued that

> the questions to ask about a country's development are: what has been happening to poverty? What has been happening to unemployment? What has been happening to inequality? If all three of these have declined from high levels, then beyond doubt, this has been a period of development for the country concerned. If one or two of these central problems have been growing worse, especially if all three have, it would be strange to call the result "development," even if per capita income doubled.

To Baran (1957, pp. 11-28), "economic development has historically always meant a far-reaching transformation of society's economic, social and political structure." Baran (1957) argued further that for economic development to occur in developing countries, they must not only terminate their ties with the DCs but must also create a socialist order that is aimed at objective reason--elimination of such unproductive ventures like the production of war gear, luxuries, advertising and so on.

In general, the socialist view of economic development subscribes to (1) the termination of exploitation of people by people; (2) the annihilation or minimization of the degree of severity of injustice in society; (3) the dismantling of every observable class system and the creation of equality in its place; (4) the alleviation or overcoming of poverty; and (5) the utilization of the central government's planning and programs of action to overcome the problems of economic underdevelopment. In a sense, the socialists view development as the transformation of the modes of production in society.

A critical review of the age-old debate between the capitalist and socialist theorists reveals that the capitalist view of economic development is totally different from that of the socialists. To capitalist theorists and scholars such as Milton Friedman, P. T. Bauer, Ian M. D. Lyttle and many others, the major objective of any economic development program must be to increase and protect free choice (McCord and McCord, 1986). Economic growth, viewed as a necessary prelude to economic development, is expected to provide humanity with more freedom and a strongly effective control over its many habitats (Lewis, 1984). McCord and McCord (1986, p. 92) pointed out that to the capitalist theorists, "an expansion in the opportunities available to mankind and a decrease in material and political limits on man's individual judgment were the ends of development." With these in mind, therefore, McCord and McCord (1986, p. 41) suggested that

> the clear task of liberal and social democrats in developing nations was to seek economic advance while stalwartly defending the rudimentary principles of a liberal polity: a rule of law independent of the whims of an elite; a tolerance for nonviolent political opposition; a willingness to consult the people's judgment; a recognition that mediating institutions--the family, the Church, unions, even the tribes or castes--have a right to function outside the state's embracing arms; a guarantee of open criticism from the press, pulpit, or assembly; and a marked hesitancy on the part of government to invade a man's privacy and to treat his work, village, family, and self as mere extensions of state power.

These must be put in place to make the whole environment safe for everyone-- even dissenters--to participate fully in the economic development program. The existence of these conditions creates courage and commitment on the part of citizens and enables them to function as expected. Bernstein (1973, p. 13) observed that "the aspiration to change, and institutional means for achieving it, are central to present day conceptions of development. Policy for development is a major preoccupation of the governments of poor countries; help is promised by those of rich countries."

Esman (1991, p. 5) suggested that the process of economic development must be viewed as the means of reducing and/or eliminating poverty, ignorance and disease; and achieving improvements in the deteriorating human condition. True economic development must lead to continuous transformation in the social, cultural, economic and political systems and/or conditions in every society. In the past, to many scholars of economic development theory, economic development implies either industrialization or urbanization or Westernization, or all three together and more. Todaro (1989, pp. 88-89) viewed development as a multidimensional process that effects "changes in social structures, popular attitudes, and national institutions, as well as the acceleration of economic growth, the reduction of inequality, and the eradication of absolute poverty."

Increases in employment opportunities and national income are necessary conditions but are not sufficient for economic development. Their existence does not, however, imply that economic development will be attained. The United Nations noted in 1970 that "the ultimate objective of development must be to bring about a sustained improvement in the well-being of the individual and bestow benefits on all. If undue privileges, extremes of wealth and social injustices persist, then development fails in the essential purpose." In the view of Stewart (1992, p. 312), "the major goal of development is to achieve equitable, participatory and sustained improvement in economic and social well-being."

The basic needs approach to economic development concentrates on the provision of opportunities for men and women to develop their potentialities--mental, physical and social (Streeten, 1981, 1984). In the words of Hope (1984, p. 14), "the basic-needs approach is founded on the premise that poverty in most underdeveloped countries is widespread and that action should therefore be directed at the population as a whole. . . . Actually, basic-needs policies are not restricted to the eradication of absolute poverty but extend to the satisfaction of needs over and above the subsistence level as a means of eliminating relative poverty through a continuous process of economic development and social process." (See also Lisk, 1978.) This approach encourages the participation of all citizens in economic policy development and implementation. It views the citizens as being the people who must monitor and make sure that those who execute policies and programs do not deviate from the original objectives--health care, education, clean water, nutrition and so on.

The Chinese (Maoist) view and model of development revolves around the view that the primary objective of economic development is to increase the material wealth of every Chinese citizen, terminate the huge income differentials prevalent in Chinese society and eliminate private ownership of the means of production. The Chinese were, therefore, expected to participate in the process of increasing and effectively using the productive capacity of the nation to develop modern industry. Their development program also paid much attention to the development of small- and medium-size cottage industries. These industries were to depend on the abundance of cheap labor--they were labor intensive industries. The whole development program has regional income equalization as one of its major objectives. In recent years, the Chinese position has begun to change, as evidenced in their open-door policies. Privatization is rapidly becoming an integral part of the Chinese economic development policy.

THE EVOLUTION OF THE GOALS OF
ECONOMIC DEVELOPMENT

The goals of economic development programs have evolved through many phases throughout the past several decades. For example, in the 1950s economic development was viewed as the undertaking of comprehensive capital projects, such as the building of dams, roads, hydroelectric power stations, industrial installations and many other related projects--this is modernization. These social infrastructures were usually deemed to be necessary for the achievement of economic growth, industrialization and human welfare (Leonard, 1989, pp. 19-22). Stone (1992, p. 37) noted that the World Bank's first mission to Columbia in 1950 focused on how to meet the basic needs of the people. In previous years, traditional development wisdom focused on extensive technical projects and large capital-intensive investment projects that usually neglected human welfare.

Severe foreign exchange shortages paved the way for the development of the structural perspective on economic development in Latin America. This paradigm of economic development was engineered and led by Raul Prebisch. To these structuralists, economic development involves the cooperation between production factors to increase the productivity of labor. Its features include a steadily continuous expansion in different sectors of the economy making use of advanced technology. Structuralists, however, do not view output growth alone as constituting economic development. In the structuralist view, therefore, economic development involves the transformation of the economic structure of the poor countries and their attainment of capabilities to pursue and achieve sustained economic growth: "to achieve this, it was recognized that it would be necessary to break away from complete reliance on foreign demand for primary exports as the engine of growth, switching instead to a supply-side dynamic to be provided by an expanding domestic industrial sector" (Hunt, 1989, p. 50). The structuralist paradigm gives strong support to import-substitution industrialization policies and programs. In its train are policies relating to foreign exchange controls, investment licensing, use of tariffs and so on.

In the 1940s and 1950s, European and North American economists began to direct their attention to economic underdevelopment in the least developed countries--African states, Latin American countries and many others. The scholars in this category came to believe that even though industrialization was necessary for the economic emancipation of the underdeveloped nations, such nations had several internal constraining factors. In the views of these scholars, such constraints can be overcome through growth in per capita income. This belief led many to accept the view that economic development is synonymous with increases in a nation's per capita income (Hunt, 1989, p. 51; Streeten, 1981, p. 108). Most of these scholars rejected the neoclassical paradigm and subscribed to government interventions in the economy to direct national economic development programs. Scholars who contributed to this view include Rosenstein-Rodan, Nurkse, Hirschman, Leibenstein, Myrdal, Myint, Bauer and Yamey, Lewis and Rostow (See Table 2.1).

Immediately after the Second World War, economic development was, therefore, viewed to be "a rapid and sustained rise in real output per head and attendant shifts in the technological, economic, and demographic characteristics of a society" (Easterlin, 1986). This view emphasizes physical output growth rather than changes in the human condition. These developments were expected to lead to increases in the national capital stock and to raise annual productivity. Development in this regard, according to Robbins (1968, p. 3), implies "progress towards some ethically defined goal." Robbins (1968, p. 6) observed further that "the most endless flood of pamphlets advocating development of this or that form of economic activity--the fisheries, the woollen industry, shipping, the draining of fens, the creation of roads and waterways--were doubtless often meritorious enough in their historical setting and have interest too in that context. "

In the 1960s, the major focus was on the provision of development assistance to the developing countries by the DCs. Thus, in the 1960s, when many sub-Saharan African countries attained political independence, the popular belief was that if they could receive adequate assistance from the DCs, they would prepare themselves for economic development. Although this view was not abandoned in the 1970s, the focus changed slightly to the pursuit of the principles of equity and economic growth (Dale, Carter and Norman, 1955; Stone, 1992, p. 40). Developing countries have always been encouraged to institute programs that are capable of achieving efficient income redistribution (Little, 1982). The focus of economic development programs became the eradication of poverty and its accompanying problems. Collier and Lal (1986), David (1986) and Lal (1983) discussed pertinent problems and inefficieny associated with income redistribution programs. By the 1980s, integrated rural development (IRD) became the main focus of economic development programs and assistance.

Although economic development policies and programs for the 1990s still hold this same view, an added dimension is sustainable economic development due to humanity's concerns about the environment, the protection of endangered species of plants and animals and the minimization of the thinning of the ozone layer. Every economic development policy and program is expected to take these pertinent issues into account. Feminism is also now a strong central issue in the modern development literature.

AN ECLECTIC DEFINITION OF ECONOMIC DEVELOPMENT

With these many views, one may sometimes be lost in regard to what constitutes true economic development. The various scholastic views of what constitutes economic development as reviewed in this chapter raise many unanswered questions. These include the following:

1 What does moderninzation mean when nations are able to achieve the building of several physical structures and yet these advances leave their societies with growing waves of crime, all forms of discrimination, poverty and suffering for many?

2 Why has the increasing number of government regulations, although leading to growth in incomes in some countries, not led to a drastic reduction in poverty, deviant behavior and hence positive economic development in many nations?

3 For centuries, humanity has been able to achieve great inventions and innovations that have the potential to minimize human suffering and inefficiency. Why is it that regardless of these achievements, many people, especially youth, seem to have no hope to live for and hardly any future to look forward to?

4 Why is it that even when governments throw copious financial resources

at social problems in an attempt to overcome the problems they pose to humanity, very little is usually achieved by way of improving human welfare and generally making life more worth living than before the increase in government spending occurred?

5 Can the myriad of scholarly views regarding economic development be synchronized and recast in a mode to shed more light on what a globally acceptable view of economic development may be? That is, can a more germane--and humane--view of economic development be formulated?

These pertinent queries bring us back to asking how we can know whether economic development has actually taken place or is proceeding in any particular society. Collecting all these views together, one can argue conclusively that economic development policies and programs must be aimed at the eradication of disease, illiteracy, urban squalor, malnutrition, economic injustice and inequity, poverty, all forms of prejudice and so on. It must foster the humanness in every human being and the right to freedom of choice based on universal principles of life (and/or sound ethical and value systems) and the means to peaceful human existence/coexistence. The primary objective of any national economic development program must be the development of the human factor (HF)[4]. Countries must be in a position to create fertile economic environments in which jobs can be fashioned for their people; provide adequate and affordable health services for everyone; develop and offer relevant education, training and mentoring programs for the entire population; and, above all, achieve and sustain national economic self-sufficiency.

In my view, therefore, the true acid test for successful economic development policies and programs is the effectiveness of society, not only in telling the poor and the severely disadvantaged about the various practical ways through which they can get over their predicament, but also in creating the environment within which every citizen is able to feed, clothe and shelter himself or herself and, above all, feel strongly that he or she belongs to a humane society. Increasing success in healing individual brokenheartedness in society; continuously rescuing those who are under the perpetual lure of idleness and self-destruction; lessening human ignorance and aimlessness; recognizing and correcting follies of past policies and programs; changing, minimizing and transforming the society's cultural beliefs, habits and customs of the heart that mitigate against the economic development process in order to promote positive adaptation; and the growing capacity to feed, clothe and house all people in society are therefore to be viewed as the major objects of economic development. The view of John Comenius that the welfare of humanity must be the primary objective of every human endeavor is illuminating (see Peter, 1977, p. 250). Above all, the often forgotten dimension of development, belongingness, must be fostered.

Note, however, that the process of economic development can be wisely directed through effective human factor engineering and activities that are aimed at lubricating development's wheels rather than increasing the frictional drag on its steps and power. Only a visionary group of people possesses the necessary human factor that will realize and discover how and why economic development occurs. This view suggests, therefore, that the primary object of any economic development policies and programs must first be the development of the necessary HF to educate, train and socialize members of society to undertake human-centered development as they learn to know their real positions in society and community life. Truly, the successful development of the HF will lead to the realization of the human potential (Gandhi (1968). The effective use of the appropriately developed HF must assist society to advance forward and achieve the objectives of the economic development program.

The attainment of improvements in human welfare can be facilitated by increasing human wealth through increased average labor productivity. The question, however, is "How can a country attain economic growth and development?" Attempts to provide solutions to this question have led to the development of economic theories whose foundational constructs, assumptions, value presuppositions, resulting policies and programs are reviewed and discussed in chapter 2.

NOTES

1. This aspect of human life is always either forgotten or relegated to the backyard corridors of development planning and programs in most countries. Economic development literature has very little to say about the fact that human beings are social beings and therefore desire to feel that they are a part of a group. In advanced countries, countless millions of people are lonely and depressed daily either because they fail to feel that they belong or because they are classified as minorities and treated as such. Due to the social structure of these societies, some people do not have long-lasting friends and family toward whom they can direct their love and be loved in return. The absence of belongingness in the lives of many people, especially young people--has led to great difficulties such as identity crisis, loss of self-esteem, drug-related crimes, teenage rebellion and many others for advanced countries. Today, in the DCs, many lonely, severely depressed, and emotionally troubled individuals (especially, youth, singles--unmarried, divorced, etc.) resort to escort services, international computer networks (i.e., the Internet and many others) to search for short term friendships, love, acceptance, and/or lasting relationships. Yet in many cases, most of these people experience fraud, abuse in its many diverse forms, deceitfulness, and severe brokenheartedness. In rare cases some, however, find partners for life. I am convinced that true economic development must not neglect this aspect (i.e., belongingness) of human life; otherwise, society cannot claim to be totally developed.

2. *The Bible*, King James Version, Micah 6:8.

3. For a more detailed analysis of this issue, see Lerner, D. 1968. "Social Aspects of Modernization." In D. L. Sills, ed. *International Encyclopedia of the Social Sciences* Vol. 10, pp. 225-226.

4. For a detailed definition and discussion of the HF, see Chapter 3.

2

Conventional Approaches to Economic Development in Sub-Saharan African Countries

INTRODUCTION

Since independence in the 1950s and 1960s, many sub-Saharan African countries (ACs) have aimed at economic development and welfare improvement for their people. Although efforts were made in many directions, there is still much to be done to achieve every desired goal. These efforts were based on principles, policies and programs drawn in line with orthodox economic theorizing. The objective of this chapter is, therefore, to present a detailed review of conventional economic development policies and programs that have been used in the past to facilitate economic development in sub-Saharan ACs. This chapter points out how orthodox economic development theories led development economists and African leaders to concentrate on irrelevant premises and, by so doing, fail to recognize and focus policies and programs on factors relevant to the economic development process in sub-Saharan ACs.

One of the main starting points is a critical examination of existing economic development theories, which have hitherto gained a monopoly position in economic policy making and economic development planning in sub-Saharan Africa. The main goal of this exercise is to isolate relevant pitfalls that can serve as useful pointers toward the direction in which sub-Saharan African countries must head.

The organization of the rest of this chapter is as follows: The following section focuses on the themes of orthodox economic development philosophy, and the subsequent section points out how orthodox economic development theory has produced a countless number of policies and programs for sub-Saharan ACs. Although the content of the chapter is not exhaustive, it presents a bird's eyeview of the many economic development theories that have shaped development planning, policy and programs in sub-Saharan ACs. The summaries and conclusions draw attention to the outcomes of the applications of these policies in sub-Saharan ACs.

CLASSIFICATIONS OF CONVENTIONAL
DEVELOPMENT THEORIES

The literature on the origins of economic development theories and their classifications is voluminous and often confusing since many scholars have attempted detailed classifications and have, unfortunately, arrived at different groupings. The intention of this chapter, however, is not to undertake another detailed review or classification. The intended goal is to present the evolving policy recommendations of these varying divergent paradigms of economic development. For those who are interested in detailed works that classify these theories, excellent classificatory reviews can be found in Chenery (1975), Forster-Carter (1976), Killick (1978), Seers (1979), Love (1980), Hirschman (1981), Streeten (1981), Kitching (1982), Little (1982), Preston (1982), Chilcote and Johnson (1983), Meier (1984), Leeson (1988) and Hunt (1989). Oman and Wignaraja (1991) have grouped orthodox economic development theories into four main categories: capital accumulation and industrialization, dualism and agricultural-centered development, open-economy development and neoclassical resurgence and the reformist development theories.[1] These theories are summarized in Table 2.1. Additional ideas about development policies, theories and myths are discussed in Berger (1974, pp. 9-31).

An extensive study and analysis of each of these paradigms of economic development reveals the varying policies to which these paradigms have led. Table 2.2 presents a summary of the most frequently used of these policies in sub-Saharan ACs and other developing countries. Each of these policies, as noted earlier, has been put forward to help deal with the economic underdevelopment malaise in developing countries. The information presented in Table 2.2 is self-explanatory and therefore needs no further discussion. It must, however, be observed that the hundreds of policies forthcoming from the various paradigms of economic development are often conflicting and confusing. This, in itself, has posed one of the greatest challenges to sub-Saharan African policy makers regarding how to select the most appropriate policies from the existing pool. The effectiveness of these policies is discussed in Chapter 3.

The theoretical musings of the great economists have brought to light what many of them have individually classified as being the major hindrances to economic development in the underdeveloped nations. Table 2.3 lists the varying reasons why economic progress can sometimes be either self-destroying or self-limiting. The pessimism of some of these economists can be summarized in a few words, as in Table 2.3. The usual view about achieving economic development is that if only these hindrances can either be removed or minimized, economic development will ensue in the underdeveloped nations. Sub-Saharan ACs have tried all these policies during the past three or more decades.

In what follows, I present a more detailed discussion of how various governments, leaders and organizations have pursued these policies in sub-Saharan ACs.

TABLE 2.1
FOUNDATIONS OF ORTHODOX ECONOMIC
DEVELOPMENT THEORIES

Theories About Capital Accumulation and Industrialization		
Scholars	**Theoretical Foundations**	**Year**
Harrod Domar	Role of savings and investment	1936/1939/ 1948 1946/1947
Rosenstein-Rodan	The Big Push	1943
Nurkse	The balanced growth strategy	1952
Lewis	The theory of economic growth	1955
Galenson & Leibenstein	The view that unequal income distribution will increase the savings rate and hence promote investment (rich save more than the poor)	1955
Kuznets	Substantiated the view of Galenson and Leibenstein	1955
Perroux	Growth poles theory	1955
Hirschman	Unbalanced growth strategy	1958
Rostow	Stage theories of development	1960
Chenery/Bruno	Analyzed relationship between saving and investment growth in the LDCs	1962
Chenery/Strout	Foreign aid and acceleration of the rate of investment in Rostowian models	1966

TABLE 2.1 CONTINUED

Dualism and Agriculture-Centered Development		
Boeke	Development programs in the LDCs revolve around social rather than economic needs	1953
Lewis	Economic development through unlimited labor supplies	1954
Higgins	Rejected Boeke's sociological dualism theories in favor of technological dualism	1956
Ranis/Fei	Labor migration from the traditional to modern sector will foster development	1961
Myint	Enclave dualism	1964
Tinbergen/Bos	Focused on the role of education and humanpower	1965
Jorgenson	The role of technical progress in agricultural development	1967
Harris/Todaro	Rural-urban migration	1970
Kelly, Williamson and Cheatham	Dualism and production technology	1972
Open-Economy Development and Neoclassical Resurgence		
Ohlin	Neoclassical trade model	1933
Kravis	Trade-handmaiden of growth	1970
Haberler	Structural adjustment	1950

TABLE 2.1 CONTINUED

Open-Economy Development and Neoclassical Resurgence		
Viner	Structural adjustment	1953
Bauer and Yamey	Structural adjustment	1968
Little, Scitovsky/Scott	Export Development	1970
Heckscher	Neoclassical trade model	1933
IMF and its scholars	Structural adjustment	N/A
Reformist Development Thinking		
Seers	Wealth redistribution	1969
Myrdal	Wealth redistribution	1970
Morris	Wealth redistribution	1979
Hayter	Wealth redistribution	1981
Note: The reformists also argued further that the developing countries must develop industry and agriculture simultaneously.		
Nonorthodox Development Thinking		
Emmanuel	Structuralism and dependency theory	1972
Prebisch	Structuralism and dependency theory	1959
Singer	Structuralism and dependency theory	1950

ECONOMIC DEVELOPMENT POLICIES AND PROGRAMS IN SUB-SAHARAN AFRICA

In this section, the discussion focuses on the economic policies of different organizations that have participated in the sub-Saharan African economic development program. The reasons for their successes or failures are discussed in the subsequent section.

The hopes and aspirations for political independence were very high in sub-Saharan ACs in the 1960s. These hopes were supported up by the availability of many different economic development theories, which served as the basis for economic development planning and policy. Orthodox economic development theorizing has generated a pool of theories that has served as the basic foundation underlying economic policy making and program formulation in many sub-Saharan ACs. Frequently, newly independent sub-Saharan ACs religiously adhere to the various prescriptions of these orthodox theories in dealing with problems of economic underdevelopment. For many years, the use of orthodox economic development theory as the main foundation of economic development planning and policy formulation in sub-Saharan ACs has led to the institution of hundreds of economic policies and programs (See Table 2.2).

THE INTERNATIONAL MONETARY FUND AND THE WORLD BANK POLICIES AND PROGRAMS

The International Monetary Fund (IMF) and the World Bank have shown the keenest interest in sub-Saharan African economic development. Although their main reasons and interests are not fully known, their apparent intentions have been interpreted in different ways by different individuals and/or groups of people. Their main policy prescriptions are discussed next.

International Comparative Advantage and Specialization

The pursuit of international comparative advantage theory and international labor specialization is key in the IMF and World Bank stabilization and structural adjustment policies. The IMF and the World Bank school of thought believes in international specialization and division of labor in that these organizations encourage sub-Saharan ACs to continue to invest in cash crop production and other primary agricultural products. The main argument is that since ACs possess comparative advantages in the production of certain primary products, they can produce them at lower costs and exchange their proceeds for other commodities for which they have a comparative disadvantage.

Structural Adjustment and Stabilization Policies

Every sub-Saharan AC that appeals to the IMF and/or its cousin, the World Bank, for loans or any other type of economic development assistance is usually required to put its fiscal house in order first. For example, government subsidies, price controls, income policies and many other such policies are the usual targets attacked first by the IMF. For any further assistance to sub-Saharan ACs, additional conditions are usually imposed. Those countries that genuinely

TABLE 2.2
SPECIFIC POLICY PRESCRIPTIONS
AND TARGETS FROM ALL PARADIGMS

* Remove impediments to private saving and investment
* Adopt noninterference with the operation of the free market
* Accumulate and maintain capital in the private sector
* Make huge investments in sectors with both forward and backward linkages
* Attract foreign capital
* Increase free trade with the DCs
* Encourage agricultural development
* Adopt government planning and deliberate intervention with market forces
* Protect infant industries
* Control population growth rate
* Dismantle government-imposed price controls and incomes policies
* Build infrastructure and investment in large-scale projects
* Invest in human resources
* Redistribute incomes
* Raise capitalists' share of national income--they have higher marginal propensity to save
* Pursue structural transformation and increase per capita income
* Institute import-substitution industrialization programs
* Diversify the structure of domestic production
* Use labor-intensive technology
* Rehabilitate and build new social infrastructure
* Pursue environmental conservation and energy development
* Meet basic needs
* Increase the savings ratio
* Pursue privatization--to weaken statism; reform the civil service; decentralize government and democratize the political process; improve and enhance public sector efficiency and effectiveness
* Pursue policies for achieving technological self-reliance
* Invest in R&D
* Write off all debts
* Control imports and promote exports
* Control inflationary pressures
* Reduce wages and free hiring
* Remove subsidies and direct wage/price controls
* Reduce current account imbalances by cutting back on public spending

TABLE 2.3
THE VIEWS OF THE GREAT ECONOMISTS ABOUT
PERTINENT HINDRANCES TO ECONOMIC DEVELOPMENT

Economist	Perceived Hindrances
Ricardo	The law of diminishing returns
Malthus	Malthusian principle of population growth and the law of diminishing returns
Marx	Exploitation and declining purchasing power
Schumpeter	The continuing impairment or the weakening of the entrepreneurial spirit
Keynes	Diminishing marginal efficiency of capital; insufficient capital; low levels of consumption; idling resources; stagnation
Hayek	The pursuit of socialism
Jevons	The depletion of natural resources
Smith	The size of the market and the extent of government intervention
Mill (Jr.)	Despotic customs; cultural homgeneity; ignorance; capital and land deficiencies
Myint	Unskilled peasant workers
Rosenstein-Rodan	Small size of the domestic market; the inability of firms to internalize the values of their own created external economies; the failure of firms to perceive the size of the external economies created by the investment of others
Nurkse	Low per capita incomes and the inability to create huge savings to finance the required investment
Leibenstein	Low-level equilibrium trap
Myrdal	Low levels of per capita output and savings; high rates of population growth; low levels of skills; poor health of the labor force

TABLE 2.3 CONTINUED

Emmanuel	Unequal exchange
Hirschman	A binding agent--the lack of organizational ability to be used in combination of latent factors to generate growth
Bauer/Yamey	Traditional institutions--the determination of wages; the nature of the extended system; political instability; unsettled monetary conditions
Baran	Low per capita incomes--failure to use the surpluses productively
Frank	The extraction and transfer of the surpluses from the LDCs to the DCs; the inability of the dominant classes to use these surpluses effectively

desire assistance must comply with all stipulations or run the risk of being denied desperately sought financial assistance. Specific policies of each of these institutions, as noted by Mosley (1987), include the IMF-induced stabilization program and the World Bank's structural adjustment (loans) policies. Additional policies and programs are listed in Table 2.2.

The Price Mechanism

The IMF encourages sub-Saharan ACs to yield to the operation of the free market system through the price mechanism. With the removal of government-imposed restrictions on the freedom of the market mechanism, the IMF and the World Bank believe that existing demand and supply bottlenecks will correct themselves over time.

Devaluation and Export Promotion Policies

These are "darling" policies for IMF and World Bank experts, who argue that devaluation policies and export promotion strategies will make imports more expensive and exports cheaper. In this way, sub-Saharan ACs may step up the production of domestic products for foreign consumption. Cash cropping to feed industrial programs in the developed countries (DCs) is strongly encouraged.

Accelerated Economic Development Program

To this list must be added the World Bank's "Accelerated Development in Sub-Saharan Africa: An Agenda for Action Program," often referred to as the Berg Report. In its 1984 document, *Toward Sustained Development in sub-Saharan Africa: A Joint Program of Action*, the World Bank's policy objectives for sub-Saharan Africa included, among other things, domestic reforms, appropriate pricing policies and the control of the population growth.[2] (See also Table 2.4.)

THE POLICIES PURSUED BY FIRST-GENERATION AFRICAN LEADERS

Independence produced high expectations for welfare improvements in most sub-Saharan ACs. Political freedom gave birth to African leadership and nation-building attempts. Many ambitious economic and social policies and programs were attempted by the first generation (i.e., Africans who fought for political independence) of African leaders. The policies and programs discussed next are included in this repertoire.

Accelerated Development Planning and Policies

After achieving independence, sub-Saharan ACs were in a hurry to industrialize. This was clear in presidential speeches and economic development plans and policies. The focus was on development planning (Green, 1967). For example, Kwame Nkrumah of Ghana suggested that what took the DCs hundreds of years to accomplish could be attained by sub-Saharan ACs in a few years. These aspirations led sub-Saharan African leaders to focus their attention too often on the dream of an economic promised land rather than on how to get there in reality. Almost every one of these dreams wilted and decayed. Although plans, policies and programs were initiated to help facilitate the process, most of them were not relevant to the sub-Saharan African condition and/or environment (see Tables 2.1 and 2.2). Almost every sub-Saharan AC has gone through this fad of unrealized economic development because of inappropriate and/or inadequate planning and unrealistically accelerated industrial policies. A properly developed labor force that had acquired the human factor (HF) necessary for implementing the program was lacking.

Import Substitution Industrialization

Perceiving clearly that the DCs have arrived where they are today due to accelerated industrial development programs, postindependence sub-Saharan African governments felt that the human condition in Africa could improve if sub-Saharan ACs could process their agricultural produce at home. Moreover, it has been and is still a popular orthodox belief that industrialization would lead sub-Saharan Africans to add more value to their primary products. In this way, they would not only establish their own facilities to process primary products, but they would also enhance sub-Saharan African welfare and living conditions. Prebisch (1971, p. 6), for example, noted that "although it is not an end in itself, [industrialization] is the principal means at the disposal of those countries for obtaining a share of the benefits of technical progress and/or progressively raising the standard of living of the masses."

In terms of sub-Saharan African economic development, the afforementioned proposition has not only been misleading but is also inappropriate as a foundation principle on which the sub-Saharan African economic development program should be based. This is the case because it fails to realize how fundamental the role of the HF is in the economic development of nations. However, sub-Saharan African leaders and their policy advisors and planners chose to go with Prebisch.

Development Planning

Every independent sub-Saharan AC came to view economic development planning as one of the major prerequisites for and keys to economic and industrial success. Thus, in the 1960s and 1970s, Ghana, Nigeria, Kenya, Ethiopia, Mali, Liberia, Senegal and several others pursued accelerated economic development through planning. These countries believed that a state-planned economic program had the power to spearhead sub-Saharan Africa's program of economic recovery. Yet it was only recently that most sub-Saharan ACs realized that economic development planning did not represent the key to economic progress in sub-Saharan Africa.[3]

MARXIAN POLICY RECOMMENDATIONS AND PURSUITS

Marxist economists have always maintained that economic underdevelopment in sub-Saharan Africa is due to colonial exploitation by the DCs and their lack of concern for African welfare (Nzula et al., 1979). They therefore maintain that decolonization must lead to self-government, which in turn would promote equal opportunities and equitable income distribution. The propagation of Marxist philosophy in sub-Saharan Africa has encouraged nationalistic policies that led to mass nationalization of foreign assets and business ventures in some countries in the past. In addition, the pursuit of business indigenization led to the exclusion of foreign capital and business from certain vital sectors of sub-Saharan African economies. Marxian economists encourage economic development planning and state-controlled economic development programs. Sub-Saharan African leaders acquiesced without any further questions and did as they were told.

TABLE 2.4
SELECTED POLICIES OF SPECIFIC INSTITUTIONS

I. IMF-Induced Stabilization Policies
1 Control of the money supply
2 Minimization of government spending
3 Enhancement of efficiency through the market
4 Provision of incentives to facilitate the switching of
   resources from nontradeables to tradeables (through devaluation,
   prices and wages control policies)

II. Goals of the World Bank's Structural
Adjustment Loans
1 Promotion of the free market system
2 Mobilization of resources through fiscal and monetary policies
3 Reform of industry
4 Reform of social policy
5 Liberalization of trade

III. The Economic Commission for Africa
1 Development of agriculture, food production, industry,
   transport and telecommunications systems
2 Development of human resources
3 Promotion of science and technology
4 Creation and development of effective institutional structures

IV. The Final Act of Lagos (FAL)
   Development of procedures for implementing the
   Lagos Plan of Action (LPA). Its policy concerns include
1 Establishing intracontinental solidarity
2 Harmonizing plans, policies and programs in all areas
3 Establishing and promoting bilateral and multilateral cooperative
   programs.
4 Synchronizing financial and monetary policies
5 Promoting intra-African trade

V. The African Development Bank (ADB)
1 Control of population
2 Reform of education
3 Control of budgetary and pricing policy
4 Control of finances
5 Promotion of small farm holdings
6 Institution of private sector incentives to boost job creation

TABLE 2.4 CONTINUED

---

7   Enlargement of foreign exchange earning capacities and/or sources
8   Pursuit of economic integration

VI. The Abuja Statement of Economic
Recovery (June 15-19, 1987)
1   Development and sustenance of domestic reforms
2   Improvement of economic management
3   Reduction of the debt burden
4   Development of a solution for the continuing commodity problem
5   Facilitation of the flow of development assistance to Africa
6   Encouragement and support of intra-African trade
7   Pursuit of self-reliance and regional cooperation
8   Pursuit of R&D, scientific and technological innovation
9   Development of entrepreneurship
10 Promotion of relevant political, social and administrative conditions
    for economic development

Other relevant programs designed to create African economic development include Africa's Priority Program for Economic Recovery (APPER) (1986-1990) and the Arusha African Charter for Popular Participation in Development (see the additional list of policies in Table 2.4).

UNITED NATIONS PROGRAM OF ACTION FOR AFRICAN ECONOMIC RECOVERY AND DEVELOPMENT

There are two central elements of the United Nations Program of Action for African Economic Recovery and Development (UN-PAAERD):

1   The commitment of ACs to pursue national and regional economic development progams as specified in *Africa's Priority Program of Economic Recovery--APPER (1986-1990)*.
2   The international community's support for the African development initiatives and programs. The focus of APPER includes

i   Revitalizing agriculture and its productivity
ii   Achieving efficiency in public sector management
iii Dealing directly with human resources development
iv   Finding ways and means for overcoming pertinent hindrances to sustainable economic growth.

STRATEGIES OF CORNIA, VAN DER HOEVEN AND MKANDAWIRE

Cornia, van der Hoeven and Mkandawire in Cornia and de Jong (1992), discussed the weaknesses of structural adjustment policies and made several policy suggestions regarding how economic development could be accomplished in sub-Saharan Africa. Their suggested economic development strategies include the following:

1   An agrarian strategy focused on small farmers
2   A strengthening of agriculture-nonagriculture linkages
3   An industrialization strategy: small scale, labor intensive
4   An emphasis on relevant and efficient human capabilities development
5   Improvement of income distribution
6   Development of trade policies.
7   An increase in aid and a forgiving of debts.

In recent years, other scholars have also suggested that establishing task forces and intensive negotiations at the regional levels regarding issues of special interest may help in achieving economic progress in sub-Saharan Africa (Onitiri, 1991, p. 482). Amin (1991, pp. 559-560) proposed an alternative, auto-centered model strategy. This model of development highlights the need for supporting an agricultural revolution with industrialization. Schematically, the auto-centered model relates to (1) production of the means of production; (2) production of goods for mass consumption; (3) luxury production/consumption; and (4) exports. The auto-centered model emphasizes the link between (1) and (2). In Amin's model, labor incomes need to increase as productivity grows. Amin maintained that development cannot occur by merely adapting the developing country to meet the requirements of the international division of labor. Instead, the developing country's economy must be disconnected from the international division of labor. To Amin, "the achievement of auto-centered development will require nationalist regimes and democratic and popular participation."

Hundreds of other policy and program suggestions for economic development in Africa can be found in the following documents:

1   *The United Nations Transport and Communications Decade for Africa, 1978-1988 (UNCTACDA)*
2   *The Addis Ababa Declaration on Africa's External Indebtedness*, which was prepared by the African Ministers of Finance in June 1984
3   *Second Special Memorandum by the ECA [Economic Commission for Africa] Conference of Ministers: International Action for Long-Term Development and Economic Growth in Africa,* which was produced by the ECA Conference of Ministers in 1985
4   *Recommendations of the ECA Conference of Ministers Concerning the Economic Issues on the Agenda of the Twenty-First Ordinary Session of the Assembly of Heads of State and Government of OAU [Organization*

of African Unity]

5   *Africa's Submission to the Special Session of the United Nations General Assembly on Africa's Economic and Social Crisi*s, which was prepared jointly by the ECA and the OAU

6   *The United Nations Program of Action for African Economic Recovery and Development, 1986-1990 (UN-PAAERD).*

7   *Adjustment in Africa: Reforms, Results, and the Road Ahead* (A World Bank Policy Research Report, 1994).

8   Adedeji, A., Teriba, O. and P. Bugembe, eds., 1991. *The Challenge of African Economic Recovery and Development.* London, England: Frank Cass.

Table 2.4 lists policies pursued by specific institutions in regard to economic development in Africa. Although the list is not exhaustive, it reveals that many policies have been prescribed for dealing with Africa's economic problems.

CONCLUSION

It is obvious from the policy review presented in this chapter that sub-Saharan Africa's problems of economic underdevelopment are not due to a lack of economic policies. The discussion in this chapter reveals that there are hundreds of economic policies from which these countries can easily choose according to their beliefs and ideological leanings. Thus, one wonders what went wrong in the midst of all these policies based on sound economic theorizing. This is discussed in Chapter 3.

In view of these policies and programs for overcoming the problems of economic underdevelopment in sub-Saharan ACs, every scholar of economic development theory will agree that these countries did not lack policies. These policies were not all created by Africans themselves. Foreign experts and international economic advisors have all participated in the design and implementation of sub-Saharan Africa's economic development program. It is clear that the evolution of economic development theories has paved the way for the various economic development policies made for sub-Saharan ACs. Most of these policies were pursued with fervency and commitment. Yet they have not been very successful in dealing with the problems of economic underdevelopment in sub-Saharan ACs. This result brings to mind the question, "What went wrong?"

A person cannot be successful without taking frequent stock of his or her available resources and carefully planning how best to employ them. In the planning process, it is crucial to identify the most important issues and concentrate one's efforts and resources on them. If sub-Saharan ACs hope to achieve progress, it is time to reevaluate what has been done in the past and reconsider every theory on which they have based their policies and programs. Although orthodox and heterodox economic development theories are not necessarily wrong, their premises do not seem to reflect objectively the actual social, economic and political conditions in sub-Saharan Africa.

Chapter 3 presents in detail, from the HF perspective, analyses and discussions of why these policies have failed to solve the problems of economic underdevelopment in sub-Saharan ACs.

NOTES

1. For a detailed description and analysis of each of these theories, see Oman and Wignaraja (1991). A summary of these theories and models is also presented in Adjibolosoo (1994c, pp. 205-218).

2. Details on the World Bank's programs of action regarding economic development in sub-Saharan ACs can be found in their documents entitled (1) *Accelerated Development in sub-Saharan Africa: An Agenda for Action, 1981*; (2) *Sub-Saharan Africa: Progress Report on Development and Prospects and Programs, 1983*; (3) *Toward Sustained Development in sub-Saharan Africa: A Joint Program of Action, 1984*; and (4) *Adjustment in Africa: Reforms, Results, and The Road Ahead, 1994*.

3. Several other documents that discuss in detail economic policy development and planning for ACs include those of the Lome Convention; the Casablanca and Monrovia groups; the Economic Commission for Africa (ECA); the Lagos Plan of Action (LPA); the Final Act of Lagos (FAL); the African Development Bank (ADB); the Abuja Statement on Economic Recovery; the United States Assistance Strategy for Africa, as discussed by Haynes and Haykin (1991, pp. 254-269); and the Monrovia Declaration of Commitment (July, 1979).

3

The Human Factor and the Performance of Economic Policies and Programs in Sub-Saharan African Countries

INTRODUCTION

For many years, sub-Saharan Africans have desired to use their resources to improve welfare conditions. Many sub-Saharan African economic development plans, policies and programs have been based on existing orthodox economic development theories. Although similar policies have been effective in the DCs, the results of their application in sub-Saharan African countries (ACs) are discouraging. Orthodox economic development theories have led development economists and sub-Saharan African leaders to concentrate on irrelevant premises and variables and, by so doing, fail to recognize and focus programs and policies on factors that are relevant to the economic development process in sub-Saharan Africa.

The beginning of the 1960s raised hopes for sub-Saharan African economic development since many sub-Saharan ACs achieved political independence. The mood, aspirations, expectations and hopes were high and alive at that time. Research in social, economic and political issues in sub-Saharan Africa was mainly concerned with problems of economic development and cultural change. Attention was focused on economic development planning, political emancipation, economic development programs and social policies. These were expected not only to lead to structural transformation of underdeveloped sub-Saharan African economies but also to facilitate their economic development. Unfortunately, these programs have failed to achieve their intended goals. The objective of this chapter is, therefore, to explore and explain why the failure occurred.

CRISES IN SUB-SAHARAN AFRICAN ECONOMIC DEVELOPMENT

To date, regardless of the intensity of many development programs, very little has changed in sub-Saharan African economies. Food aid and technical, financial and other humanitarian assistance continue to flow in from the developed countries to sub-Saharan African nations. Yet problems of drought, famine, inflation, international debt and unemployment continue to escalate. The existing social infrastructure facilities such as health, education, transportation and many other institutional structures are relatively weak and inadequate. The sub-Saharan African international debt situation, in addition to other problems, has placed those economies in a vicious cycle of economic underdevelopment (on the issue of debt, consult Culpeper (1988); refer to Cheru (1990) for a discussion of debt, development and democracy; see also Akeredolu-Ale (1991) for an analysis of the human situation in Africa today). Worst of all, existing conventional economic development theories seem to be ineffective in providing relevant policies and corresponding programs for dealing with the problems.

Sub-Saharan African economic development is, therefore, in crisis. Failed rapid economic development planning; industrial projects, economic, social and political programs; and many other strategies paint a dismal picture. Sub-Saharan ACs have done poorly and run the risk of falling behind previously attained social, political, intellectual and economic standards.

The crucial questions, therefore, are as follows: Why have economic development and cultural change been so difficult to attain in many sub-Saharan ACs? What might have gone wrong? Is the diagnosis of the problems of sub-Saharan African economies by conventional economic development theorists wrong? Or have conventional economic development theorists applied the right medicine to the wrong disease, or vice versa? Or is this failure due to other factors that have not yet been fully identified and dealt with appropriately (Adjibolosoo, 1994c, p. 213)? "Where then does Africa go from here?" (Brokensha, 1974).

To conventional economic development theorists, the economic development process is a set of theories which, if diligently applied, must yield expected positive outcomes--economic growth with development. To sub-Saharan ACs, however, economic development still seems to be elusive and slippery regardless of their evangelical pursuit of policy and program prescriptions based on orthodox economic development theory. The application of conventional economic development theories in sub-Saharan African countries has, therefore, achieved very little success in accurately identifying the real underlying economic malaise plaguing sub-Saharan Africa. Economic, social and political policies and programs based on these theories have therefore not provided true and lasting solutions to sub-Saharan Africa's problems of economic underdevelopment. The pursuit of socialistic policies and programs has also not brought any lasting gains. Recent events regarding socialism in the dismantled Soviet Union have revealed the plight of the socialist model of economic development (McCord and McCord, 1986, pp. 91-92).

Although orthodox economic development theories are not necessarily wrong, the fact remains that their resulting policies have apparently failed to solve sub-Saharan African economic problems. In my view, however, if the premises of conventional economic development theories are modified to incorporate and reflect the social, economic, intellectual and political conditions that actually exist in sub-Saharan ACs, a pathway to economic development and cultural change may be opened to them (Adjibolosoo, 1994c, p. 215). The pertinent question, however, is "How can this be successfully achieved?"

To be successful in this process, such reformulated theories must concentrate on the essential role of the human factor (HF), which has hitherto been ignored by orthodox economic development theorists, in economic development planning and policy making in sub-Saharan Africa.

THE DEFINITION OF THE HUMAN FACTOR

Every society has its business, political, economic and social goals and objectives. These objectives may be defined and enshrined in social, economic and political institutions. The procedures for executing these are usually specified in national economic development plans. The organization of these institutions, however, requires the appropriate human qualities and/or characteristics (i.e., the HF) to function as expected.

The HF term, as used in this chapter, "refers to a spectrum of personality characteristics and other dimensions of human performance that enable social, economic and political institutions to function and remain functional, over time. Such dimensions sustain the workings and application of the rule of law, political harmony, a disciplined labor force, just legal systems, respect for human dignity and the sanctity of life, social welfare, and so on. As is often the case, no social, economic or political institutions can function effectively without being upheld by a network of committed persons who stand firmly by them. Such persons must strongly believe in and continually affirm the ideals of society" (Adjibolosoo, 1994a, p. 26).

The HF term is, therefore, defined as those unique characteristics and qualities of the human personality that determine whether the labor force will or will not be successful in accomplishing set goals and objectives. These unique charateristics include those listed in the preceding paragraph and the human ability to use effectively and apply acquired knowledge and information to identify and solve everyday problems. In this process of knowledge and information acquisition and its application to achieve results, the people must exhibit responsibility in leadership, dedication through commitment, resourcefulness in the use of available resources, resilience and tolerance in adversity, inventiveness, innovativeness and imagination in relation to their chosen vision and accountability through service. The absence of this knowledge and other relevant components of the HF makes it extremely difficult for sub-Saharan ACs to grow and develop in the social, economic and political sense. When people of sub-Saharan ACs search for and acquire the relevant knowledge and act on it, they will be placed on a sound footing for social, economic and political maturation and economic growth and development (Adjibolosoo, 1993a, p. 143).

This implies that the development of human qualities and/or characteristics does not necessarily refer to mere human resource development and human capital acquisition through education and training. To be productive, the people of a nation must also acquire unique human qualities and/or characteristics that encourage and promote economic progress (such as integrity, discipline, dedication, responsibility, diligence, insightfulness, accountability and the like). It is these attributes and many others akin to them that contribute to a successful or unsuccessful utilization of acquired knowledge and skills--human capital--for articulating and fostering the economic development process of nations. Human capital is, therefore, a small segment of the HF. Yet sub-Saharan ACs have emphasized human capital acquisition rather than HF development. This costly mistake must be corrected immediately to avert any further disappointments and/or permanent social, economic and political disaster in the region.

THE COMPOSITION OF THE HUMAN FACTOR

Societies that wish to achieve economic development must assist their people to acquire the whole HF necessary for economic progress. In what follows, I present a detailed discussion of the various components of the HF. The six primary components of the HF are spiritual capital, moral capital, aesthetic capital, human capital, human abilities and human potentials. Each of these aspects will be defined and explained through relevant examples. As has been pointed out elsewhere, the HF constitutes the intangible asset or liability of humanity. A properly developed HF animates, guides and encourages people to perform specific functions that are required of them in their tasks assigned by society.

Spiritual Capital

Spiritual capital is the aspect of the human personality that possesses the capability to be in tune with the universal laws and principles of human life. These laws and principles state the truth regarding how humanity must live if it is to achieve the "good and abundant life" in every regard. Spiritual capital provides insights into the human condition that the five senses are unable to grasp and bring forth. It furnishes the individual with more advanced capabilities to create, to invent, to innovate and to develop techniques and/or procedures for dealing with the limitations of the human intellect. The human spirit, when in tune with the universal laws and principles of human life, will neither be broken nor denied the power to reach out to its vision, goals, ideals, etc. In his bestselling book *The Seven Habits of Highly Effective People*, Stephen Covey (1989, p. 292) noted that "the spiritual dimension is your core, your center, your commitment to your value system. Its a very private area of life and a supremely important one." It is the seat of human efficiency and effectiveness in job performance and task accomplishment. A poorly developed spiritual capital due to either conscious or unconscious neglect can deny a society the ability to create a humane and productive environment for its inhabitants. James and James (1991, p. 34) noted that

> increasing numbers of people are becoming aware of how they have ignored, denied, or been out of touch with the spiritual part of themselves and other sources of power available to them. They have lost the sense of curiosity and wonder about the spiritual dimension of life. It's almost as if they were standing on the shore of a crystal-clear stream, thirsty yet not knowing how or where to quench their thirst.

Spiritual capital furnishes the individual with the will to pursue and carry out what is true in order to complete tasks effectively. Sandin (1992, pp. 232-235) noted that "doing the truth is the identifying mark of spiritual wholeness. The goal of spiritual education is obedience to the truth; its outcome is living the truth. . . . A society that fails to grasp the significance of the spiritual dimension of life, as Paul Nash warns, will achieve only a stunted humanity. . . . If education does not result in spiritual [capital] formation, it is [a] bad investment."

Moral Capital

Moral capital represents habits and attitudes of the human heart that are based on principles relating to right or wrong. It refers to the qualities individuals possess that lead them to conform or not to conform to ethical principles and standards of conduct. The voice of the human conscience usually functions as part of a person's moral capital. The constituents of moral capital are diverse and include integrity, humility, sincerity, charity, courtesy, patience, faithfulness, sensitivity, purity, honesty, kindness, justice, tolerance, forgiveness, flexibility, collegiality, truthfulness, fidelity and many others. Moral capital is crucial to the economic development process in that it furnishes the individual with the ability to perceive principles and universal laws as the primary foundation for acceptable or unacceptable human behavior and action. Both spiritual and moral capital humanize humanity.

Aesthetic Capital

Aesthetic capital implies the possession of a strong sense of and love for beauty. It includes a strong passion for music, drama, dance and for other artistic capacities (imagination, inventiveness, innovation and creativity are strong components). Aesthetic capital, like the other components of the HF, requires the continuing renewal and development of the human mind and the nurture of human perceptiveness. When fully developed, it furnishes people both with the ability to be appreciative of beauty and truth and the skills to judge between what is good and acceptable and what is not.

Human Capital

From the human capital theory perspective, human capital is usually defined as the know-how and the skills that are acquired by men and women, are used to enhance human productivity, and have market value. Human capital is made up of technical, conceptual, intellectual, analytic and communications skills. An example of properly developed human capital is the individual with knowledge (gained from the study of academic disciplines, human experiences, revelation, etc.), understanding, astuteness and intelligence or aptitude. Physical well-being and emotional health are integral parts of human capital, as well.

Human Abilities

Human abilities constitute the power or capacity of an individual to undertake projects competently or effectively perform tasks requiring mental and physical effort. These are the acquired or naturally endowed human abilities necessary to, but not alone sufficient for, successfully performing assigned tasks and/or effectively undertaking and engaging in productive activities. Human abilities enable people who possess them to execute excellently given duties and functions when these abilities are working in conjunction with other components of the HF. They are a necessary component of the effective and efficient utilization of acquired human capital. Human abilities include wisdom, vision, commitment, devotion, dedication, determination, diligence, courage, accountability, judgment, responsibility, reasoning, competence, interest, motivation, credibility, human energy, optimism, perseverance, endurance, self-control, objectivity, reliability, adaptability, alertness and many other such human attributes.

Human Potentials

Human potentials are the human talents that may or may not be harnessed and employed for human-centered development. These may be referred to as the unused dimensions of the HF. Through imagination, humans can visualize uncreated worlds of potentials. Covey (1989, p. 107) suggested that "through conscience, we can come in contact with universal laws or principles with our own singular talents and avenues of contribution, and with the personal guidelines within which we can most effectively develop them." The human potential can only be developed to its fullest degree when the individual has acquireded significant levels of both spiritual and moral capital. Its role in the economic development process is critical.

It is critical that nations see to the total development of the HF. As pointed out elsewhere in this book, human-centered development will not happen in the absense of the relevant HF.

THE RELEVANCE OF THE INTERACTION
AMONG HF COMPONENTS

These human qualities and characteristics are concepts in motion. Individuals will either accumulate or decumulate each quality through the various stages of their lives. Although the death of an individual may terminate the existence of the individual's qualities and characteristics, their indirect influence may remain perpetually.

Although there may be a tendency to view moral and spiritual capital as one, they must be separated because although a strongly developed spiritual capital will automatically imply the acquisition of a significant amount of moral capital, the reverse is not necessarily true. That is, acquired moral capital does not necessarily imply spiritual capital. This view implies that spiritual capital encompasses moral capital in its entirety within the individual.

Spiritual and moral capital must be present for both human and aesthetic capital to function well. Although spiritual capital can be sufficient alone for the effective use of both human and aesthetic capital, moral capital is not always sufficient alone. The acquisition of both spiritual and moral capital may lead the individual to identify the necessary principle-centered rather than feelings-centered value system. It is often the case that those whose lives are built around universal ethical principles and standards are individuals who are able to work and successfully complete tasks without extensive supervision. In the words of Swindoll (1987, p. 123), these are people "who model excellence when no one is looking or for that matter when half the world is looking."

A society whose labor force has developed the HF will achieve significant levels of resource productivity without necessitating the use of extensive resources for monitoring the labor force or for productivity enhancement techniques. This labor force will be driven by the universal principles engendered by and embedded in the society's acquired spiritual capital, moral capital and human abilities. The mere acquisition of human capital is insufficient to equip the individual to be always effective in this regard; thus, we sometimes observe people who are rich in human capital yet are not able to function effectively and efficiently.

Excellence in the use of both human and aesthetic capital requires the acquisition of both spiritual and moral capital. Although some individuals may be able to perform without spiritual and moral capital (probably due to their richness in human capital), their performance levels will be suboptimal; their levels of productivity and their performance records will fall short of their expected potentials. The presence of both spiritual and moral capital creates an environment in which human abilities can excel; this is crucial for HF effectiveness. Human abilities can rarely be fully developed in the absence of both spiritual and moral capital.

The preceding discussions reveal that the mere acquisition of both human and aesthetic capital may not necessarily lead to the high human performance required for economic development and industrial progress. Societies that are wealthy in human and aesthetic capital and yet are bankrupt in the areas of spiritual and moral capital will not develop a labor force rich in human abilities. Without properly developed spiritual and moral capital, acquired human abilities can be misused. Spiritual and moral capital cannot be accurately measured; they may, however, be experienced by individuals and observed in those who possess them.

The whole development of the HF is, therefore, necessary for continuing human progress and survival and is required for long-lasting economic development and established business success. The neglect of any one of the components of the HF may lead to severe problems of economic underdevelopment and frequent business losses and/or failures. Many developing countries have in the past concentrated on the development of both human and aesthetic capital while neglecting the other components of the HF. Economic development has, therefore, been limited. In past years, the United States, Canada, Britain and many other Western developed countries paid serious attention to HF development and were successful in attaining high levels of economic growth and development. Advanced countries that are presently depreciating both their spiritual and moral capital will fail to maintain their human abilities and will be faced with the danger of economic and industrial decline in the long run. In this regard, the United States, Canada, the United Kingdom, Japan, Germany and many others run the risk of falling victim to the syndrome of HF underdevelopment unless they take the necessary steps to ensure that HF development remains a priority in their industrialization programs.

The direction an individual's economic behavior will take will be impacted by his or her personal level of both spiritual and moral capital development. Those who are poor in spiritual and moral capital are the people whose behaviors (social, economic, political, etc.) are strongly affected and propelled by selfish interests in personal riches and fame; these types of behaviors, however, lead to economic underdevelopment for their own society. Although the many variables that influence human behavior can include money, culture, prestige and self-actualization, people poor in spiritual and moral capital usually focus on money and prestige. Thus, as an individual acquires more and more spiritual and moral capital, his or her thinking, character and actions (behavior) will be based more and more on the long-lasting principles of human life (such as integrity, justice, equity, fairness, love, sanctity of life, etc.) rather than on temporal self-aggrandizement. In societies in which the basic necessities of life are not easy to acquire, human behavior is usually driven by the desire to satisfy these needs. When the satisfaction of these needs is pursued solely with self-gratification in focus, the economic development program may suffer severe setbacks, especially when the environment and opportunities for negative rent-seeking attitudes are created and people engage in activities that would exert a negative impact on efficient resource allocation and hence the general economic growth and social welfare.

It is possible for people to spend large amounts of financial resources to acquire human capital yet become unwilling to participate in the labor market. Although explanations of this observed phenomenon may vary from person to person and from culture to culture, it can be argued in general that such people, *ceteris paribus*, are usually severely bankrupt of several other components of the HF. In a few cases, people experience physical handicaps that may lead to the observed behavior. An improperly developed HF will create hindrances on the road to human progress.

The competitive advantage of such countries as Japan, Germany, the United States, Hong Kong, Singapore, South Korea, Malaysia and many others is determined by the existing level of the HF acquired by the labor force. The abundance of capital, skilled labor, advanced technology, sound economic policies and/or programs and other natural resources does not necessarily imply that a country will simultaneously experience economic growth and development (see a detailed discussion of this issue in Chapter 5).

The developed countries have for many years concentrated on the development of the necessary human qualities and/or characteristics. The pursuit of HF development in these countries suggests that the DCs realized very early the important role the people of a nation must play in the nation's economic development program. As I have discussed elsewhere,

> Requirements for economic development include primary and secondary factors. The secondary factors are natural resources, human resources, capital, and infrastructure. The primary factors are the Human Factor needs: honest and law abiding people, with self-discipline, vision, and dedication to development. While the availability of secondary factors is necessary, but not sufficient, for development, the existence of primary factors is necessary and sufficient for development. The DCs are rich in primary factors and are developed; ACs are rich in secondary factors but lack the primary factors, and are underdeveloped. (Adjibolosoo, 1994c, p. 215)

Sub-Saharan African countries have not been able to prepare their people for the desired economic development program. The main reasons for this failure are discussed in Chapter 4. As pointed out earlier, the primary question of major concern is "What is the relevant HF possessed by the people in the DCs and the Newly Industrializing South-East Asian countries that the sub-Saharan African labor force lacks and needs to develop?" (Adjibolosoo, 1993a, p. 143). It is my belief that the HF must be taken into account if we are to understand the complex and dynamic processes by which sub-Saharan African societies evolve and develop. We need to comprehend the role and relevance of the HF in the economic development process if the joint African-Western World effort to achieve economic development and cultural change in sub-Saharan ACs is to be successful. Evolving sub-Saharan African economic, social, and political institutions require the appropriate HF to function efficiently and effectively. Sub-Saharan African economic development policies and programs require the relevant HF that can help Africans create and innovate, take constructive and productive initiatives, diagnose correctly and determine the problems of economic underdevelopment and search for appropriate solutions. These unique human characteristics and/or qualities always influence a society's ability to achieve the goals and objectives of its economic development program. Their continuing neglect or absence will always spell doom for the economic development process.

For several decades, however, many sub-Saharan ACs and their well-known foreign expert advisors have not been successful in recognizing and developing the relevant HF for managing national resources, economic development programs, economic policies and the political process. Due to this failure, external assistance has been rendered ineffectual. This observation is hardly ever recognized and confronted. It is time to right this wrong and effectively redirect sub-Saharan Africa's economic development policy and program.

THE INTERDEPENDENCE BETWEEN THE HF AND OTHER RESOURCES

The relationship and interdependence between the HF and other national resouces is illustrated in Figure 3.1, in which the various factors that impact on economic development are grouped into two categories: the HF and economic factors. Whether a country develops economically or not is determined by the degree of continuous interaction among these factors (Adjibolosoo, 1994a, pp. 27-31). If the continuing interaction among these factors proves useful to the process of economic development, the nation will experience economic progress; otherwise, economic underdevelopment will result. Unfortunately, in planning economic development programs for sub-Saharan ACs, postcolonial African leaders and their international economic development planning experts and consultants have glossed over the crucial fact that no economic development program can be effectively executed without properly developed HF. In many cases, the focus was on human capital acquisition (often referred to as human resources development) that is encompassed in the HF.

The HF approach to economic development in sub-Saharan ACs is presented diagrammatically in Figure 3.2. This approach maintains that no sub-Saharan African countries can attain economic development without developing first the necessary HF. If the people in any country lack the necessary characteristics and/or qualities that are relevant to economic development--and this would be a liability--that country will experience extensive problems in its economic development program. As these problems increase, compound and become intricately complicated, the country will be locked in a vicious cycle of economic underdevelopment. A more detailed study of Figure 3.2 reveals that

FIGURE 3.1
THE FACTOR MIX AND COOPERATION FOR ECONOMIC DEVELOPMENT

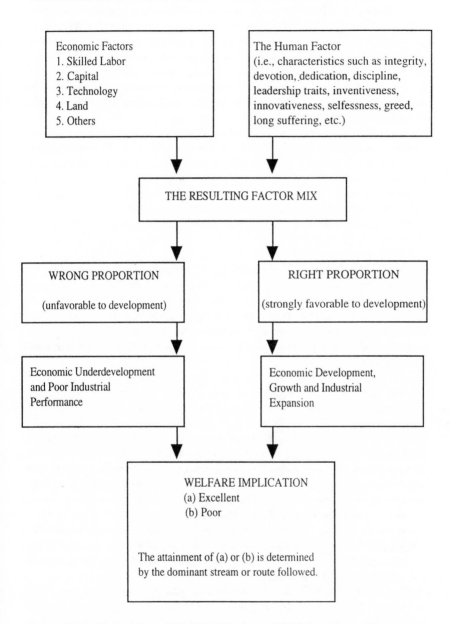

Source: Ezeala-Harrison, F. and S.B-S.K. Adjibolosoo. 1994. *Perspectives on Economic Development in Africa.* New York: Praeger (p. 28)

if sub-Saharan ACs can change the state of their poorly developed HF and are willing to channel resources into developing programs to produce the required HF, they will begin to experience economic growth and development over time.

If, however, the relevant HF is not developed, several problems will be created. These difficulties will act as severe hindrances to the economic development process. The unavailability of the necessary HF also defeats the purposes of economic development planning and policy making. This is one of the major reasons why many policies and programs have failed in the past in sub-Saharan Africa. The outcomes are usually social rent-seeking practices that destroy rather than promote economic progress. A few of these practices[1] are discussed in Chapter 4. In what follows, I discuss how the failure to focus on and develop the HF in sub-Saharan Africa led to sound but ineffective economic policies and programs.

THE PERFORMANCE OF ECONOMIC POLICIES AND PROGRAMS

As has been documented and discussed elsewhere in the sub-Saharan African economic development literature, policies pursued by various interest groups have not successfully solved sub-Saharan Africa's problems of economic underdevelopment. In what follows, a detailed analysis of why policies and programs failed (and still do fail) in sub-Saharan Africa is presented--especially those policies pursued by the IMF and the World Bank. Other policies and programs discussed are those of the first-generation African leaders and the United Nations.

The Inadequacy of the IMF and World Bank Policies

The IMF and the World Bank focus mostly on policies that would facilitate the production of tradeable items by sub-Saharan ACs for sale in the global marketplace. For decades, this policy has enslaved sub-Saharan Africans and established their economies as major producers of single agricultural cash crops for which they possess conducive climates, although they have no domestic uses for these crops. Resources are usually moved from the production of non-tradeables to the production of tradeables (Spooner and Smith, 1991, p. 14). The market system is deemed to provide the necessary price signals and/or incentives for the efficient allocation of scarce resources between the production of tradeables and nontradeables.

These IMF-World Bank structural adjustment and stabilization policies encourage and strengthen the dependency of sub-Saharan African economies on those of the developmentally advanced countries. Not only do these policies create continuous shortages of domestic staples; they also erect severe upward pressure on their prices and, therefore, exacerbate continuing internal inflation.

FIGURE 3.2
EXPLAINING ECONOMIC PERFORMANCE IN AFRICAN COUNTRIES

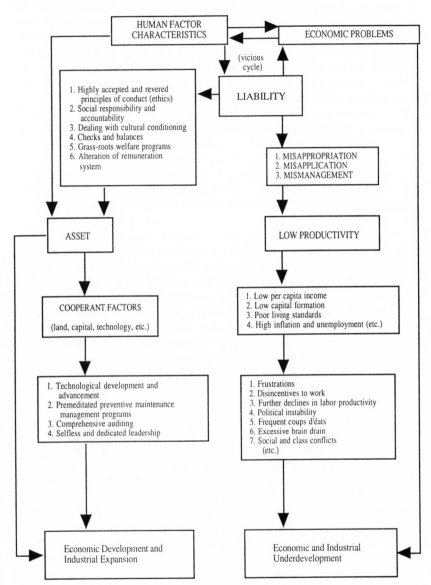

Source: Ezeala-Harrison, F. and S.B-S.K. Adjibolosoo. 1994. *Perspectives on Economic Development in Africa.* New York: Praeger (P. 29)

As long as sub-Saharan African economies continue to service the economies of the DCs, they will remain perpetual hewers of wood and drawers of water. These handicaps will continue to manifest themselves in shortages, inflation, hunger and hence sub-Saharan Africa's inability to develop. Viewing development issues from the perspective of the HF approach to economic development, therefore, Bauer (1984, p. 5) is incorrect to have argued that peasants will experience a great prosperity if they respond to market incentives and produce millions of acres of cash crops. Surely, they produce huge quantities of cash crops and yet starve not only because they receive very low prices for their goods in the world market but also because they neglect the production of staples for domestic consumption.It is now time for sub-Saharan ACs to change course and take control of their economic affairs, tailoring nationwide production and consumption activities toward the production of nontradeables for domestic use and gradually weaning themselves of the production and export of tradeables--cocoa, coffee, sisal, rubber, tobacco and many others. It is deceptive to think that sub-Saharan ACs can gain sufficient foreign exchange resources through the production and sale of a few tradeable goods. They never achieved this in the past and will not in the future if the relevant steps are not taken to correct past oversights.

The production of nontradeable goods in sub-Saharan ACs has the potential for encouraging domestic processing and manufacturing of these items for the domestic market.[2] The IMF-World Bank structural adjustment and stabilization policies turn these issues head over heels. The fruit of the sub-Saharan African labor is exported abroad and sold at prices that are far below the true value of resources and human energy spent by the peasants to produce the tradeables. This is one major source of the growing debt burden sub-Saharan ACs carry today. Their produce sold in the global marketplace is unable to fetch sufficient foreign exchange to help pay for all funds borrowed for the production of tradeables and/or to rehabilitate other existing programs.

President J. J. Rawlings' interview with *Africa Report* substantiates this point. To the question "It is common knowledge that the World Bank and IMF consider Ghana the star pupil in economic reform, but how do you see your country's economic efforts over the past decade? Would you do things differently if you could start over again?", President J. J. Rawlings replied as follows:

> No, I wouldn't do things differently, in terms of general policies and fiscal measures, but I would hope to see us maximizing the gains from all the sacrifices our people have made through stricter and more efficient management. As regards our performance over the last decade, I think we could have achieved even more if the international economic order was favorable. For example, we tripled production in certain export commodities only to earn less in revenue owing to falling commodity prices.[3]

As is obvious from the view expressed by President J. J. Rawlings, structural adjustment and stabilization policies hold little promise for economic success in sub-Saharan ACs.

This view suggests that the visible hands of the IMF and the World Bank actually promote inefficiencies in sub-Saharan African economies by creating strong artificial signals that mislead the real invisible hand whose natural objective, I am convinced, is to foster self-sustaining and self-sufficient sub-Saharan African economies. Stabilization and structural adjustment policies usually lead to the discontinuation of the production of the necessary domestic staples.

Sub-Saharan African governments have to realize that their basic mandate is to create the environment within which their citizens can produce sufficient goods to satisfy domestic demands. If all resources that have already been poured into producing tradeables (since independence) had been poured into HF development, the production and, if possible, the processing of local staples for domestic consumption, sub-Saharan ACs would not have continued until today to experience acute food shortages. Sub-Saharan Africans must view economic growth and development in terms of the increasing ability of their economies to support growing domestic need for HF development, food, clothing, shelter and belongingness. Other things will follow later.

Although international trade may be beneficial, sub-Saharan Africans must not continue to serve as mere appendages to the economies of advanced countries. My view, unlike the views of the IMF and the World Bank, is that the term *structural adjustment* implies the artifical manipulation and twisting of existing production structures of sub-Saharan African economies by the visible hands of the IMF and the World Bank to serve the advanced countries' economies better than they would those of sub-Saharan ACs. This, contrary to popular opinion, is tantamount to gross inefficiency on the part of sub-Saharan African economies because, by responding favorably to these visible draconian hands, sub-Saharan ACs fail miserably to eliminate shortages in the production of domestic staples for home consumption. In consonance with the aforementioned observations about IMF-World Bank policies, it can also be argued that structural adjustment and stabilization policies have the tendency to keep sub-Saharan ACs in perpetual debt servitude and/or bondage. Why then must sub-Saharan ACs borrow to produce commodities from whose sale they will hardly benefit? This question demands answers, and I believe that only sub-Saharan Africans can provide themselves with the true answers to it.

The IMF and World Bank are perpetually caught up in protecting their hegemony over the sub-Saharan African financial world and economic conditions and are excessively paternalistic in determining for sub-Saharan ACs what they (the IMF and the World Bank) believe is good for them (sub-Saharan ACs). They are much more concerned about the financial interests of advanced countries' financial institutions and/or creditors than they are in the recovery of stagnating sub-Saharan African economies and declining human welfare. They are, therefore, unable to perceive that their structural adjustment and stabilization policies will always fail to establish the necessary and sufficient conditions for long-term sub-Saharan African economic recovery (except that their resources are used for continuing HF development in sub-Saharan Africa).

A critical study of the various stabilization and structural adjustment policies pursued unrelentingly by the IMF and the World Bank in sub-Saharan ACs suggests that the main ingredients for economic development--the HF and the appointment, education and training[4] of African leadership--are usually not included. There is no known IMF-World Bank policy aimed at the development of the necessary HF in sub-Saharan Africa. This attitude is no different from that adopted by the colonial administrators in the colonial era (see details in Chapter 4).

A careful analysis of the IMF and World Bank policies for sub-Saharan ACs reveals that at least four major conclusions can be drawn. First, either the IMF and the World Bank are not aware of the role of the HF in economic development programs of nations; or, although they know, since the economic development of sub-Saharan African countries is neither in their short-run nor long-run interest, they do not deem it necessary to develop the required HF in the region. Second, the IMF and the World Bank are solely engrossed in how sub-Saharan ACs can generate sufficiently large domestic primary resources to sell in global markets (usually underpriced) and either pay in full (or service) their international debts or support the industrial program in the DCs. This is a feasible proposition because in all sub-Saharan ACs, output in the primary (agricultural) sector is generated by laborers who have little formal education. Third, the IMF and the World Bank's policies and programs are not good enough to bring about real and permanent improvements in economic progress and human welfare in sub-Saharan ACs. Fourth, the IMF and the World Bank have already concluded that sub-Saharan ACs must neither be assisted to achieve technological progress nor be permitted to attain domestic and/or regional self-sufficiency on their own.

It is therefore not surprising that the IMF and the World Bank always exert their paternalistic influence over sub-Saharan ACs, play one against the others and continue to impose structural adjustment and stabilization policies on them. Those who wish to dispute this argument have to explain first why these financial institutions still pursue policies and programs that will not have any long-term positive impacts on sub-Saharan African economies.

The failure of the IMF-World Bank stabilization and structural adjustment policies in sub-Saharan ACs is due to those institutions' myopia in recognizing that sub-Saharan ACs require a well-groomed people with acquired positive human qualities and/or characteristics to manage their economic development plans, policies, programs and process. Many scholars have observed that the IMF-World Bank stabilization policies have been aimed at solving fiscal deficits and current account disequilibria. As such, they are inadequate for the attainment of continuing and long-lasting economic recovery.

Stewart (1992, p. 317) noted that a detailed analysis of structural adjustment loans given to sub-Saharan Africa concentrated on policies of trade, finance of government activities and administration, public enterprises, agriculture and support of fiscal policies. Social policy was given a low priority in the 1980s. Unfortunately, the structural adjustment and stabilization policies of the IMF and the World Bank have not achieved any significant changes in health, HF development, rural infrastructure, human welfare, nutrition and so on. These results reveal that their policies in the long run defeat the purposes of economic development planning and policy making.

Examples of resulting negative impacts of IMF-World Bank stabilization and structural adjustment policies are evident in Niger, Tanzania and Burkina Faso (i.e., in the case of education); Tanzania, Zambia, Burkina Faso, Niger and Zimbabwe (i.e., in the case of health); and Niger, Burkina Faso, Ghana, Malawi and Tanzania (i.e., in the case of rural infrastructure) (Mosley and Smith, 1989; Stewart, 1992). In Ghana, Kenya, Malawi and Tanzania, financial reforms engineered at the IMF-World Bank only led to huge increases in interest rates and failed to produce increased domestic savings and investment growth (Helleiner, 1992; Stewart, 1992). Stewart (1992, p. 322) noted further that

comparison of Burkina Faso, which followed a *self-imposed* adjustment program, and Tanzania, which follwed an orthodox package, is instructive. Between 1980 and 1987 Burkina Faso raised real per capita government expenditure by 35 per cent by increasing tax and expenditure ratios, while per capita income was growing. Meanwhile, real per capita government expenditure in Tanzania dropped by 35 percent, with falling per capita incomes and a sharply falling expenditure ration. In Burkina Faso investment rose by 4.3 per cent per year between 1980 and 1988, while it remained virtually stagnant in Tanzania.

Surely, the IMF and the World Bank have not achieved great successes with their structural adjustment and stabilization policies in sub-Saharan Africa.[5] There is, therefore, the need for changes in policies and programs to develop the primary requisite for development, the HF.

Policy Failure and the First-Generation African Leaders

In the same manner, first-generation sub-Saharan African leaders have also failed to help their countries develop because they could not see clearly what is needed to be done to achieve progress in sub-Saharan Africa. Many of them were interested only in their prestigious leadership positions and did everything necessary to maintain power and yet very little to promote economic growth and development. Their efforts, policies and programs were not only misguided but also lacked purpose, direction, continuity and commitment. Unfortunately, a few years into their term of office, all first-generation sub-Saharan African leaders failed to perceive that they did not have what it takes to attain economic development. Thus, instead of relinquishing their holds on leadership roles, many of them hung onto power, hoping that by chance they would lead their nations out of existing economic stagnation. To cover their failure and gross inefficiency, most of them proclaimed themselves to be life presidents and, therefore, could neither be deposed nor challenged except through violently bloody and economically destructive *coups d'etat*. Although some of them were finally overthrown by the military, few were thrown out through ballots and the rest have reigned for no less than three decades, having little to show as their lasting achievement. They have contributed toward the continued bankrupting of their fellow citizens. The plight of their successors in subsequent years is not different. This observation seems to suggest that the current African leadership is failing to make sufficient use of the examples of its predecessors.

The Damaging Consequencies of UN Policies and Programs

Commenting on the United Nations development strategies for the last two decades for the developing countries, Adedeji (1989, p. 273) observed that

perhaps the most damaging consequence of the way the strategies for the first two decades were designed was that they lent authority to a number of dubious maxims of economic development and deferred more meaningful and realistic examination of how growth, structural change and improvements of standards of living of the mass of the populations of the Third World can be pursued within a framework of international co-operation and adjustment.

Whatever the case, the damage has already been done and sub-Saharan Africans must rise to the task of nation building and deal with the actual problems of economic underdevelopment and those created through HF decay and bad policy formulation and implementation.

QUESTIONING EXISTING PREMISES AND THINKING

Regardless of the intensity of past attempts to solve the problems of economic underdevelopment, there is a crisis in economic development policy making, planning and programming in sub-Saharan Africa. Since the beginning of the twentieth century, many sub-Saharan ACs have tried to achieve industrial progress without success. The failure of import substitution industrialization, operation feed yourself, infrastructure development, improving the balance of payments situation, reducing the size of external debt, inflation control, rural and urban job creation, increasing average labor productivity and many other programs is increasingly revealing that policies based on orthodox and heterodox economic development thinking have been unable to address the economic underdevelopment nightmare in sub-Saharan Africa (Adjibolosoo, 1994c).

This brings many questions to mind. Why have ACs found it difficult to attain industrial progress despite assistance from experts of conventional economic development theory? Are the paths of economic progress so obscure that sub-Saharan ACs cannot find them? Do the basic premises of orthodox economic development thinking inappropriately characterize the true conditions prevailing in sub-Saharan Africa? If so, what then are conventional economic development thinkers and policy makers missing? In what ways can positive changes occur?

In search of answers to these questions, it is crucial to note that orthodox and heterodox economic development theories are founded on many assumptions that are typical of Western advanced countries. These theories are formulated on the premises of certain givens, and, therefore, the "all things are equal" assumption. For example, these theories are based on Western social ethos; individual and corporate work ethics, a well-developed labor force that possesses the necessary HF; the availability of appropriate social, economic and political institutions; and so on (Adjibolosoo, 1994c). I am, therefore, arguing that the failure of economic development programs in sub-Saharan Africa is neither due to the lack of resources nor the inability to formulate and pursue economic development planning and policies. Many sub-Saharan ACs have had the privilege of inviting reputable economic development theorists from the DCs who are assigned the tasks of identifying, evaluating and prescribing appropriate action plans to pull their economies out of economic development decadence. IMF and World Bank experts and economic development gurus and policy makers are on daily economic rescue missions to sub-Saharan ACs. They have done so for several decades. Yet the challenges are not being met; nor are the problems being dealt with effectively. They are, therefore, definitely missing something of great importance: the HF.

It is often assumed "that among the most important determinants [of increased output in advanced economies] are advances in technology, improvements in organization at both the macro and micro levels (including so-called economies of scale), and especially increased investments in human capital" (Cameron, 1993, p. 13). This belief is, however, incorrect from the perspective of the HF approach to economic development. These factors have not in themselves contributed to growth in the DCs. The most important factor that made increased productivity of these inputs possible is the available HF, the highly unrecognized and terribly neglected dimension of sub-Saharan Africa's economic development program. Corina et al. (1992, p. 1) painted a picture of the African condition as follows:

After two decades of remarkable, if uneven, progress, improvements in the welfare of African children started to falter toward the end of the 1970s. The 1980s witnessed a further deterioration in the economic and social conditions of most households in sub-Saharan Africa, which was starkly reflected in negative trends in income per capita, investment rates, declining social service delivery and child welfare. Despite the radical policy reforms introduced in the 1980s, prospects for the rest of the century remain dismal in the view of most observers, not least for the continued squeeze on the external flow of resources to Africa and the rapid spread of AIDS. However, events which have occurred over the last two years and which are apparently only tenuously connected to Africa's economic fate may, in fact, be the bedrock of profound, positive changes in the environment within which policies are framed in Africa.

If one were to provide a general classification of the problems described by Cornia et al., one would be wrong if one classified them under other groupings apart from that of HF deficiencies. These problems have been viewed and dealt with from wrong angles--never before seen as results of HF deficiencies. Structural adjustment programs and stabilization policies have been ineffective because they fail to perceive properly the true sources of sub-Saharan Africa's problems of economic underdevelopment.

It is clear from the policy mosaic discussed in Chapter 2 that African governments, the World Bank, the IMF, the OAU, the Economic Commission for Africa (ECA), the African Development Bank (ADB) and many other development-oriented agencies have failed to identify the actual problem of economic underdevelopment in sub-Saharan Africa. Yes, they all have spent huge sums of resources on research, policies, planning, programs, conferences, seminars, roundtable discussions, projects and so on. *Yes,* they seem to be concerned about sub-Saharan African people's welfare and economic progress. Yet their policy prescriptions are shallow, inadequate and strongly ineffective. The resulting outcomes of such policy formulation and implementation continue to cast severe doubts on the orthodox development wisdom and strategies. They don't seem to get it right!

Why is it that, although the inescapable stylized facts and historical records are evidence of this failure, these institutions still continue to pursue similar policies and programs? Can they not perceive and understand the glaring facts and historical evidence? It is not a question of which policies or programs that will work. The real question is "What will it take to have policies, plans and programs work successfully in sub-Saharan Africa?"

From the perspective of the HF approach to economic development, the search for solutions to sub-Saharan Africa's problems of economic underdevelopment must focus on the level of HF development. Sub-Saharan African countries do not need any more new economic models and theories to explain why they are where they are today. There is a myriad of such nebulous theories already in existence. It is now time to find out why orthodox economic development modeling, policy making and program implementation have failed in the past. This search, if continued in the paradigm of orthodox economic development theorizing (as has been the case in the last half century), is bound to lead to conclusions whose resulting policies and programs will drag sub-Saharan ACs into even deeper problems of economic underdevelopment in the coming years.

Merely encouraging sub-Saharan ACs to put policies and programs in place to encourage and facilitate the inflow of overseas financial resources and other kinds of capital, to correct economic distortions, to create incentives for both domestic and foreign entrepreneurs and venture capitalists and to call for improvements in the global economic environment are all inadequate measures for dealing with problems of economic underdevelopment. To continue with these methods, which failed in the past, would demonstrate that the perpetrators are not aware of past history and that they do not know what it will take to salvage declining sub-Saharan African economies. To look continually for solutions to the problems from elsewhere is to be under a global economic delusion. Sub-Saharan Africans and other developing countries tried in the 1960s and 1970s to push for a New International Economic Order (NIEO), improved access to the markets of the advanced countries, continuing technical assistance and many other ostensibly desirable goals but have failed to achieve the goals of their economic development plans.

Since these policy attempts did not succeed in the past, what has changed in the international economic, social and political environments to prove that they will work in the 1990s and in the twenty-first century? Since every country is bound to pursue its own policies that are aimed at improving the welfare of its people, why must advanced countries pursue policies that are probably bound to defeat this purpose? Since the developed countries will not implement policies that will be perceived as having the potential to undermine the goals of their national development programs, sub-Saharan Africans must realize that any efforts made to convince them to pursue certain policies will be a total failure. It will be more effective and productive in the long run to spend existing resources to develop the necessary HF that will help these countries rise out of their economic stagnation. Progress attained in this manner will benefit the global community.

AGREEMENT AND DISAGREEMENT AMONG DEVELOPMENT ECONOMISTS

Although scholars of orthodox economic development theory seem to have reached a consensus on what constitutes economic development (refer to Chapter 1), they are poles apart regarding how economic development is achieved (see Chapter 2 and also Cameron, 1993, p. 3). Economists, social theorists and engineers, political scientists and many others seem to be confused about how nations achieved economic development in the past and how currently underdeveloped countries can also attain economic progress.

Each of these groups of scholars is caught up in the mills of mathematical model building based on hypotheses, assumptions and theoretical constructs that have very little to do with the societies whose problems they are attempting to solve. What these scholars seem to have missed is that regardless of what theories, models, ideologies and so on a nation can subscribe to, its attempts at economic development are doomed to failure if the principal foundation, the HF, is not developed to equip people to lead and direct the national economic development policy and program. The former Soviet Union and Cuba failed for this same reason. Similarly, various civilizations declined in the past due to HF decay (see Chapter 4 for details).

Progressive human-centered economic development requires continuing changes in a people's cultural mind-set and an unchanging commitment to risking change. In this process, behavior-modifying procedures must be effective and efficient both in penalizing and reinforcing all types of human behavior and/or action in society (see details in Chapter 11).

The differences in culture between many Western advanced countries and sub-Saharan ACs, however, are so varied that to achieve success, policies in each country group must not be based on identical underlying assumptions. The failure to consider and balance carefully these differences led to the transplant of identical policies and programs from the DCs to sub-Saharan ACs. Since the "all things equal" assumption does not necessarily create the required conditions for policies (be it capitalist or socialist) in sub-Saharan ACs, the results of orthodox and heterodox economic development policies have led to the current crisis in sub-Saharan African economic development programming. This crisis will continue to escalate if all misconceptions about the sources of sub-Saharan African economic stagnation are not acknowledged and corrected. The IMF and the World Bank are the weakest institutions either to appeal to or depend on to achieve economic progress in sub-Saharan Africa. ACs, therefore, need to look elsewhere--to be precise, to themselves first, before others.

Schumacher (1973) pointed out correctly that behind every human invention lies a whole gamut of human activities and efforts--education, research and many others--without which very little would have been achieved. Schumacher (1973, p. 165) noted that "all this [the foundation structure, painfully and carefully built over an extended period of time] is easily forgotten, because the modern tendency is to see and become conscious of only the visible and forget the invisible things that are making the visible possible and keep it going." Schumacher (1973, p. 165) further asked "Could it be that the relative failure of aid has something to do with our materialistic philosophy which makes us liable to overlook the most important preconditions of success, which are generally invisible?" He, therefore, argued that development begins with people's education, organization and discipline. If these are nonexistent, very little can be achieved regardless of the abundance of economic resources. It is, therefore, critical to take good care of people and assist them to develop the HF because they are the most basic sources of society's wealth. The problem, however, is that as international economic development experts and IMF-World Bank policy advisors try to help developing countries, they act as if economic development can just happen, like pressing the switch of an electric lightbulb.

CONCLUSION

This chapter has shown that when sub-Saharan ACs identify the real factor (i.e., the HF) that is necessary and sufficient for economic development, they will attain progress by concentrating their resources on developing this factor. Truly there exists a solution to the continuing economic decline in sub-Saharan Africa.

NOTES

1. Examples of such negative rent-seeking practices found in Ghana include (1) *kalabule* (cheating and profiteering); (2) palm greasing (excessive bribery and corruption); (3) ghost workers (faked names recorded on the payroll whose pay is secretly appropriated by corrupt officials); and (4) culture of silence (people's refusal to report damage, problems, the corruption of civil servants and political appointees, etc.). These problems and many others not listed here take several different forms in African countries. A more detailed analysis of these problems can be found in Chapter 4.

2. This process has great potential for economic development and industrial expansion in sub-Saharan Africa and for creating many forward and backward linkages. This is the case because as sub-Saharan ACs begin to focus on the production of nontradeables, the result will be increased production of domestic staples. This abundance will not only lead to price cuts but may also lead people to think about and conceptualize the processing and preservation of the excess. As individuals enter into business ventures to process the excess domestic staples, there will be sufficient food throughout the year. This process may lead to the creation of strong domestic canning, bottling and preservation industries. If it is always true that necessity is the mother of inventions and that practice makes perfect, then this phenomenon will lead sub-Saharan African industrialists to invent, innovate and improve the quality of their manufactured goods and will therefore place these industrialists in position to compete effectively with other companies in the global village. The success in this area will expand into such industries as pharmaceuticals, African traditional medicine, clothing and automobiles. Global markets will be acquired as sub-Saharan Africans enhance the quality of their manufactures. This will provide permanent foreign exchange sources for sub-Saharan African countries. Excessive dependence on foreign exchange may diminish in the long run as sub-Saharan ACs become more capable of producing at home their basic necessities of life. This is a strong possibility that must be pursued vigorously.

3. Read the complete interview of President Jerry John Rawlings conducted by Margaret A. Novicki in *Africa Report*, March-April 1994, pp. 23-25.

4. I am not referring to education and training at all levels to acquire human capital only. Rather, my concern is far beyond knowledge and skill acquisition. It is about the development of relevant human qualities and/or characteristics that are required for a society to produce and maintain a strongly disciplined and productive labor force.

5. To ascertain the validity of this view, refer to the World Bank's 1994 Policy Research Report, *Adjustment in Africa: Reforms, Results, and the Road Ahead* (published for the World Bank by Oxford University Press).

4

The Genesis of Human Factor Decay in Sub-Saharan African Countries

INTRODUCTION

Contrary to popular opinion, colonization, in my view, was a process of socialization used by European powers to make subservient and serviceable European aliens out of Africans. It was not just a mere attempt of Europeans to secure raw materials for European industrialization or a means of bringing both economic and political emancipation to sub-Saharan African countries (ACs). As such, colonial socialization has affected every sphere of the sub-Saharan African way of life. Its extensive impact on sub-Saharan African thinking, character and actions has not been favorable to HF development.

The main objective of this chapter is to discuss how the colonial socialization process, through various agents, has contributed to HF underdevelopment and decay in sub-Saharan ACs. In this chapter, I use historical evidence to explain why, after experiencing successful development of human qualities and/or characteristics in precolonial sub-Saharan African societies, modern sub-Saharan ACs are experiencing continuing decline in the HF and seem to be failing to achieve economic development and improved human welfare. These proposed explanations are used as foundation principles on which policy recommendations are made to sub-Saharan African governments for the creation of successful HF development programs.

BACKGROUND INFORMATION: BEFORE EUROPE ARRIVED

Africa's intellectual enlightenment preceded Europe's by many centuries, even millenia. For example, Egyptian civilization was far ahead of European enlightenment for many centuries prior to the industrial revolution in the 1700s. In those earlier years, the Egyptians were more literally advanced and educated than Western Europeans. The Greeks always admired Egyptian wisdom, knowledge, science, architecture and many other developments in ancient Egypt (Welch, 1965, pp. 5-6). Egyptian priests knew and viewed the Greeks as less advanced than Egyptians. Welch (1965, p. 5) noted that one Egyptian priest once said "O Solon, you Greeks are Children." This saying is evidenced in the fact that Cairo and Fez developed and operated excellent universities and many other well-known centers of higher learning and science. The Greeks frequently sent their scholars to Egypt to study and learn the secrets of Egyptian knowledge, understanding, wisdom and successes. Although Greek philosophers borrowed a great deal of knowledge, understanding and wisdom from Egypt, little credit has been given to Africa for what they (the Greeks) had learned and gained from Egypt. This form of plagiarism and academic dishonesty in ancient times has not ceased even until today. In modern times, while Africa is often acccused and smeared falsely as being the source of deadly diseases and problems, little credit is given to African achievements, discoveries, artistic designs and patterns (i.e., *kente* designs), African drumbeats and musical rhythms that are being adapted and adopted in music elsewhere, African choreography, military intelligence, political forms, legal systems, medicine, and many others. At the prime of colonialism and slavery, many of these were either criticised or discredited and in some cases, said to be devilish and barbaric.

Egyptian educational developments were several hundreds of years ahead of Western European conceptualization. Timbuktu, in the heart of sub-Saharan Africa, was well known for its academic excellence and advanced educational developments. Welch (1965, p. 272) observed that "education was a stern business for those peoples who had books, just as it was for the bookless, whose harsh initiation systems for the young have been mentioned." Studying was made challenging, and children were encouraged to participate in it in Timbuktu. All these developments came to an abrupt halt when Western Europeans arrived at the shores of the great continent, Africa. Welch (1965, p. 350) argued that African peoples are no dull human beings. They have a long and constructive historical past that has often been neglected. Not only do they have the ability to learn and acquire knowledge, but they also possess the capacity to think and create, as is evident in their art work, music, handicrafts and more. Their leaders in the past successfully administered huge empires. They maintained law and order and kept alive vital economic and business activities.

Before colonization, nation-states in sub-Saharan Africa had already developed their own culture in relation to social, political, economic and business life. Embedded in these varying cultures were their own technologies crafted for adapting to their environment and solving pertinent problems. Medicine, law, ethics, poetry and fiction (see Awoonor, 1976, pp. 54-145), military strategy and intelligence, philosophy (as evidenced in their proverbs, riddles and stories) and many other areas of human life were advanced (Awoonor, 1976, pp. 49-53). Like many non-African societies, African societies did not only have needs and problems but were also faced with massive challenges regarding how to overcome existing hindrances to human progress. These nation-states therefore developed capabilities with which to confront problems of everyday social, political, economic and business life. Pre-colonial African nation-states developed a strong community spirit and reverenced the dignity of labor. They practiced division of labor and specialization in all areas of human endeavor. McCord and McCord (1986, p. 32) noted that "the original societies of the Egbas and Yorubas in Nigeria were vigorous *village republics*, subverted by colonization; the peasants of [the] Ivory Coast, Taiwan and Korea have adopted immensely productive agricultural techniques as they responded to land reform and market incentives; Sikhs in the Punjab and their Hindu cousins in Haryana and Uttar Pradash carried out a revolution in agriculture within six years."

The agents of education in these nation-states made effective use of many formal and informal education and training procedures, which took several forms of learning by doing on the job. Story-telling programs were used as agents for spiritual, moral and ethical development, courage building, inculcation of integrity, devotion, dedication and commitment to accomplishing what was expected of the individual in society. For example, every African story was carefully constructed to teach some moral or work ethic or philosophy of life or spiritual prowess, or all four and many others. In some cases, the period of training and learning was long and intensive. For example, the art of divination took seven or more years to acquire in Dahomey and Yorubaland. It was an extended period of higher intellectual learning, spiritual development, critical thinking and skillful examination of natural phenomena and other available evidence. This extended duration of education and training for traditional medicine men and women matches the one modern doctors and lawyers go through in the Western World. One wonders what the results of the African procedures would have been if colonialism had not occurred.

The youth were trained in various areas of community life and were often taught to have a deep reverence for God, the elderly and for work and leisure. Among the Ewes of Ghana, for example, much pleasure was derived from hard work, whose fruits always brought greater zeal and encouragement for developing better skills with which to accomplish other related tasks that could enrich the individual's family life in particular and that of the immediate community in general.

Indigenous techniques existed for ensuring social control or overcoming sicknesses and diseases, and evolving legal systems made it easier to deal with disputes and problems of interpersonal and economic/business relationships. Similarly, advanced political structures were in existence which facilitated effective local administration. Since there were frequent disputes over territories and challenges to jurisdictions, each nation-state had in place its own war machinery and well-crafted procedures for fighting battles with recalcitrant enemies. For example, the Akans,[1] Ewes, Kushites, Yorubas, Zulus and many other nation-states in pre-colonial sub-Saharan Africa had every necessary system developed and available for maintaining law and order, peace and successful business life. Could it have been the case that had colonization, external slavery and the artificial partition of Africa by European powers not occurred, African kingdoms could have developed into modern nation-states as was the case in Western Europe? And if this had been the case, could the current plight of Africa have been averted? Answers to these searching questions are complicated and require an extensive research that is beyond the scope of this chapter.

Rights of passage were used to groom citizens to acquire the HF for a life of service to humanity through selfless devotion, dedication, integrity, honesty, responsibility, accountability and so on. Precolonial African peoples also practiced capital punishment and involved themselves in certain negative religious practices--their culture had both positive and negative aspects, just like any other ancient or, for that matter, modern Western culture.

After colonization, most of these achievements were lost. The colonial era of administration served as a great dividing line between the state of HF development in pre- and postcolonial African nation-states. The initiation of colonial rule served as the starting point for the disintegration of the HF in previously independent African states. In their helplessness, African nation-states waited and watched the destruction of their existing programs aimed at HF development and the attainment of economic progress. The loss of morale and human will during colonization led to the decline in the strength of the human spirit in Africa. The already acquired HF in the region began to wear away, leading to a gradual impairment of its original wholeness. This degeneration of human qualities and/or characteristics--decline in physical, spiritual and ethical systems and mental and moral qualities--of the African peoples paved the way for the creation of deeply rooted problems that today have made void all efforts made in the last half century to put African states back on a sound economic footing. The failure in this regard is, no doubt, due to the inability to restore the long-lost HF in the African labor force.

Although this phenomenon (i.e., the failure of Africa's development plans, policies and programs) has a lot to do with HF decay and/or underdevelopment in ACs of modern times, very little research work has been done on it. This failure to look more critically at the impacts of colonialism on the state of human characteristics development in Africa has led to the pursuit of economic, political and social policies and programs that have for many years failed to bring economic progress. Thus, the root cause of Africa's economic underdevelopment has not been correctly deciphered and directly addressed. To achieve any positive changes and progress in ACs, the true causes of the decline in the HF must be carefully researched, studied and dealt with properly.

THE GENESIS OF HUMAN FACTOR DECLINE

How did it all begin? Given the preceding discussion, one will expect that African countries could have developed the required HF for their development programs. This, however, was not the case. In the following discussion, a series of presentations are made to provide relevant answers to the observed phenomenon of HF disintegration in ACs. The discussion is aimed at isolating pertinent factors that African governments must pay extensive attention to if their goal is to achieve economic development--especially the necessary HF. The factors that feature prominently in the HF decline process are classified under either internal or external causes.

The External Factors

Lack of trust in colonial administrators

At the time of colonization, African countries were plunged into a state of continuous flux. Their own indigenous programs were abruptly terminated, and they were forced to adopt a substitute culture that little understood existing African ways of life. This phenomenon created much confusion and many misconceptions. The strong suspicion and doubts generated opened wide doors of animosity and resulted in colonizer and colonized being unable to work together. There was no unity of purpose. Whereas the colonized just wanted to regain their lost freedom and get on with their disrupted lives, the colonizers were more engrossed in how to harness and use the colonized to foster their own interests. However, the colonizers had the power and authority to force the colonized to do what was expected of them. Africans, therefore, never had any reasons for trusting the colonizers. This lack of trust quickly filtered into everything they were asked to do.

Africans who had the privilege of working as clerks in the colonial administration and other sectors of the economy, where they represented the European rulers, did not see anything wrong with taking items and/or property belonging to foreigners, who, in cunning ways, took Africans' land, culture, freedom to rule and other types of property--even the essence of their lives-- away from them. This philosophy of life was based on the view that one cannot be labeled as a thief when one takes away from a thief what he or she had stolen. Thus, colonization both created and continuously fueled the practical application of this philosophy of life and paved the way for the erosion of certain elements of the qualitative HF in Africa. The escalation of the application of this view of life can be viewed as the birthing of political corruption, an entrenched negative rent-seeking behavior.

Values that were well established in African states began to erode. Africans had to be reeducated to fit properly into new social, economic and political systems under European hegemony. Cockcroft (1990, pp. 63-64) noted that

confronted with reality, the rapid establishment from the 1920s onwards of key Western institutions in the fields of law, education and agriculture created great conflicts within African society. . . . These conflicts were triggered by the European administrators and missionaries who in the first decades of the colonial period adopted a stance of rejection of the social and cultural values which they confronted. . . . Consequently, to *progress* within the colonial state, younger Africans had to accept the new values, or face the prospects of rural stagnation.

The moral, ethical and spiritual struggles between the colonizers and the colonized turned out to be destructive to HF development in Africa and other parts of the World--the native Indians of North America, the aboriginal people of Australia and New Zealand and many others. These people became aliens in their own lands of birth. They lost both the will and the spirit to live, work and excell in everything they were thereafter engaged in.

Colonial educational thinking was based on mission accomplishment

In the initial stages of the colonial program, many cooperative societies were formed and encouraged to help develop and produce the necessary raw materials for the factories being established in Western Europe (Nzula et. al., 1979, pp. 20-35; Orde Browne, 1967, p. 25). Thus, the kind of education and training given to the local farmers was designed to provide them with adequate knowledge to function as effective cash crop producers. The cash crop business was ubiquitous in ACs. Africans were therefore forced to discontinue already existing organized modes of production and farming to concentrate their human and land resources on cash crop production.

Since the colonial administrators needed local clerks to serve in many different capacities, government-fincanced kangaroo English schools[2] were established in British colonies to help produce such clerks and to facilitate the British agenda. Examples of such schools were also common in the Malay states of Perak and Selangor in the 1880s and 1890s in Asia (see Rudner, 1987, pp. 193-209 for details). Berg (1965, p. 235) observed that

acute scarcity of trained and educated manpower is typical of African countries. In the final balance sheet that will be drawn up on the colonial experience, long neglect of the development of African human resources will surely weigh heavily on the debt side. This is particularly true in French-speaking Africa for two main reasons, the nature of the preindependence educational system and the special political circumstances binding French Africa to its metrople.

French educational policy in Africa was primarily aimed at assimilation. Africans were to be tranformed into French people (Kimble, 1960, p. 108). Berg (1965, p. 238) noted further that

The French conception of their educational mission did not include the systematic preparation of Africans for positions of major responsibility. In a curiously distorted way, French educational thinking was rooted in a notion basic to modern manpower and educational planning--that the educational system should be intimately related to the needs of the economy. Thus, vocational agricultural training received major emphasis in the village schools of the interwar period. Education in the liberal professions was discouraged.

Yet a society cannot effectively prepare its citizens for a meaningful life of work and play without having designed and successfully implemented an effective liberal arts education. Africans were denied real opportunities to develop further the HF they acquired in the pre-colonial era.

In the 1950s, human factor development was not a French concern in French West Africa. The French administration rejected secondary education, which is a *sine qua non* for high-level humanpower development in any country. The French administrators failed to foresee that in the long run Africans would be needed to work at jobs usually reserved for the French in ACs (Berg, 1965, p. 245). Since the needs of European economies did not include those of Africans, Africans were prepared only to serve as assistant artisans, clerks, agricultural technicians and so on, always in subservience to Europeans (Berg, 1965, p. 239). The higher level manpower jobs were reserved for Europeans only. There was no pressing need to open higher education to Africans under colonial administration. These policies and programs made it impossible for the colonial administration to prepare Africans to manage and administer rule under the political structures handed over to them after the colonizers were gone. Most ACs were catapulted into the eve of independence only to realize later that they were ill equipped to step into the vacant administrative shoes of those who had once colonized them. They became like square pegs in round holes.

In South Africa, guidelines for Bantu education were restrictive. Education given to the Bantus was not only different from that given to white South Africans but was also intentionally designed to provide the Bantus with the most basic knowledge they needed for rural life. To the Bantus, according to the adherents of apartheid, life does not exist beyond their own homeland. This being the case, they needed to know no more than their own surroundings. Bantu education therefore emphasized to the Bantus that they neither had any rights to nor the need to receive education of the same magnitude and quality as provided for white South Africans--they could not have equal rights with the white people (Davis, 1972, p. 14). Clearly, the South African government's educational policies and programs for the Bantus were a propaganda ploy to foster and perpetuate its apartheid policy. It rarely ever encouraged HF development in the Bantus. It is hoped that this situation will change for the better in the new South Africa.

Colonial education and African antipathy toward manual labor

In the words of Dumont (1969, p. 91), "French education also develops an antipathy toward manual labor, with which it is concerned little if at all. France is training cripples as far as their fingers; no entirely celebral knowledge, which ignores manual dexterity and the experience of the five senses, can be complete." This kind of treatment meted out to the African peoples was prevalent all over Africa. Much harm was done by making work, especially manual labor, become distasteful to many Africans just as the Greeks detested manual labor and scorned it. In most cases, mismanagement and mishandling of African workers led them to develop a disaffinity for work. They resented European domination and work simultaneously. The treatment meted out to slaves by their owners led to the development of lethargic work behavior--strong aversion to work and sluggishness in duty--in the African labor force. It can hardly be denied, therefore, that colonization and slavery created a mental state that led the African to view work as something to be engaged in out of compulsion. Africans therefore endured work rather than enjoyed it. Orde Browne (1967, p. 28) observed accurately that "slave mentality thus injuriously affected not only the freedman but also the employer and society generally; its baneful effect in lowering efficiency and sanctioning waste will probably take long to disappear completely." This disappearance can only happen when relevant education and training policies and programs are put in place to help Africans develop the necessary HF.

My own experiences of the fruits of this are still fresh in my mind. While I was in elementary school in the 1960s, the most frequent kind of correctional punishment dished out to pupils who flaunted school regulations and/or authorities was to send them to work in the school garden. Thus, regulation offenders dug beds and trenches, watered seedlings, weeded plots, built fences, carried several bucketfuls of clay or sand, administered manure, transplanted seedlings and performed other similar tasks. These types of measures produced a disaffinity and hatred for manual labor in pupils while they were in school, and this disaffinity is often carried into adult life. In the secondary schools and colleges in most ACs, the story was no different.

This phenomenon was one of the many acts of colonialism that opened the door for the disintegration of human qualities and/or characteristics in African countries. The hatred and dislike created for work in the African psyche encouraged shirking and absenteeism in independent Africa. In this regard, Dumont (1969, p. 82) noted that "work was often pushed to excess. . . . In underdeveloped countries, laxity and profligacy are too often seen. A typist for the Dakar government types an average of six to seven pages, double-spaced, a day, less than a quarter of what an average French typist accomplishes, for a salary that is equal if not higher." Truly, this is indicative of the African feeling and behavior under the colonial administration that it is insane to work conscientiously for someone who once usurped your own inalienable rights and became lord over you in your own homeland. This attitude, unfortunately, became so ingrained in the African that even after colonialism, many Africans continued to view postindependence African-led governments as the foreigners who once dealt falsely with them. The new African governments have been treated almost exactly the same way as the colonial administration was in terms of allegiance and work behavior. The devolution of the HF and the genesis of its decay in ACs began at the commencement of colonial administration.

The behavior of the colonial administrators in regard to how Europeans who had acquired formal education were treated led to the creation of a warped African view about the goals of formal education and training. It produced the attitude that those who acquired European knowledge through formal education did not have to involve themselves with intensive manual work. Herskovits (1962, p. 224) noted that "the Africans also soon observed that in the African setting the Europeans, who could read and write, did no manual labor, but enjoyed higher status and remuneration than the Africans who could not. The obvious conclusion was that literacy was a prime factor in permitting a man [or woman] to become the manager, the supervisor over those who did not know how to read and write." University education in the postcolonial era reinforced rather than terminated this false perception. Although it was designed for human resources development, its programs proauce academicians who lack the required HF. African universities produced many intellectuals who have been unable to apply their acquired knowledge to solve domestic problems.

Porterage: Beast of burden

Porterage was another vicious attack on the African labor force by colonial administration and merchants (Orde Browne, 1967, pp. 39-42). Africans were used as beasts of burden. They traveled many kilometers, accompanying merchants and carrying their goods and wares. Being on these journeys, continuously carrying heavy luggage under terrible weather conditions and always watched keenly by those they labored for, was not only extremely distasteful to them but also deprived them of the necessary time, energy and health required to think and learn and thus to improve on their own technology and human welfare. These physically exhausting activities drained Africans mentally and psychologically decimated their self-confidence and humanness. Their true names were changed to others that were easier for their owners and masters to call them by. There was very little they could achieve in terms of technological creativity (i.e., invention and innovation) during and after colonization.

The provision and impacts of colonial handouts on HF development

The continuing decay in the required HF led many Africans to look to the colonial administration for handouts. Work was no longer palatable. In the words of Dumont (1969, p. 94), "the peasant is accustomed to receiving everything free, and is encouraged in this attitude by the spectacle of innumerable privileged civil servants. It is hard to persuade him to make the great efforts necessary for agricultural development. His leaders have chosen the easy way out, preferring to make liberal promises, rather than get down to work." This impact can still be seen in how African leaders move around the world looking for foreign aid, technical assistance and all types of help from elsewhere. It is hard for them to perceive that much progress can be achieved in Africa without necessarily receiving help from abroad.

The lack of Africanization policies and programs

French African leaders were not encouraged to talk about political independence from France. They therefore could not initiate any Africanization programs. The French were encouraged to take up jobs in French Africa--thus blocking the opportunities for French Africans. This prevented the institution of programs to develop the required skills, responsibility and accountability in Africans (Berg, 1965, pp. 246-247). To place Africans in positions where they would be required to give orders and/or instructions to Europeans was a heresy. Thus, even after independence, expatriates still controlled the African job market in French ACs. African leaders therefore failed to develop the HF necessary to their economic development programs for independence and beyond. Neither leadership nor entrepreneurial skills were developed. African politicians had power and authority but lacked the relevant HF for which there existed no *quid pro quo* for a national development program.

The failure of the colonial administration to develop the HF perpetrated continued HF decay and/or underdevelopment in African countries. At independence, many African leaders were possessed, and probably blinded with, the idea of accelerated economic development and therefore channeled huge proportions of existing economic resources into economic development planning, policies and programs. At that point in time, little did they know that the foundation of any economic development program is properly developed HF. Their programs therefore ignored effective development of human qualities and/or characteristics. When the new leaders decided to encourage the education and training of indigenous Africans, the programs pursued were based on either unsuitable or irrelevant colonial patterns. Education and training programs followed existing colonial curricula that did not reflect domestic needs. Rote learning rather than understanding and critical analysis and thinking was encouraged. African leaders failed to prepare their own citizens for postindependence economic development policies and programs. In my view, if intelligence were synonymous with wisdom, no society in history would have attempted to roof buildings whose foundations and structures have neither been conceived nor laid down in reality. Those who attempted to do so in the past failed. If Africans desire to achieve economic progress, they cannot continually afford to commit similar mistakes by neglecting to develop the required HF in the African labor force.

At best, colonial education and training policies and programs were crafted to produce educated African elites who were expected to serve as instruments (political stooges) for furthering the colonial administration's agenda. Their expected role was to facilitate the achievement of colonial objectives (Thompson and Adloff, 1958, pp. 518-521). These education and training programs were not only handicapped in the sense described earlier, but were also offered to a select few in Africa (Hailey, 1938). Education and training programs also failed to go to higher levels of learning. Africans were not considered to have any need for higher education and training. Besides, they were just being trained to serve as garden boys and girls and domestic servants for their European administrators. Higher education for Africans was, therefore, strongly discouraged. The curricula used in these schools scarcely had anything to do with African environments. British education and training programs in ACs were no better than those of the French because their objectives were no different.

These experiences are similar to those of Asian countries under the colonial administration. For example, Myrdal (1963, pp. 1737-1741) observed in this regard that "in its social conception and economic utility, Malay vernacular schooling constituted an immobilizer of roles, and entailed a veritable *education for poverty*." These education and training programs were operating in poor facilities, had poor instruction quality and irrelevant curricula, and turned out graduates who were not properly trained to meet the growing development challenges of newly independent nation-states. Ingham and Simmons (1987, p. 207) noted that "at the end of the colonial period Malay[sia] was still acutely under-educated in relation to the country's level of economic attainment. This lag in educational development was to leave its imprint on high-level manpower constraints, on social and ethnic inequality, and on regional disparities for some time afterwards."

The worker's self-interest and work behavior

In Western Europe, workers obeyed and fulfilled the terms of their work contracts because their individual livelihood depended on the amount of time they put into work in the labor market. They also knew that as free citizens, their employers were obliged to pay them some remuneration for their work hours. Western European workers were also aware that through their work, they could make money from which they could obtain property. Moreover, many European workers belonged to labor unions and had their interests, rights and welfare protected. These opportunities, however, were not available to African workers. In many cases, penal sanctions were erected against them. Workers who absented themselves from work were fined or flogged or imprisoned on breach of contract convictions--workers' conditions not excepted. Unlike Western European workers, African workers lacked both personal freedom and effective unions. How then could we have expected them to have developed the necessary HF for the postindependence economic development program?

The dormancy of the African creative urge

If necessity is truly the mother of invention, then Africa's inventive urge was lulled into slumber by the colonial administrative spirit. It was colonialism that fought hard to replace all African indigenous technologies with Western European surrogates or clones. During its era, European colonialism provided Africans with almost everything except the appropriate technology they needed. They were furnished with wine, tobacco, medicine, guns, processed food, clothing and many other things. When all this was going on, traditional African industries that originally supplied these items gradually lost their existing markets to imported Western European substitutes. Over time, African indigenous engineers and technologists allowed their creativity and tools to lie dormant and rarely ever pursued any serious future inventive and/or innovative programs. The loss of opportunities to manufacture items for local markets, therefore, led to the inability of Africans to develop properly the technical aspects of their human characteristics. Africans were turned into people who most often looked for handouts from their colonizers, who, in turn, were more than glad to supply them since doing so promoted their objectives both at home and abroad. Before colonization, most African states manufactured their own clothes, wine, guns, fishing nets, canoes and so on. Most of these technologies and/or arts, however, were lost when such commodities were introduced from Western Europe.

At the conclusion of the colonial administration, Africans still lacked knowledge about European know-how (inventiveness and creativity) and were unable to return to their own indigenous technologies and skills, which were suspended at the inception of colonial administration. In their desire to achieve rapid industrial development after having gained independence, African leaders began to dig deep into funds left for them by the outgoing colonial administration to purchase Western European equipment for the fulfillment of their lofty industrial dreams. Yet the expected mosaic and/or miracle of development did not happen. What went wrong? The continuing pursuits of newly emerging African political leaders entailed few premeditated plans and programs to develop relevant human qualities in their own people. Postindependence educational curricula and programs were rarely different from the faulty and limited types pursued by the outgoing colonial administration. Thus, instead of correcting the mistakes of the colonizers, first-generation African leaders perpetrated and contributed further to the extensive underdevelopment of the HF. They tried feverishly to put roofs on imaginary buildings that lacked proper foundations and structures--the relevant human characteristics and/or qualities. Since then, their dreams have either collapsed or shriveled.

The absence of opportunities

During the era of colonial administration, true opportunities were lacking. Africans, therefore, were not frequently placed in sensitive positions of trust whereby they could be confronted on a regular basis with decision-making powers and authorities,[3] where their social ethos and ethical systems could be called into question and challenged. The whole duration of Western European administration in Africa denied Africans the necessary opportunities to accomplish tasks for themselves. Indigenous Africans, therefore, could not even learn by doing. For example, radio and television programs were either made in the colonies by actors and actresses imported from Western European countries or were brought from abroad--electronic colonialism (McPhail, 1987). Textbooks and story books also came to ACs from similar sources. This evidence substantiates the argument that Africans were denied the relevant opportunity to develop either directly or indirectly the necessary HF. Above all, cultural imperialism (Hamelink, 1983) was destructive to the development of the HF in Africa.

The education and training curricula

As noted earlier, Western European education and training programs designed for ACs were aimed at the production of clerks and other types of assistants to European administrators. In the beginning, therefore, these education and training programs solely emphasized the three Rs--reading, writing and basic arithmetic. The curricula intentionally excluded the major liberal arts core subjects. Above all, philosophy, the classics, African ethos and ethical systems, African history and culture, citizenship education, the natural sciences and technology, management theory, business administration and many others were not taught until recently--and even that is still not across the board. Herskovits (1962, pp. 221-222) noted that there was

> the tendency to write off aboriginal beliefs, moral codes and other regulatory social devices, along with material culture and native technology, as being of a quality that desired little or no attention in planning curricula or classroom procedures for African schools. . . . What the European brought to the African was schooling which, however important it may be, constitutes but a portion of the total process of social and cultural learning. The schooling brought to the African, moreover, was European schooling, with curricula and objectives that, drawn from the background of the Metropole, incorporated curricula and aimed at objectives which were oriented toward the experiences of children there.

The education and training program encouraged and perpetrated rote memory learning rather than critical thinking, analysis and comprehension. Berg (1965, p, 261) pointed out that

> particularly in Senegal and the Ivory Coast, the schools are poorly adapted to local conditions and needs. The structure of the system remains almost wholly based on the French model: hours of instruction, arrangement of the school year, degrees, examinations, etc., all parallel the French. No real attempt has been made to organize rural education differently from urban education or to transform the content and direction of the primary school, which have nothing to do with preparing for an agricultural life. . . . Education remains literary, bookish, remote from African reality. Rote learning predominates, and preparation for examinations is the major concern.

Although precolonial ACs employed their indigenous means of social control and other related institutions to teach, train, educate and inculcate values in their citizens, postcolonial African states have been less successful in developing the required foundation, the HF, for economic development and cultural change.

The Internal Factors

Overemphasis on personal wealth

Personal wealth is held in high esteem in ACs. It does not only accord the rich with prestige but also creates many opportunities for them and their siblings. The unrelentless pursuit of personal wealth usually leads to the neglect of the development of long-lasting values, the dignity of labor, the sanctity of human life and respect for fellow citizens in many societies all over the world, not solely Africa. Just like any other people in the world, many Africans have learned to do business in a way similar to playing to win a sporting game at all costs. This behavior diminishes respect for dedication, accountability, responsibility, integrity, trustworthiness and many other similar qualities.

Excessive abuse of the existing cultural welfare system

Just as has been the case in many other countries (i.e., both developed and developing), Africans have abused one of the best yet least costly social welfare systems the world has ever known. A system that was devised for and aimed at the maintenance of human welfare and dignity has been misused by individuals who have forgotten about the dignity of labor and the joy of work. Many people prefer to depend on the mercies of the extended family system and the benevolence of friends without necessarily contributing toward the maintenance and continuation of the welfare system. It has apparently become more fashionable and dignifying for individuals to coast through life living on handouts from other members of the family and other people. This has, however, led to the unwillingness of some to participate in the labor force, hence living a life that depreciates their HF.

These and many other factors have contributed significantly to Africa's barrenness in qualitative human qualities and/or characteristics. The outcome of these developments are usually social rent-seeking practices that destroy rather than promote economic progress. A few of these practices are discussed in the next section.

RESULTING SOCIAL PRACTICES AND ATTITUDES

In what follows, an extended discussion of a few of such social rent-seeking practices and attitudes is presented. ACs must realize the debilitating impacts of these social rent-seeking practices on the success or failure of economic recovery programs and develop relevant education and training programs to deal with them successfully.

Kalabule

This term, as used in Ghana, refers to cheating and profiteering. It is a common practice in every African country. It involves all business undertakings that use foul means to achieve excessive economic profits. The practice of *kalabule* involves the extortion of money from consumers. Businessmen and women sometimes create artificial shortages by hoarding their merchandize. Consumers, therefore, pay excessively high prices. Sellers team up to pursue this policy and thus raise their profit margin. *Kalabule* thrives mostly when there are many middle men and women in the sale of essential items. It is encouraged by government price control policies involving the sale of essential items (i.e., drugs, baby food, milk, detergents, etc.). Designated store managers receive items from government depots at stipulated prices, sell a few to the public and merchandize the rest at cut-throat prices to consumers under the table. Managers profit by charging higher prices than have been allowed by government. Vending outlets sell essential items to other stores, which in turn sell them in the open market at inflated prices.

Kalabule in this form is an indirect way of income redistribution in ACs. It distorts the actual form of income distribution because consumers who pay these exhorbitant prices transfer their meager incomes to rich businessmen and women. *Kalabule* therefore has the power to make the rich richer and the poor poorer. It negatively affects resource allocation. It is therefore necessary for Africans to take a closer look at its practice and devise procedures that will educate businesses to realize its destructive impact on economic development.

Fairness in business activities and undertakings will prevail when the necessary HF is developed.

Palm Greasing

Palm greasing is either a direct or indirect form of bribery and corruption. It refers to situations in which a government employee performs his or her duty only after having extorted illegal payments and/or benefits from service recipients. For example, if an individual has to travel abroad and needs travel documents, the official in charge of issuing these documents will issue them only after he or she has been paid some amount of money. The practice does not relate to money alone. Sometimes gifts in kind are given and accepted. Some officials openly demand such payments. If not paid, they delay the processing of the required documents. In most cases, once the palm greasing process is accomplished, the required service is performed immediately. The crucial question therefore is "Why do some government officials and employees not perform their duties without accomplished palm greasing?"

This practice creates unnecessary delays in an already cumbersome bureaucracy. Like *kalabule*, it puts an unnecessary burden on the poor. Poor people who cannot grease the palm of officials may not be assisted at all. Usually only those who grease the palm get served quicker. It can, therefore, be argued that palm greasing is not only an inefficient way of income redistribution but is also a means of delaying the process of human-centered development. The ultimate results are low productivity and low economic growth and development. In the long run, this leads to declining living standards. Public officials who behave in this manner leave their duties undone and discourage high labor productivity. This observation explains why there are always struggles for power and positions of influence and decision making in African countries (Adjibolosoo, 1994b, pp. 123-132). People who vie and strive for certain positions know that once they attain these positions, they can amass wealth for themselves. Palm greasing is therefore a destructive social rent-seeking practice. It does not only hinder economic growth but also delays and destroys the incentive for hard work. It negatively affects government policies, programs, projects and so on. For success, ACs must deal with this destructive social rent-seeking practice.

Ghost Workers

The practice of using ghost workers and their names to claim money illegally from the government treasury is probably an age-old practice in many countries. Its caricature in Western advanced societies is welfare fraud. It was not until the era of the December 31, 1981 *coup d'etat* that it became more obvious in Ghana. It is destructive because it encourages fund mismanagement, misapplication and misappropriation (the three Ms). The ghost worker practice involves goverment officials who add many artificial names to the payroll. These names are not real (i.e., names of deceased or imaginary people). When the official in charge of payroll receives all the required funds from the government treasury and pays actual workers, he or she appropriates the rest of the money. This practice has been widely used by headteachers, headmasters, principals, bursars and principal secretaries in every African country. During the wake of the excessive exodus of teachers from Ghana to other African states and the rest of the world, those who indulged in the practice did not strike off the payroll the names of teachers who vacated their posts. They claimed the excess monies for their own use. When the government finally uncovered the scam, most people who indulged in it had already fled the country. Although some were arrested, tried and jailed, others had already died. Since this practice drains and misuses scarce public resources, Africans must develop procedures for dealing with it.

The Culture of Silence

The culture of silence is an age-old social problem in ACs. It was during the era of the December 31, 1981 revolution in Ghana that it also came into the limelight. It refers to the phenomenon in ACs whereby most citizens revert to an attitude of passivity. That is, when some people observe any practice which is inimical to economic policies and development plans, they decide to be silent about it. Similarly, in cases of public property destrution, some citizens decide to be silent since the item is seen as government property. When government officials take bribes, no reports are made to the appropriate authorities.

This culture does not only perpetrate low productivity but also hinders the process of economic development. Its practice militates against effective preventive maintenance management programs. It destroys the continuity of human-centered development. Since economic development is, therefore, a cumulative process, the culture of silence is its real enemy. If ACs desire to develop they must participate effectively in programs designed for dealing with this practice. A nation that is consumed by the culture of silence may find it difficult to make successful breakthroughs in the economic development process.

Genetics has not contributed to the poorly developed HF in colonized Africa, as motivational theorists sometimes suggest. Anyone who understands what the colonial African labor force went through--subjection to forced labor, heavy tax burdens, being made beasts of burden, and so on--will correctly not label modern Africans as being stupid and lazy. The current condition and work behavior of the labor force are the direct fruits of a senseless and primitive colonial mentality. Thus, instead of writing modern Africa off as a basket case, it may be better to spend appropriate resources to disabuse and decolonize the African mind-set developed under colonial torture--or at least make efforts to educate and train Africans to acquire the wisdom required for economic development. Although this will not be an easy task, it is probably the best way of starting HF development in Africa--without which every other economic development policy and program will fail.

CONCLUSION

If the colonial administration had seen into the future and realized that Africans would one day have the opportunity to rule themselves, and if the administration was willing and ready to help Africans become successful, it could have developed, instituted and operated relevant education and training programs that would have produced the required HF in the African people. This, unfortunately, was not the case. Thus, for many years African potentials were untapped and unused by colonial administrators, who were more eager to bring in the colonies' expatriate personnel to work for them.

NOTES

1. For a comprehensive discussion of the Akan political organization, judicial processes, ritual and medicine, refer to Chapters 6, 7 and 8 in Brokensha, D. 1966. *Social Change in Larteh, Ghana.* Oxford, England: Clarendon Press.

2. Colonial education and training interests were mainly concerned with making good European citizens out of Africans. Thus, the establishment of institutions of higher learning (i.e., University of Ghana at Legon, University of Ibadon in Nigeria, *Ecole* William *Ponty* in Senegal and many others) during the colonial administration was aimed at achieving this goal.

3. In many areas in colonial Africa, the European administrators instituted indirect rule. This was a form of administration in which the colonizers ruled the indigenous Africans indirectly through their own chiefs. The chiefs were accepted as representatives of the colonial administration and had to report to it. In this way, the chiefs did not have any definitive prerogatives to act on urgent matters without permission from the colonial administration. This system did not, therefore, provide viable conditions in which the chiefs could learn to administer rule efficiently and effectively. In most cases, the chiefs were no more than political stooges and/or puppets. Thus, although an opportunity to rule existed, it did not contribute to appropriate HF development in terms of political leadership and administration.

5

The Human Factor: The Engine of Growth and the Handmaiden of Economic Development

INTRODUCTION

It is often said that a nation's greatest resource is its people. In my view, this statement is only partially true and somewhat flawed. To achieve universal validity, it should be restated as follows:

> The greatest resource of a nation is a well-disciplined labor force that has achieved required human qualities and/or characteristics that are critical for articulating a national vision, developing the capacity to initiate, plan, organize, manage and control the national development program to foster social progress, economic growth and development, political maturation and many others.

In this chapter I argue, not only that the true engine of growth and handmaiden of economic development is the HF[1] but also that developing countries wishing to achieve progress need to educate their people to acquire the necessary human qualities and/or characteristics, without which neither institutions nor institutional structures can function efficiently and effectively. This chapter explains why the HF is the key element of every development program.

Throughout time in every civilization, humanity has struggled to deal with either naturally or artificially created problems. One of the first and oldest problems that confronted humanity was scarcity, which is still the basic concern of modern economic analysis. Economists view all human endeavors as attempts to deal with the scarcity problem. Efficiency in scarce resource utilization--the primary concern of economics--is always lauded. Such resource use attempts lead to the evolution of new ideas and techniques that are used to further humanity's efforts to conquer its environment and in turn subdue scarcity. In the past, many such attempts have led to progress in different areas of human life in some countries. Confronted with an ongoing scarcity problem and varying acts of nature that create human discomfort, humanity has used its reasoning faculties to evolve and develop solutions to the difficulties. The industrial revolution, developments in medicine, the initial unrelenting attempts to fly, shipbuilding and shipping, the development of the railway, motor vehicle manufacturing, computerization, global communications and transportation systems and many other inventions and innovations have helped humanity overcome some of its pertinent hindrances to progress.

Although these developments speak clearly and loudly for themselves regarding the role of people, some economists have for many years viewed capital as the main engine of growth, whereas others have enthroned trade as the handmaiden of economic development. Institutionalists argue that the existence of efficient institutions and well-defined property rights is vital to the economic development process. Other scholars of the economic development theory view the role of ideologies (especially capitalism or socialism) as being crucial to the economic development process. In recent years, continuing attempts have been made by Western scholars to establish a positive relationship between democracy and economic development. In the debate about the usefulness of ideological strands, the battle between capitalism and socialism has been fierce for many years. Although socialists believe that it is the system that corrupts people and must, therefore, be controlled, capitalists maintain that when left on their own, the market forces have the capability to create sufficient wealth for society. What these economists often gloss over is that human progress could not have been achieved without appropriately developed HF that is astute and entrepreneurial--creative, inventive, innovative, responsible, resourceful, resilient, trustworthy, accountable, problem solving and many others.

The main goal of this chapter is, therefore, to argue from the perspective of the human factor approach to development that the HF rather than capital accumulation, international trade, institutions and ideologies is the true engine of growth and handmaiden of economic development.

ORTHODOX CONCEPTIONS ABOUT CRITICAL FACTORS IN ECONOMIC DEVELOPMENT

Many scholars of economic development theory have identified certain factors as critical to the economic development process. Some have emphasized capital and its accumulation; others have emphasized labor (Fei and Ranis, 1961; Haberler, 1959; Heckscher, 1950; Hicks, 1965; Kravis, 1970; Kuznets, 1959; Lewis, 1954; Meier, 1963; Nurkse, 1958; Ohlin, 1933; Solow, 1956; Vaizey, 1981; Viner, 1952). Many institutionalists have also maintained that the role of institutions is vital to the process of human progress and economic development (Chamberlain, 1963; Clark, 1952; Commons, 1990; Langlois, 1986; Mitchell, 1937, 1969; Veblen, 1921, 1934).[2]

The Harrod-Domar pioneering economic modeling work in the 1940s portrayed growing savings and investment (i.e., capital accumulation) as the major determinants of economic growth. This view, often referred to as capital fundamentalism, has guided development policy, planning and programming for many decades in the developing countries (Gillis et al., 1992, pp. 267-268). In their work, Harrod (1939, 1948) and Domar (1947) maintained independently that the output of any economy depends on the magnitude of capital invested, implying that to achieve continual growth in the national output, capital must grow.

Since the view expressed by the Harrod-Domar model of economic growth seems to be too narrow, many other scholars attempted in many different ways to show that there are additional factors that cause growth. This class of scholars is usually more concerned with the contribution of each factor to the production process and to technical progress. Some of this research expressed doubts about the central position accorded to capital in increasing the national output. Prominent among these are Cairncross (1955), Solow (1956), Schultz (1961), Hicks (1965), Jorgenson and Grilliches (1967a, 1967b, 1972), Denison (1972, 1974), Johnson (1976), and Jorgenson, Gollop and Fraumeni (1987). Johnson (1976) argued that economic development is a generalized process of capital accumulation that involves many different investment inputs. Jorgenson and Grilliches (1967) attributed technical changes to increases in other inputs such as research, education, training and many others.

The arguments made in favor of international trade are based on the theory of comparative advantage or costs. Countries are said to be in a better position to increase domestic incomes when they spend most of their resources to produce commodities in which they have production and cost advantages. Although the concept was originally developed by David Ricardo, many other scholars have built on his initial views. Some of these scholars include Heckscher and Ohlin (1933), Heckscher (1950), Myint (1959), Leibenstein (1966), Kenen (1967), Meier (1968), Kravis (1970) and many others. Kravis (1970), for example, viewed trade as being crucial to economic development. The popular belief is that developing countries need to acquire capital and engage in international trade and specialization to grow economically. A review of scholarly work aimed at critiquing this view is found in Kitamura (1968), Myint (1969), Greenaway (1967) and many others.

Whereas to Furtado economic development is "initiated and sustained by an internal supply-side dynamic" (see Hunt, 1989, p. 124), Fei and Ranis (1961) maintained that it is rising agricultural productivity that accelerates the process of development toward the attainment of the take-off stage, as postulated by Rostow (1960). In the view of Prebisch (1959, 1971), rising labor productivity is the engine that fuels the process of economic development.

The result of these views is the orthodox policy prescription that the developing countries pursue a drive for capital accumulation and expand international trade. Stone (1992, p. 37) noted that the orthodox view of the 1940s and 1950s was that development planning and projects in developing countries must focus on "capital intensive investments in large projects--dams, roads, power stations, and industrial installations."

Traditional neoclassical economic development theories have maintained that national output (Q) requires a sufficient amount of capital (K) and total existing labor force (*L*). A common procedure used to capture the relationship between output, capital and labor is specified in a general (implicit) functional form as

$$Q = f(K, L) \tag{1}$$

The more specific forms of equation (1) are usually referred to as the Cobb-Douglas production functions.

SOME RELEVANT QUESTIONS

If this relationship between output and inputs is always valid, why is it that some countries have huge quantities of labor and small quantities of capital and yet fail to develop? On the other hand, why do others have huge capital resources and fewer labor force resources and yet are developed? Although some scholars may argue that this may be due to the varying degrees of factor substitution, I wonder whether any such substitution exists in the first place in the sub-Saharan African case. Alternatively, if one argues that the differences may be due to inefficiency, the pertinent question therefore becomes "Why does this inefficieny exist, how is it created and where does it come from?"

If it is true that capital and labor can be easily substituted for each other, should it not be the case that regardless of the variations and/or combinations of these two factors, economic development should proceed as expected in every nation? Do historical stylized facts support the orthodox characterization of the relationship between output and the inputs of capital and labor? It is, however, encouraging to note that recent growth literature is beginning to realize that there exists some magnitude of total output that both capital and labor neither explain nor account for. The following sections address these questions from the HF perspective.

THE HUMAN FACTOR: THE PILLAR OF PROGRESS

Many achievements throughout human history have been significantly influenced by acquired human ingenuity. The Industrial Revolution; the Egyptian civilization and its inventions; the Reformation; the Age of Enlightenment; the development of the telegraph, telephone, computers and airplanes; and many other achievements would not have been possible without a well-educated people who have acquired the relevant HF.

In the era of the Industrial Revolution, many new developments were brought about by people who did not necessarily have any extensive formal training in science. What is common to most of these inventors and innovators was their obsession for the development of new techniques and tools that could be used to deal with hindrances to human progress in their time. Table 5.1 lists inventors

TABLE 5.1
EIGHTEENTH-CENTURY INVENTIONS

Inventor	Invention	Function	Year
Jethro Tull	Seed drill	Sowing seeds	1674-1741
de Reamur	Incubator	Incubating eggs	1683-1757
Cuthbert Clark	Draining Plough	Draining land	1777
Andrew Meikle	Threshing machine	Threshing cereals	1719-1811
Denis Papin	Steam pump	Pumping water out of deep mines	1647-1712
Thomas Newcomen	Atmospheric steam engine	Pumping water out of very deep mines	1663-1729
Jacob Leupold	Steam Engine	Mechanically moving a piston in a cylinder	1674-1727
Robert Barker	Water turbine	Grinding corn	1745
John Smeato	Tidal pump	Supplied water to subscribers in London	1724-1792
John Wyatt	Cotton spinning machine	Spinning cotton	1700-1766
John Kay	Flying shuttle	Weaving	1704-1764
James Hargreaves	Spinning Jenny	Spinning cotton	1778
Edmund Hilary	Diving bell	Exploring the world beneath the sea	1656-1742

TABLE 5.1 CONTINUED

Inventor	Invention	Function	Year
Claude de Jouffroy	Steam boat	Transporting water	1751-1832
Robert Fulton	Submarine	Traveling undersea	1765-1815
Claude Bertholet	Machine for bleaching and dyeing textiles	Bleaching	1748-1822
Clark Tennant	Bleaching powder	Bleaching cloth	1768-1838
Abbe Nollet	Electric light	Producing electric light	1700-1770
William Watson	Electrical conductor	Using wires instead of chains to conduct electrical circuits	1715-1787
Benjamin Franklin	Lightning conductor	Protecting buildings from lightning	1706-1790
Charles, Third Earl of Stanhope	Printing press	Printing	1753-1816
James Watt	Copying machine	Copying letters	1736-1819

Source: Rowland, K. T., 1974. *Eighteenth Century Inventions*. New York: Barnes and Noble.

and their various inventions. As is obvious from Table 5.1, behind every invention was an individual who was committed to finding better solutions to pertinent problems or discovering better and more efficient ways of accomplishing tasks. Had these individuals not devoted their lives to working on each of these programs, humanity would probably not have been blessed with these inventions. All through history, men and women who committed themselves to finding solutions to problems relating to human progress and welfare developed relevant procedures and machines. Many inventors worked on problems involving agriculture, mining, oceanography, steam power, textiles, electricity, medicine, scientific instruments, civil engineering, aeronautics, printing, paper making, pottery and glass, ordnance, chemistry, clocks and compasses and many others. No other factors of production could have made all these developments and inventions possible without the availability of the required HF.

National success in any society depends on people who are well prepared and determined to find solutions to existing problems. In the ancient empires of Greece, Rome, Ghana, Mali and many others for example, royal soldiers were expected to do and act as they were trained to do. They were expected to perform their functions with precision. These soldiers were, therefore, meticulously trained to perform with courage, devotion and commitment. They were efficient, effective and precise in everything they did because they were groomed to be steadfast of mind and to endure all hardships on the battle ground. Their daily service required a long and thorough preparation. This process weeded out individual soldiers who might fail to meet required performance standards. All of these empires were successful and flourished as great civilizations because they spent huge resources to prepare people to protect and defend the empire.

In view of this ancient experience, a society's human resources require a goal-oriented programming that will bridle them for the economic development task. A strong leadership with proper vision to initiate and train others to participate effectively in the development program is required.

In attempting to develop their economies, societies must perceive that it is people who create ideas, develop appropriate technology and use them to make progress happen. Plans, policies and programs are made, executed and monitored by people. When people lack the will to do and the determination to accomplish, the goals of social, economic, political and intellectual development may not be achievable. It can, therefore, be argued that the foundation stone to successful economic development planning and policy is the HF. Economic development programs must be based on available disciplined human resources and not a mere abundant labor force that is not adequately prepared for the task. In this regard, the HF approach to economic development views the HF as the primary engine of growth and the handmaiden of economic development. If labor fails to operate effectively and efficiently in conjunction with the other factors of production, these cooperating factors cannot by themselves furnish society with what it needs for life (see Figure 3.1).

Adam Smith emphasized the role of individual preparation to acquire wealth and achieve prestige and power. He argued that Britain contributed to the economic development of the American colonies by making available to them people who possessed the relevant HF to lay the proper foundations for economic progress.[3] Similarly, according to David Ricardo, the magnitude of capital formation is contingent on the productive capabilities of a nation's labor force.[4]

John Stuart Mill maintained in his *Principles of Political Economy* that "successful production . . . depends more on the qualities of the human agents than on the circumstances in which they work." It was Mill's view that economic progress leans heavily on continuous expansion of humanity's knowledge of the laws of nature and its ability to get rid of every human-imposed hindrances--beliefs, customs, opinions, habits of thought and so on. In addition, Mill believed that men and women must keep in motion every factor/force that is favorable to human progress.[5]

The acceptance of the view that a nation's labor force is more heterogeneous[6] than homogeneous suggests that each labor unit possesses unique and specific human qualities and/or characteristics that differentiate it from others. Ely (1889, p. 146) noted that "moral and intellectual qualities influence its [labor's] productiveness." In his discussion of the role of labor in the productive process, he maintained that alertness, skills, temperance, trustworthiness, the ability to perceive and other related qualities are critical. This view reflects the heterogeneity of the labor force.[7]

LABOR FORCE HETEROGENEITY AND ITS IMPACT ON PRODUCTION

Assume for the sake of simplicity that human qualities and/or characteristics can be grouped into two categories as (1) productivity augmenting (HF^+) and (2) productivity diminishing (HF^-) characteristics.[8] The alternative characterization of the production function can, therefore, be accomplished by observing that the effectiveness of a nation's labor force is determined by the proportion of each of the two HF. This mix will render the labor force either effective or ineffective as an input in the production process (see Figures 3.1 and 3.2).

When a nation's labor force fails to acquire productivity-enhancing human qualities and/or characteristics (HF^+), then the total expected unproductive labor force will exhibit mostly productivity-diminishing characteristics (HF^-). Similarly, if the whole labor force has attained productivity-increasing human qualities, the magnitude of the expected productive labor force will be high with the required human qualities and/or characteristics (HF^+). In real-life circumstances, since these two dichotomous extremes may not be realized, the expected labor force must be viewed as a mixed bag of productive (HF^+) and unproductive (HF^-) labor force (Adjibolosoo, 1993c). The HF is, therefore, a composite variable that is made up of either productivity-enhancing or -reducing characteristics or both (see details in Chapter 3). To increase national output, the expected labor force rather than the absolute magnitude of the labor force is the more relevant variable.

Thus, in attempting to maximize productivity growth and human welfare, each country must maximize the productivity-enhancing human qualities of the labor force (i.e., HF^+) while at the same time minimizing its productivity-reducing human characteristics (HF^-). To evaluate the impacts of the HF on output, it may be useful to determine how it affects the magnitude of the marginal and average productivities of every other input. Although this can be accomplished through quantitative and econometric techniques, it is not the main concern of this chapter and therefore has not been pursued any further (see

Adjibolosoo, 1993c, for the mathematical model in this case).

If we assume that the labor force is homogeneous, then the total expected ouput will be higher (when all the labor force has acquired common productivity-enhancing qualities) than when the entire labor force exhibits productivity-diminishing characteristics. However, as noted earlier, this dichotomous view of labor force productivity is not appropriate in that the labor force is more heterogeneous rather than homogeneous. Therefore, by taking into account the influences of the human qualities of the labor force, the true expected national output will be produced by the total combined labor force.

Given this, the magnitude of the national output will be determined by the effectiveness and efficiency of a country's educational system and training programs (and any others in which the citizens are involved elsewhere) in turning out people who have acquired productivity-enhancing human qualities and/or characteristics. This substantiates the HF view of economic development that output growth is not only determined by huge accumulations of capital alone but also by the acquired HF of the existing labor force. Of crucial importance to economic development planners and policy makers is therefore the knowledge of how to use the educational machinery effectively to train the labor force to acquire productivity-enhancing HF and thus to increase the average productivities of all inputs.

For every country, the race to increase national wealth must be preceded by the development of positive HF in its labor force. If a country's labor force possesses mostly negative human qualities and/or characteristics, regardless of the magnitude of external assistance and the availability of domestic resources, it will not achieve higher productivity.

In light of these factors, whether or not a particular country attains economic growth and development simultaneously with a given amount of capital (both financial and physical) and other cooperating factors will be contigent on the state of its available HF. Thus, the single most important determinant of economic growth and development is the HF. This view, therefore, installs the HF as the true engine of growth and the handmaiden of economic development. Capital cannot always play a substitutionary role in the initial stages of the development process in any country to the neglect of the invaluable role of the necessary HF. Rather, its role must be viewed as complementary to that of the relevant HF. It is the effective combination of existing capital resources, institutions and the available HF that will increase national productivity.

David Hume argued extensively in his essays that it is the energy and industry of people that facilitate economic growth. Since international trade requires large quantities of domestic output whose magnitude depends on the people's effectiveness, it can be argued that the volume of a country's international trade may not increase if its people are not capable of raising its productivity. Large gains can only be made in labor productivity when the people have acquired the HF necessary for the exploitation of gains from international specialization and comparative advantage. At the moment, most least developing countries (LDCs) are not rich in the positive HF and hence may not enjoy the full benefits from international trade; although they may produce sufficient output to service their foreign debt, their continuing debt bondage situation may not change.

THE HUMAN FACTOR: THE INTEGRATING CORE

Figure 5.1 illustrates the relationships and interactions between the HF, institutions and the process of economic growth and development. It is the people of a nation who create institutions, develop and assign property rights. When effectively worked through the acquired HF, these institutions evolve and become aids to the economic development process. The evolutionary process is cyclical (either pro or counter or both) and, when poised in the right direction, can create positive snowballing effects on the development of positive HF, institutional maturity and the acceleration of the economic development process. The crucial point is that the availability of relevant HF provides the necessary leadership and followership qualities for the efficient operation of institutions. The acquired HF generates the necessary leadership that makes it possible to plan, organize, manage and control institutions and human behavior. The courage, resourcefulness and integrity that result from acquired HF also make it possible to create rules and regulations that guide human behavior and action, the production process, exchange, social contracting and the many other aspects of human endeavor. These rules specify how rewards and sanctions should be meted out.

The cyclically complicated processes illustrated in Figure 5.1 suggest that both the existing human qualities and institutions together play an indispensable role in the economic development process. Each factor either bolsters and magnifies or reduces support and diminishes the other's effectiveness. Just as much as all institutions need a well-groomed HF to be effective, so also do people require efficient institutions to perform. However, since institutions are inanimate, they may never be functionally effective without the ingenuity of the nation's citizens. A society may develop institutions and institutional arrangements and/or structures to help in the economic development process, but if the necessary HF is not available to ensure that rewards and sanctions are effectively enforced as stipulated in institutional rules and regulations (i.e., the people's ability to achieve and maintain the rule of law and equality before the law), every national institution will be ineffective and inefficient. This will create conditions for strong diverse social rent-seeking (negative) behavior that will pose problems to the economic development process (see a detailed discussion of this issue in Chapter 4).

It can be argued, therefore, that the initial outcome of this cyclical symbiotic interaction between HF and institutions is what has become known as culture, the sum total of a people's way of life. Its purpose is sevenfold according to Harrison (1972, pp. 119-128). That is, the organizational culture

1 States items of primary importance and the standards against which to measure success and failure.

FIGURE 5.1
IMPACT SEQUENCE OF THE HF AND INSTITUTIONS ON DEVELOPMENT

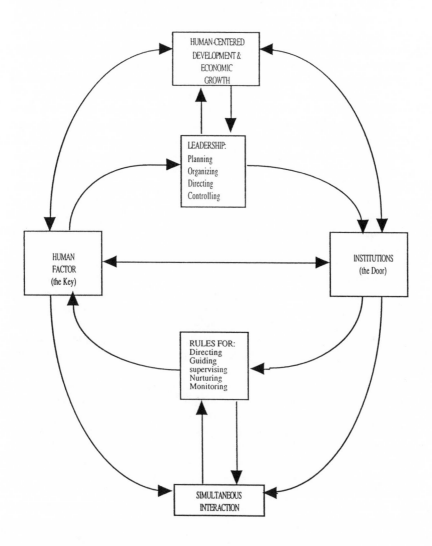

2 Determines how to allocate and use resources depending on goals being pursued as end products.
3 Outlines what is expected from all participating agents.
4 Establishes the rules and regulations regarding legitimate and illegitimate behavior--it places power where it belongs.
5 Specifies behaviors that are approved and disallowed and suggests procedures for rewarding and punishing observed behavior accordingly.
6 Clarifies how interaction and relationships between members should be conducted and how each member should relate to outsiders (i.e., competitively, collaboratively, honestly, distantly, or hostilely).
7 Educates people in how to deal effectively with the external environment (i.e., aggressively, exploitatively, responsibly or proactively).

Commenting on these seven points, Beach (1993, p. 12) suggested that "the culture is the essence of what is important to the organization. As such, it prescribes and proscribes activities, and it defines the *dos and don'ts* that govern the behavior of its members." Neither the HF nor institutions can be neglected or played against each other. Successful economic development programs must have as their foundation the unifying cooperative and coordinative strengths of the available HF and institutions. At every new level of interaction, better results and improved procedures for doing things emerge (this issue is discussed in detail in Chapter 6). In view of this, it becomes clear that those who argue that developing countries need to develop effective institutions and incentive systems to achieve economic development have failed to perceive that there can be no efficient and effective institutions and incentive systems without the appropriate HF that is required to keep them functioning as expected of them.

As I have discussed elsewhere,[9] people with well-developed HF are, therefore, the principal foundation and supporting pillar that uphold and sustain the development process. That is, a well-developed HF is the cornerstone of human progress just as notes are to music, the alphabet is to reading and writing, numerals are to counting and mathematics, oxygen is to life, hydroelectric currents are to light bulbs and so on. The functional role each of these elements plays in the activity it is involved in is indispensable. These activities will never commence successfully in the first place without these essential inputs.

Thus, to be effective and efficient in carrying out their expected functions and to help societies achieve the goals of their economic development program, existing institutions require people who

1 Have the ambition and the imagination to search for clues; have the intent always to perform and are of one mind[10]; have the willingness to search for, and insist on discovering, solutions to existing national problems.
2 Are determined to search for and acquire understanding about current problems, existing levels of available skills and the additional abilities required for the enhancement of productivity, and have knowledge about

what must be done and how and the wisdom to use acquired knowledge to solve problems. These people will facilitate the rate at which solutions are carved for overcoming hindrances to the economic development process.

3 Have the zeal and the willingness to give liberally their best in contributing to the national economic development program. The industry brought to the reconstruction process by each person must grow out of individual free will and commitment to self-interest insofar as it is consonant with national economic development goals.

4 Provide the required leadership that is apt to facilitate the process of providing the opportunities for every citizen to contribute freely to the success of the national program for economic progress.

5 Have the assurance that courage, resourcefulness and hard work will not only increase the wealth of their society but will also lead to the continuing enjoyment of the fruits of their munificence.

6 Possess a sense of purpose, insight, vision and direction; are skillful in wisdom and scientific knowledge; are steadfast in commitment to risk taking; and are dedicated to personal integrity. These are the people who possess relevant human qualities and know what is good and required for human progress (i.e., effective and efficient maintenance of law and order, respect for the rule of law and property rights, the promotion of hard work and social welfare and an unrelenting respect for the sanctity of human life and the dignity of labor).

The existence of people of this caliber will lead to the creation of a society that will be rich in the positive HF necessary for judiciously fashioning meaningful national economic development policies and programs. Such a well-disciplined labor force will possess the capability to institute, develop and manage efficiently all evolving institutions and institutional structures that are expected to serve as the cornerstone for each society's economic development program (see Figure 5.1).

Merely creating institutions and institutional structures that do not have people with the required HF to manage and direct them would be like installing lamps in a house that has no electricity: The fixtures would be there but there would still be no light! I argue, therefore, that the existence of institutions and institutional structures, capital (both physical and financial), ideologies, huge trade surpluses, etc. is not necessarily the key foundation to progress. Although they are necessary for economic development (i.e., they are the door), they are not sufficient. It is the availability of relevant HF (i.e., the key) that constitutes the true engine of growth and the generator of economic development (see Figure 5.1); these HF are the sufficient characteristics that are required for economic development.[11] A country may have every possible institution, institutional structures, well-defined property rights and other required materials and yet fail to attain progress because it may have been unable to produce the HF required to provide the requisite supervision of the national economic development program.

This is one area into which all developing countries have put very few resources in the past. It is now time for each of these countries to recommence the economic development process by building this necessary foundation structure through education, training and mentoring.[12] In view of this, it can be argued that many economic policies and programs in the past in the LDCs were either misplaced or misdirected. The LDCs need to know this and devise schemes to deal successfully with it.

Henry Marshall Tory, who was appointed president of Carleton College on June 18, 1942, observed that "I learned very early the lesson that it is people, not buildings, that make an institution; and if we can put our hearts to it we can do something worthwhile" (see Carleton University, 1992). Most advanced countries have perceived this philosophy in the infant stages of their industrialization process. Therefore, they committed a lot of resources to educating, training and developing the needed human qualities and/or characteristics. People like Henry Marshall Tory, with vision, devotion and commitment, are what it takes to spin the wheels of economic development for cumulative improvement in societies.

I also surmise that the root cause of the decline of any civilization and the growing institutional inefficiency and ineffectiveness is HF decay (see Chapter 4 and Adjibolosoo, 1995, pp. 3-14). National productivity, wealth and living standards have positive relationships with the nature of the existing HF. A detailed study and critical analysis of the destruction of ancient civilizations such as those of Rome, Greece, Ghana, Mali, Songhai, Israel and Kush Meroe, just to mention a few, reveals that the collapse was mainly the result of HF decline. In the same way, the rise of these civilizations is attributed to the invaluable role of the positive HF. In all these cases, although there were other external secondary factors that contributed to the initial success and later decline of these civilizations, it is unquestionably clear that the primary contributing factor was the lack of the appropriate HF.

THE HF AND SYSTEMS EFFICIENCY AND DEVELOPMENT

A more relevant yet complicated way of looking at the problem of low productivity and economic underdevelopment is to recognize that technological efficiency (or the system's effectiveness) depends on the level of HF development. Poorly developed HF will reduce the system's efficiency.

In Figure 5.2, a system's effectiveness (SE) is viewed as being dependent on the level of HF development (HFD). When a one-to-one correspondence between SE and HFD is assumed with a given initial design, the positive relationship between the two variables is represented by the 45-degree diagonal line. For example, when there is a 1 percent improvement in the HF, one would expect that there must also be a 1 percent improvement in the system's effectiveness. Although the positive linear relationship is the ideal or expected relationship between SE and HFD, it will not be realized because of existing hindrances in the system which militate against the realization of any expected one-to-one correspondence between SE and HFD.

FIGURE 5.2
HUMAN FACTOR DEVELOPMENT AND SYSTEM EFFECTIVENESS

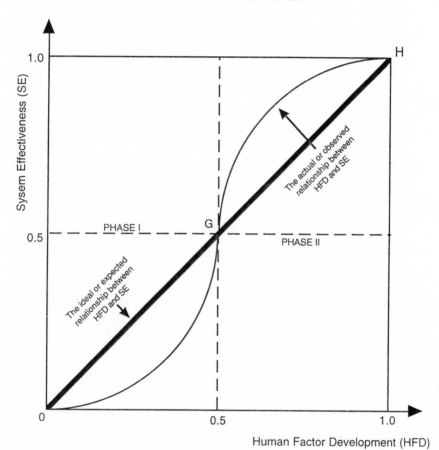

The possibility of these hindrances in the system suggests that the empirical growth relationship between SE and HFD can be best approximated with the logistic function, which is the S-shaped curve drawn from point 0 through G to point H in Figure 5.2. Regardless of how efficiently a system is designed to function, if the labor force fails to acquire the HF necessary for its application, a country will find itself operating in phase I (see Figure 5.2). This will mean low productivity and economic underdevelopment. Countries that will make it into phase II will be those that have attained continuing successes in HF development.

THE HF AND THE SYSTEMS FALLACY SYNDROME

Contrary to popular belief, low productivity and economic underdevelopment are not necessarily due to poor systems and inefficient technology (or techniques). Systems, technologies, equipment and so on are created by people. Thus, regardless of their artificial intelligence, they are also, like institutions, inanimate. Their performance and efficiency levels depend on the HF. Thus, any attribution of human deficiencies and failures to systems or technology is hereby referred to as the systems fallacy syndrome. Countries that are concerned about raising input productivity to achieve economic development need to recognize and avoid becoming victims of the systems fallacy syndrome.

SOME EXAMPLES

Examples of the role of the HF in human progress and successes abound. In what follows, a few examples are presented to illustrate the importance of the HF to the human enterprise.

The HF and Nonprofit Organizations

The research findings of Knauft, Berger and Gray (1991) conclusively point out that the successes of many nonprofit business activities are due to positive HF. The prominent human characteristics and/or qualities that have contributed to the successes of each of the companies studied are presented in Table 5.2.

The data in Table 5.2 reveal that the success of the companies listed depend on the HF. The most common and frequently recurring human qualities include dedication, commitment, vision, leadership, management and administrative skills, responsibility, knowledge, industry, communications skills and creativity. It can, therefore, be concluded that no human institution or business venture can be successful without the availability of these relevant human charateristics. Essentially, people who have developed self-control, a relevant work ethos, rules of orderliness and efficiency in everyday activities and a disciplined labor force

TABLE 5.2
EXCELLENCE IN ACTION: OUTSTANDING
NONPROFIT ORGANIZATIONS

ORGANIZATION	AREA OF STRENGTH	HF
Atlanta Historical Society	Adapting to changing times	Character, ethos, communication skills, accessibility, leadership skills, administration
Baxter Community Center	Getting an agency back on its feet	Dedication, commitment to mission, dynamic leadership, industry, loyalty, foresight, management style, adherence to values, sincerity and decisiveness, performance, responsibility
East Bay Asian Local Development Corporation	Entrepreneurship at the grass roots	Understanding, vision, ambition, youthful vigor, devotion, assuming ownership, commitment, leadership skills, sensitivity, purposefulness
Guadalupe Center	Leadership that heals	Education, taking responsibility, values, desire to help, hard work, persistency, dedication, tenacity, integrity, commitment, leadership skills

TABLE 5.2 CONTINUED

Indian Health Board	Challenging the status quo	Knowledge, vision, drive to succeed, administration, initiative, leadership skills, responsibility, determination, dreams, dedication
Interlochen Center for the Arts	Unswerving dedication to mission	Dedication, vision, talented youngsters, experience, leadership skills, management, persistency, responsibility
Northside Center for Child Development	Managing leadership transitions	Direction and support, vision, knowledge, dreams, understanding, responsibility, self-determination, foresight, commitment, perception, dedication, leadership skills, administrative efficiency, loyalty
San Francisco Education Fund	A pioneer in managing the problem of success	Industry, management, commitment, leadership, responsibility, passion, self-assessment, devotion, administration, knowledge, creativity, motivation, enthusiasm, persistency, vision, experience

TABLE 5.2 CONTINUED

Seattle Emergency Housing Inc.	Building partnership	Ability to learn, vision, passion, experience, creativity, leadership skills, industry, persistency, interpersonal skills, commitment, motivation, sense of purpose, consistency, knowledge, zeal, enthusiasm, understanding, verbal communication skills
Upward Fund Afterschool	Leadership for independence	Commitment, industry, vision, leadership and administrative skills, management

are necessary for human progress. Similar results hold true for most of the advanced countries' transnational corporations (i.e., IBM, Ford Motors, GE, GM, Chrysler, Sears, Boeing, Goodyear, Chase Manhattan and many others).[13]

The Role of the HF as Portrayed in Movies

In a 1991 movie called *Sister Act*, the value of the HF in human success was demonstrated. After witnessing a mob murder, Whoopi Goldberg, one of the two stars, is pursued by the killers, who wish to silence her by killing her. She is later taken to a nunnery to be hidden from her assailants. While in the nunnery, she realizes that the nuns cannot sing well. By combining other human qualities with her musical talents and/or skills, she is successful in teaching the nuns to sing beautifully. Her success is so great that even the Pope makes a visit to the nunnery. The role of the HF in human progress and success has also been demonstrated in at least three other movies: *Sister Act II, The Sound of Music* and *Lean on Me*. These examples show clearly that very little can be achieved by societies that do not possess an adequately groomed labor force that possesses the HF.

Every economic development effort and/or program in a society must, therefore, begin with vigorous HF development plans. The right to live, be free, enjoy peace and tranquility, coexist with other people who are different from you and be human cannot be achieved and maintained in its absence.

Government legislations, bylaws, regulations and such cannot be substituted for HF development which is a major vehicle for the attainment of economic development in every regard in all societies (Adjibolosoo, 1994d). It is the only cure for ethnic and/or racial intolerance and international aggression. Very few government and organizational programs and/or regulations can achieve their goals without the availability of the relevant HF.

WHAT OF IDEOLOGY?

In my mind's eye, I saw capitalism and socialism go to a small claims court for a hearing. Adam Smith and Karl Marx began to argue about the usefulness of capitalism and socialism to humanity. Aristotle and Plato and all their students were in attendance. The debates and arguments of both parties were so heated that they had to reappear before a renowned supreme court judge within three months. When the court was finally called into session, the judge called on the counsel of each camp to present its closing statements and/or arguments.

When Karl Marx rose quickly to his feet, he stared deeply into Adam Smith's eyes and said "Humanity has been milked like cash cows by capitalists, who finally forced the downtrodden to worry themselves into economic anemia and/or amnesia. Their hopes for a better life are dashed and they continue to remain in continuing poverty, with lots of day-dreaming. Friends, you the jury have to quarantine all capitalists and banish them to a far-away planet so that humanity can breathe and live a peaceful communal life once again."

With a smile beaming on his face, Adam Smith rose up slowly and retorted, "Whereas capitalism is the window of financial ventilation to a world of economic success and is, therefore, environmentally friendly, socialism is isolation and, therefore, leads to human degradation and economic stagnation. I think that you the jury need to know these pertinent facts." To all other court attendants, the debates and recent historical events seem to be suggesting that although capitalism has apparently presented the best arguments and may win, socialism seems to be in disarray and may lose.

Just as the judge was about to ask the jury for its verdict, a HF approach theorist popped up in the center of the courtroom and blurted out, "Whether or not capitalism is the window of financial ventilation and socialism is a continuing process that leads to human degradation and economic stagnation is immaterial. Similarly, the milking and the impoverishment of some members of the human race by both capitalism and socialism cannot be denied. What is crucial to know is that it is the available or absent human qualities and characteristics (i.e., the HF) that cause each ideology to succeed or fail. Ideologies have never achieved anything and will never. It is people who make things happen regardless of their ideological leaning, assuming the availability of the appropriate HF. You the jury must be conscious of this view too."

Upon hearing this, the judge laughed and said to the court, "I am convinced that we have all heard the verdict! Court is adjourned." To the surprise of all observers and contenders, everyone went home feeling that there is economic hope for humanity, especially sub-Saharan Africans.

To the sub-Saharan African country, it is useless to focus on ideological debates. What is needed at the moment is to identify the real hindrances to economic development and devise techniques to deal with them.

IMPLICATIONS FOR SUB-SAHARAN AFRICA

This chapter suggests that unless the required HF is properly developed to help people perform their entrepreneurial functions, a country can rarely ever develop economically. No society has ever developed without having groomed the relevant HF in its labor force. Thus, sub-Saharan ACs cannot be expected to be the first to do otherwise. It is not possible and will never happen. At this point in time, when sub-Saharan ACs are still in the infant phase of the economic development process, the African people must be educated and trained to gain the positive HF that are necessary for economic development.

Today is the time for sub-Saharan ACs' governments to create education and training programs that will prepare their human resources and transform their lacks into positive HF to support the economic development program. Since a nation's past influences its present and probably its future, a current policy of creating and equipping the labor force for productivity growth will have positive and long-term implications for progress in sub-Saharan Africa.

From the perspective of the HF approach, countries that have achieved economic development possess a labor force that has attained high levels of HF development. The orthodox view about the critical factors that make economic development happen seems to have failed in sub-Saharan Africa. Many of these countries have done almost everything possible to increase domestic savings and the volume of international trade and yet have not achieved any significant success in economic development.

Nigeria, for example, with huge oil resources in the 1970s and 1980s, failed to use the oil revenues to make economic development happen. The destructive effects of HF decay can be seen in the Nigerian case (McCord and McCord, 1986, pp. 38-39). Nigerians have been less successful in trying to deal with their pertinent problems of economic underdevelopment because they have not yet produced the necessary HF in themselves. The days of growing oil revenues in the late 1960s and the 1970s have come and gone with very little economic development. In Nigeria today, a few hundred dollars offered as a bribe to a customs officer will induce him or her not to prevent contraband items from being brought into the country. McCord and McCord (1986, p. 45) noted that in 1981, someone set ablaze the foreign ministry to destroy any evidence of poor construction. Similarly, arsonists burned down the telecommunications office building. In many other cases, individual contractors will do everything possible to destroy any evidence that may convict them in courts of law if they are apprehended and tried. This phenomenon is not typical of Nigeria alone. It is common all over sub-Saharan ACs. Similarly, Ghana, the Ivory Coast, Kenya and many other countries have missed golden opportunities to develop.

Although orthodox explanations for these failures abound, I argue that they are not the real reasons for the failure (Adjibolosoo, 1994a). The true cause for these failures is that sub-Saharan ACs lack the HF necessary to use the existing resources effectively and efficiently to achieve economic development. External assistance in its many forms has been ineffective in turning the sub-Saharan African economic underdevelopment around because the domestic labor force does not possess the qualities required for the efficient use of resources from both domestic and foreign sources. In view of this, it is time we stopped using orthodox economic arguments to explain the failure of economic development planning, policy and programs in sub-Saharan Africa (see Chapter 3 for a detailed analysis). Kiros (1992, p. 40) argued that although commercialization and industrialization are critical to Africa's material development, this may not happen unless technically and morally responsible Africans become available. This is why sub-Saharan ACs need to pay extensive attention to HF development.

Sub-Saharan African leaders and all African peoples who are interested in and concerned about social, economic, political and ntellectual development must begin to alter their existing education and training programs to meet their HF needs as we enter the twenty-first century. It is important to realize that continued dependence on the developed countries through aid packages and other forms of humanitarian assistance will merely perpetuate the economic underdevelopment in sub-Saharan ACs. If possible, it is now time for these countries to focus on HF development and thus to set the stage for future economic development in sub-Saharan Africa.

I am convinced that neither the strength of the European Economic Union nor the apparent collapse of Eastern European socialism will spell disaster for sub-Saharan ACs. If at all, these phenomena, in addition to the expected marginalization of Africa, must be viewed as windows of opportunities for catapulting sub-Saharan African economies into high gears of economic growth and development. This catapulting, however, will not materialize until the HF necessary for the economic development process becomes available in the region. For many decades, sub-Saharan Africa has been treated like a helpless, cranky and crying baby. Every time it cries, a long and ugly feedingbottle is shoved into its mouth. When signs of being soothed begin to show, the feedingbottle is pulled out. As more discomfort begins and sub-Saharan Africa resumes crying, shouting and kicking, begging for another feeding, it is provided with all alacrity (i.e., recall international response to the recent problems in Somalia, Ethiopia, Rwanda, etc.). Sometimes, sub-Saharan Africa is threatened by being told that if it does not pursue democracy, respect human rights and preserve the tropical rainforests, the supply of future feedingbottles will be denied.

As long as this attitude continues, Africa, the poor, hungry and helpless baby, will not have the true opportunity to develop and prepare its own feedingbottle in the future. A more critical thinking and careful evaluation of the effects of foreign aid and assistance packages to Africa will reveal that if they are discontinued, Africa will not be totally annihilated. Instead, it will force Africa to develop its own alternative sources of sustenance. Recall, for example, that about fifty years ago, when China initiated the cultural revolution and was experiencing hard times, the U.S. and the rest of the Western world refused to provide any forms of assistance to the Chinese. Today, what do we see? A nation that is gradually overcoming many odds and obstacles and working hard to turn its crises into windows of opportunities. My continuing observation and study of this nation make me believe that Africa will have a better chance of developing if it is left alone. Although foreign aid is necessary, it is not sufficient for development, especially when the donors determine the terms and decide on how the funds provided must be used. Sub-Saharan ACs can develop without it.

NOTES

1.   See Chapter 3 for a detailed definition of the HF.

2. A more detailed bibliographical reference on institutional economics can be found in Commons, J. R. 1990. *Institutional Economics: Its Place in Political Economy*. Vol. I. New Brunswick, NJ: Transaction Publishers.

3.   See the *Wealth of Nations*, p. 576.

4.   See the *Works and Correpondence of David Ricardo*.

5. See his essay "Nature," in *Three Essays on Religion*, pp. 28-36; and the *Representative Government*, pp. 190-191 and 214-217.

6. See, for example, Solow (1957), Ehrenberg (1973), Denison (1974), Bellante (1979), Kumar and Coates (1982), Oi (1983), Garen (1985), Heywood (1986), Jorgenson, Gollop and Fraumeni (1987) and Farber and Newman (1989) for discussions of a *nonhomogeneous labor force*.

7. In more recent growth literature, economists have begun to model labor heterogenity into the production function. See relevant references in note 6. Their approach is, however, based on the narrow human capital theoretic view. The human factor approach maintains that other human qualities and/or characteristics that are different from human capital be also included in this analysis to make it more complete.

8. This implies that equation (1) must be re-specified as: $Q = f(K, N)$, where N is the composite expected labor force made up of varying combinations of HF^+ and HF^-. The model can be complicated by recognizing that even in each of these two classifications, there exist varying elements. Although some positive HF will be more productive than others, negative HF can also exert differential negative impacts on the magnitude of national output. This approach has not been pursued in this chapter. The interested reader should refer to Adjibolosoo, 1993c).

9. See, for example, Adjibolosoo, S. B-S. K. 1993a. "The Human Factor in Development." *The Scandinavian Journal of Development Alternatives*, XII (4):

139-149; Adjibolosoo, S. B-S. K. 1995. "The Significance of the Human Factor in African Economic Development." In S. B-S. K. Adjibolosoo, ed. *The Significance of the Human Factor in African Economic Development.* New York: Praeger.

10. Being of one mind does not necessarily mean that people must be identical in every regard. It, does imply, however, that to achieve success and excellence in the economic development program, the people in every AC must develop their own development mission statements, leadership skills, guidelines for enhancing average labor productivity, planning, policy and programs to be pursued. In a sense, there must exist a consensus on these issues (that is, minds must meet).

11. Similar arguments regarding the relationship between the HF and institutions can also be made for how the HF and capital, trade, ideologies, etc. must interact to achieve economic progress in countries.

12. I am referring to an education, training and mentoring program that is capable of producing the necessary HF rather than mere academic intellectuals whose heads are swollen with ideologies they cannot use to solve sub-Saharan Africa's problems of economic underdevelopment.

13. For more details on these issues, see Loomis, C. J. 1991. "Can John Aker Save IBM?" *Fortune*, July 15, 1991, pp. 40-56; Caminity, S. 1991. "Sears' Need: More Speed." *Fortune*, July 15, 1991, pp. 88-90; and many other articles in various *Fortune* issues.

6

Economic Development as a Dynamic Learning and Discovery Process: A Human Factor Theory

INTRODUCTION

For many years, the process of economic development has not been fully excavated by scholars of economic development theory. Historical evidence and stylized facts about problems of economic underdevelopment in developing countries attest to this. Many resources that have been poured into these nations have led to insignificant changes in the well-being of people in these societies. The state and the process of economic development have not been properly distinguished and defined in the past.

The failure to do so may be due to several reasons. One reason is that most economists seem to be more interested in states (i.e., stable equilibria) than in processes. Yet when one looks outside and observes individual economic agents act on and react to market forces, there is little evidence to suggest that continuing stable equilibrium exists. Another reason is that it is easier for economists to quantify states than processes. Thus, even though economic historians such as Schumpeter, Hayek and many others sought to examine economic processes in the past, their efforts and results were considered marginal to economic development theory and never became accepted and fully integrated into mainstream economic development thinking and modeling. There exists little differentiation between the two concepts. The result is that the state and the process of economic development have been lumped together and viewed as economic development, thereby obscuring the meaning of the two concepts and how economic development occurred. It is, therefore, important to disentangle the meanings of these terms to understand the nature and dynamics of the economic development process. The hope is that this differentiation may help scholars of economic development theory identify and propose workable solutions to the problems of economic underdevelopment in sub-Saharan African countries (ACs).

In this chapter, I argue that the progress of any country requires the following: (1) there must be the ability to acquire and use knowledge; (2) what has been learned must produce positive attitudinal changes regarding people's choices between old and inefficient and new, more effective ways of solving problems; (3) the people must use the acquired HF to develop and evolve new procedures that have greater promise for creating more effectiveness in social progress and to solve pertinent problems subsequently through the discovery process; and (4) the people must view the economic development process as a continuous problem-solving and discovery process that happens over time (Ofori-Amoah, 1995, pp. 15-24; Schumpeter, 1961, pp. 58-66). The argument, therefore, is that economic development is a dynamic learning and problem-solving process. I view learning not only as an activity of knowledge acquisition alone but also as a process that leads to positive attitudinal change and the creation of constructive problem-solving procedures.

THE VARYING STATES AND PROCESSES OF ECONOMIC DEVELOPMENT

The state of economic development refers to the level of progressive attainment of society's hierarchical goals, ideals and aspirations at   specific points in time, whereas the process of economic development refers to the means whereby those goals, ideals and aspirations are achieved. The varying states and processes of economic growth and development are higly intertwined and therefore cannot be separated easily into distinct stages. Economic growth and development proceed from one point in time to another. This phenomenon can exhibit an upward linear trend (i.e., continuing economic growth and development), a downward linear trend (i.e., economic growth without development and/or perpetual economic decay) or a combination of both, in which case the phenomenon will follow patterns of cyclical fluctuations (i.e., the flow and ebb of economic development processes from one state to another over a long period of time). In the case of a long-lasting stagnation, no cyclical movements are observable.

Human progress is a continuous process that can be likened to the growth and tending of plants in gardens. The farmer sows the seeds and provides them with moisture and other nutrients required for the process of growth. This process must be sustained by plant food, water and sunlight. Nature supplies the appropriate amount of sunshine necessary for effective photosynthesis. Over time, the changes that occur in each individual plant will be determined by several factors, including the farmer's ability to learn and utilize new knowledge and/or technology. This natural process is reminiscent of economic development. Schumacher (1973, pp. 164-165) wrote as follows:

Let us imagine a visit to a modern industrial establishment. Through all its fantastic complexity, we might well wonder how it was possible for the human mind to conceive such a thing. What an immensity of knowledge, ingenuity, and experience is here incarnated in equipment! How is it possible? The answer is that it did not spring ready-made out of any person's mind--it came by a process of evolution. It started quite simply, then this was added and that was modified, and so the whole thing became more and more complex.

Progress occurs through hard work over time. It neither happens by chance nor through the mere pushing of an electronic button or switch on the wall.

ECONOMIC DEVELOPMENT AS A LEARNING PROCESS

For the purposes of this chapter, I define learning as becoming sufficiently informed about or acquainted with knowledge that creates the potential for producing permanent behavioral change and/or at least encourages potential behavioral change. Learning is, therefore, viewed as a discovery process whereby the individual uncovers hidden or previously unknown ideas and/or information. The learning process must be designed to aim at ascertaining knowledge through intensive analysis or inquiry. Its impact is to affect attitudinal change either positively or negatively. Learning has the power to alter human behavior and cultural mind-sets through training, experience or practice. In general, behavioral scientists have agreed that "learning is a relatively permanent change in behavior or potential behavior that results from reinforced practice or experience" (Swanda, 1979, p. 110 and Hammer, 1974).

In the view of Luthans (1973, p. 362), central to this definition of learning are four major points:

1 Learning entails either a positive or negative change.
2 To be perceived as learning, the change in behavior must be permanent. This point excludes temporal changes that may come as a result of adaptations to changes in physical and/or emotional conditions surrounding the individual.
3 Learning requires training, practice or experience.
4 Reinforcement of training, practice or experience must also happen to render learning effective and useful.

Swanda (1979, pp. 110-111) observed that

the learner, through learning, intellectually and conceptually understands something he never understood before. He is potentially able to enlarge his skills and engage in activities that enhance his expertise. He is also able to organize individual items of information into a whole concept. These whole concepts can be arranged into interrelated units. In effect, learning results in expanding one's ability to use and apply various new combinations of skills, concepts, and behavior. Learning makes possible the attainment of new behavior. When a person can make responses that he previously could not make, he has learned.

This view of learning suggests that learning involves more than gaining knowledge. It involves the ability to apply acquired knowledge. That is, the acquisition of knowledge is a necessary but not sufficient condition for problem solving and successful attainment of technological progress. The sufficient condition requires the people's ability to apply what has been learned (i.e., knowledge gained) to existing problems and difficulties. It is through the application of this ability that existing technologies are improved and/or new appropriate technologies can be evolved by a society whose inhabitants possess the HF necessary to overcome the major hindrances to the development process (see Chapter 9 for further discussions of this issue).

Two classic learning processes most often discussed in the economics, business and psychology literature relate to learning from examples/experience or observation or modeling and learning by doing.[1] Learning by doing is prominent in the economic and business literature. It is usually discussed in terms of the learning curve. Learning by example and doing leads to the acquisition of knowledge that becomes useful for the enhancement of performance effectiveness and efficiency on the job. The more learning that takes place, the more effective people become in doing their jobs. Thus, the more relevant knowledge people have about their prevailing circumstances, the better prepared they will be in attempting solutions to pertinent problems.

For example, to the human race, there exists an unlimited stock of relevant information that has not yet been accessed and decoded. Although this reservoir of knowledge is necessary and sufficient for meeting human needs, effectively solving problems and overcoming human ailments (i.e., curing cancer, AIDS, racial intolerance and many other ills), it must be discovered and learned to affect attitudes and/or cultural mind-sets that form the bedrock for all human action and/or activity. This assertion can be illustrated with a hypothetical example.

Suppose for the sake of argument that there are three different societies. In the first society, there is neither knowledge production nor extensive communication systems (i.e., living at the mercies of nature: a passively inactive community). In the second society, although people do not possess knowledge production or extensive communication systems, they are able to generate just the knowledge necessary to maintain what they have already achieved (i.e., living within the bounds of reason: a functionally active community). In the third society, there exists a growing knowledge and telecommunications industry that is not only capable of generating the information necessary for solving current problems but is also able to find solutions in advance to anticipated future problems (i.e., creatively producing more than required for present existence: a community of people who possess intense emotional drive and/or fervor to conquer, transcend and live above existing environmental circumstances). The crucial question that arises, therefore, is "How will the people's learning ability, discovery processes and attitudinal changes impact human progress in each of these three societies?" In relation to these societies, it can be argued that since economic development is a continuing process, the society that is capable of continuously gaining more knowledge about the process of economic development will be the one that will achieve success in its pursuit. It is, therefore, crucial for every society to perceive that learning is indispensable to the economic development of nations. When no learning occurs, continuing economic underdevelopment may result.

PROBLEM-SOLVING PHASES OF THE ECONOMIC DEVELOPMENT PROCESS

Figure 6.1 illustrates three phases (levels) of problem solving in the economic development process. In phase I (primary level), basic (simple) problems of economic development are confronted. A society that successfully develops techniques and creates effective methodologies to deal with these problems may successfully catapult itself into phase II (the secondary level) over a period of time.

Since there may exist many unknown intervening variables, progress may be relatively slow. Societies that are able to overcome phase I problems will be ready to advance to dealing with phase II problems and/or hindrances to economic development. If nothing stalls this process, the society will finally move into phase III, where it will be confronted with more advanced, complex and abstract problems. In this phase, it is likely that the attained level of the economic development process may plateau when the available HF is not able to help the people develop solutions to complex problems. As long as humanity inhabits planet earth, this dynamic problem-solving saga will continuously repeat itself in every society. This problem-solving procedure is what Ofori-Amoah (1995, pp. 15-24) referred to as the Saturation Hypothesis.

Four of the existing millions of possible trajectories of the phases of problem solving and the levels of economic development are shown in Figure 6.1. These trajectories exhibit diversity in the problem-solving abilities of the three phases and the levels of economic development for different societies. At the primary level, each of the four societies represented in Figure 6.1 is at the lowest level of its economic development process. As time moves on, the problem-solving abilities of each society diverge from those of others. Those societies that discover more accurate solutions faster than others are able to attain higher levels of economic development and are able to enter subsequent phases faster than others. For example, in phase I, society C is able to deal more effectively with its hindrances to economic development than all the other societies. Similarly, in phase II, society B is able to solve problems more efficiently than A and D. However, as each society enters phase III, its ranking changes. In this phase, society A has attained the highest level of economic development. Trailing A from behind are B, C and D, in that order.

This theoretical observation explains the present economic conditions of the United Kingdom, United States, Japan, Spain, China, Italy, Egypt, Ghana and many others. The theory also sheds further light on the economic decline of nation-states. As noted in Chapters 4 and 5, HF decay plays a crucial role in a nation's economic development process.

FIGURE 6.1
PHASES OF PROBLEM SOLVING AND THE LEVELS OF ECONOMIC DEVELOPMENT

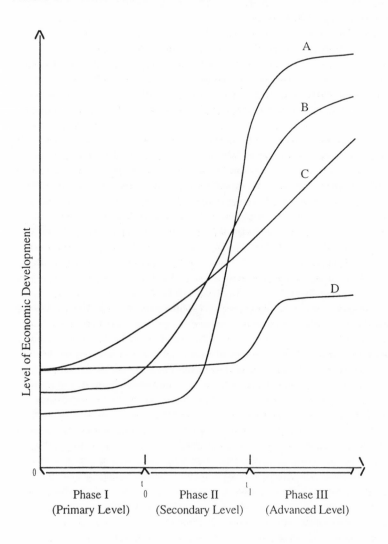

Phases of Problem Solving

The rate at which each society is able to unravel intricately complicated problems is determined by the intensity of the advances made by its people in fostering learning and positive attitudinal change. Although the rate of problem solving may be rapid in some nations, it will be slow in others. The time it takes to overcome pertinent problems in each of the three phases is not only determined by the complexity and novelty of the society's problems but also by the rates at which learning, discovery and positive attitudinal change take place in the people and by their existing human qualities and/or characteristics.

This observation suggests that the rate of acceleration of the economic development process is therefore determined by the rate at which problems are solved in each society. Such solution techniques may be unique and/or specific to societies. They may not be successfully transferred and adopted, as done by their inventors in their own societies elsewhere. That is, it is equally unlikely that the application of techniques being used by country A to solve phase III problems will work for country B, which is looking for solutions to its phase II problems. These may not work even if both societies are trying to solve phase III problems since each may be faced with unique difficulties and yet have attained varying levels of HF development. Similarly, these techniques will neither work for country C, which is still battling with phase I problems of economic development, nor for country D. This explains why approximately half a century of economic development planning and policy implementation has failed in sub-Saharan ACs and other developing nations. These countries have always been dragged along to pursue policies that the advanced nations knew would serve their (the DCs') interests best (Ofori-Amoah, 1995, pp. 15-24).

There are no shortcuts to the economic development process. Even when we are made to believe that they exist, we need to be wary about their adoption. Hirschman (1958, p. 29) noted that it is important to be suspicious of any suggested shortcuts because theories in the social sciences are not necessarily neutral. That is, these theories were developed in relation to specific conditions pertaining to the societies under consideration. They must be viewed as ways of shedding light on pertinent problems in these societies. They focus on variables that are typical of the society being studied. They may, therefore, be less applicable to other societies. Hirschman (1988) argued further that "an attempt to *apply* them nevertheless may turn out to be a lengthy detour rather than a short cut. For, as we have become used to looking at reality through certain theoretical glasses, we may for a long time be unable to see it as it really is."

Sub-Saharan ACs have paid dearly for trying to use shortcuts. They have made a long detour and, even now, no one is sure whether they will achieve economic development in the future if they continue to pursue and apply orthodox economic development theories and policies that are irrelevant to their unique circumstances. Ghana is struggling to achieve economic development in sub-Saharan Africa. What is required at the present,however, is the development of the HF in Ghana, and progress will ensue. Any sub-Saharan African country that wishes to achieve economic progress must do likewise.

A relevant policy conclusion to be drawn from this theoretical analysis is that to be successful, economic development policies and programs must not only be based on each society's ability to deal with its initial pertinent problems before advancing naturally into the next phase of the economic development process but must also be properly guided. When a society that is battling phase I problems is dragged along by those that have already attained phase III, its economic development process may be stalled. This, in fact, has been the real-life experience of countries that economic development theorists have labeled as economically underdeveloped. As one problem is solved and additional knowledge and wisdom are gained, a society will be better placed to confront more complex problems (Ofori-Amoah, 1995, pp. 15-24). The economic development process may plateau in any of the three phases at any time when that society fails to attain positive attitudinal changes through the development of the HF and/or finds it too difficult to generate the necessary wisdom and/or skills for problem solving (see details in Chapter 9). In this case, it could be argued that the learning and the discovery processes and attitudinal changes may have leveled off in such a society.

In view of these observations, it seems to me that macroeconomic policy and economic development theory and/or policy must not be quickly generalized since they are usually designed to deal with internal problems of the economic development process in a specific society. There can, therefore, be no global macroeconomics in the existing world order, despite what some economists try to make the rest of the world believe. This view does not, however, rule out global policy synchronization as every nation begins to experience economic development based on the HF approach. In the modern world, nations attempting to attain higher phases of economic development pursue their own self-interest. They therefore devise problem-solving techniques to contain their difficulties.

Neither humanity in general nor any specific society in particular will experience violent and destructive revolutions and/or wars if humankind has come to terms with the truth that no single individual or society wields total control or monopoly over the knowledge that makes economic development happen (Jewkes, 1958). This observation suggests that the growth of knowledge that has the potential to solve problems can be arrived at through dialoguing processes, which may lead to the synthesis of several ideas into new knowledge that works. Cato, for example, has been reported to have argued that the Roman legal order

> was based upon the genius, not of one man, but of many: it was founded, not in one generation, but in a long period of several centuries and many ages of men. For, said he, there never has lived a man possessed of so great a genius that nothing could escape him, nor could the combined powers of all men living at one time possibly make all the provisions for the future without the aid of actual experience and the test of time. (quoted in Bartley and Kresge, 1991, p. 85)

Bartley and Kresge (1991, p. 5) observed that "it is the significance of knowledge and information that leads to the evolution of understanding. Indifference cannot produce the sort of inquiry, the criticism and dissent that is necessary for the growth of knowledge." (An extended discussion of this issue is presented in Chapter 9.)

In the economic development process, new inventions and/or innovations may come either as a result of solving a problem when people are ready for doing so or as an outcome of growing human needs and demands[2] in relation to a previously created consumer and/or producer item. In the first case, through the process of developing solutions to problems, new items may be stumbled on (i.e., these inventions and/or innovations are nothing more than unexpected byproducts of the pursuit of the solution process[3]). In the second case, people's cravings, needs and/or demands may stir inventors and/or innovators to think about how to create products to satisfy the demand. In this case, the development of new items is a direct response to growing human needs and effective demands. In both cases, these will lead to economic development.

However it commences, each society's economic development process or experience is unique regardless of where it leads. The pursuit of the economic development process implies an ardent and relentless search for a path of progress that can create conditions in a society's existing environment for improved human welfare. Each society's trajectory is influenced by societal attitudes, learning capabilities, creativity, problems, difficulties, events and so on. Whatever trajectory comes as a result, the society must act to influence it in the desired direction. This may be achieved by dealing with pertinent problems, unexpected events and forces that exert pressures of magnitudes strong enough to deflect the expected direction of the trajectory. Whatever the artificial and/or natural dynamics are, positive human efforts made to control the evolving direction of each trajectory must produce relief from factors that diminish human welfare and enhance the human condition in society. These efforts must be aimed at social engineering to develop the necessary HF.

In the economic development process, all subsequent difficulties may not be predicted or perceived with perfect foresight. There will always be room for surprises. Thus, it will always be the case that at each point in time, society may devote its time, energy and material resources to dealing with more pressing and/or prominent concerns and/or problems. The proportion of resources assigned to dealing with such drawbacks will therefore vary from period to period and from society to society due to varying circumstances. Among these pressing issues are human attitudes and cultural mind-sets. Since these usually exert significant impact on economic variables and the development process, there must be programs designed deliberately to effect appropriate positive changes in them. This issue is discussed in detail in Chapter 10.

LEARNING AND DEVELOPMENT: SUCCESSES AND FAILURES

Attempts in any society to promote economic development must therefore be viewed as being akin to those used for hunting treasures hidden in a maze.

Every effort to reach the treasure of economic development may lead a society into experiencing initial setbacks and then further difficulties and problems, the solutions to which will move society closer to a higher phase or state of economic development and its corresponding improvement in human welfare. That is, going through the economic development process may be likened to the running of gauntlets. Since the maze may be complicated and the gauntlets severe and harsh, societies that get to the treasures of progress will be those that are able to deal successfully with pertinent hindrances.

The economic development process must, therefore, be viewed as a dynamically integrated phenomenon that is continuously propelled by the interaction of traditional and modern ideas, which create new circumstances and environments within which learning and knowledge acquisition are progressively and cummulatively achieved and used to deal with both original and newly created impediments. Among all the factors of production, only acquired human qualities and/or characteristics will empower people and render them capable of apperceiving and managing these intricately intertwining and complicated processes through ingenious applications of acquired knowledge, skills and experiences to achieve the cherished goals of society.

Whether or not economic development occurs will be determined neither by the magnitude of existing capital stock nor technology, but rather by how effectively the acquired HF potential of the society furnishes the people with the capability to harness and apply these resources to problem solving techniques, and by the creative processes already unleashed and in progress. As the society whose HF is well developed uses its capacity to develop innovative technologies for solving problems, this whole process will lead to further discoveries through ingenious applications of acquired knowledge (Gordon, 1980, p. 12). This ongoing process continually gathers momentum and leads to new discoveries and developments. In this process, capital, technology and many other factors are cooperative.

All nations aspiring to accelerated development must not only continuously refine and/or discard old methodologies that may have already lost their sharpness in solving the problems of society, but they must also introduce new ones. In each society, the learning process must be properly articulated to engender the required attitudinal development. Problems of economic underdevelopment may not be solved in situations wherein a society is not able to change and/or discard institutions and cultural mind-sets that have lost their primary usefulness and relevance. Societies that hang onto conventional institutions and cultural mind-sets or refuse to deal with new problems will continue to remain stagnant (if not slip into decline) at one phase or state of the economic development process. Desired progress requires that the whole culture of a people evolve dynamically rather than remain stagnant. That is, progressive economic growth and development require continuing cultural dynamism, which is brought about by a people who have achieved total HF development. In a world of frequent and continuing changes, societies that are unable to cope with global changes will experience decaying economic, political and social conditions.

Problems of economic underdevelopment may linger because not only is the society's necessary HF not properly developed, but the people may also have failed to differentiate correctly between the actual causes of the problems and the apparent symptons. In addition, this phenomenon may be a result of the failure and unwillingness of the members of that society to perceive the inability of existing cultural norms and sanctions to overcome present hindrances. To overcome these problems, the process of economic development must therefore not only be viewed as a search for opportunities that have not yet been discovered and used up, but also it must be carefully guided to lead to the evolution of new procedures and the advancement of existing problem-solving technological knowledge.

At every point in time, the acquired HF must help the people pay astute attention to existing problems, ideas, opportunities and problem-solving mechanisms. Concern must not only be focused on intraphase issues but also on interphase concerns and linkages. To deal successfully with the changing phases and concerns of the economic development process, the people must have their focus sharpened and maintained by constantly asking the following questions: "What actually determines and propels the economic development process?" "If these are clearly identified, what must be done to harness and promote their continuous propulsion?" "If they are nonexistent in the domestic economic environment, how can their presence be assured and/or acquired?" Finally, it is crucial to ask "What abilities (i.e., human qualities and/or characteristics) does the available labor force already have, or need to acquire, to blend the smooth working of all variables operating in the process of economic development?"

It is appropriate to reiterate that the people's initiative, resourcefulness and ability to cope with changes in the domestic and global economic, political and social environments will foster the economic development process. The successful use of the acquired HF in dealing with these variables will reduce the impacts of growth-diminishing variables. Very little will escape the attention of a society whose HF is well developed and is capable of tapping into nature, discovering its laws, problems and difficulties; and instituting education and training programs to support the economic development process. Schumpeter (1961, p. 61), for example, argued that "the entrepreneur is merely the bearer of the mechanism of change." Bartley and Kresge (1991, pp. 186-187) noted that Hayek once argued that "even mere maintenance of the existing level of incomes depends on adaptation to unforeseen changes. . . . The point to keep constantly in mind is that all economic adjustment is made necessary by unforeseen changes." The intellectual hands and compass of the society's labor force that possess the relevant HF are capable of leading to the appropriate knowledge, which can unlock the solutions to problems for the resolution of conflicts before they degenerate into more complicated difficulties.

The question that remains unanswered is "How can all these be accomplished?" The answer to this question can be found in learning, discovery and attitudinal and/or cultural/intellectual mind-set changes--made possible through the acquisition of the HF necessary for economic development. Hayek in Bartley and Kresge (1991, p. 189) observed that "required changes in habits and customs will be brought about only if the few willing and able to experiment with new methods can make it necessary for the many to follow them, and at the same time to show them the way. The required discovery process will be impeded or prevented if the many are able to keep the few to the traditional ways." Hayek (1937, 1945b) discussed economics of knowledge and the use of knowledge in economic. Truly, economic development is both a dynamic learning and discovery process.

CONCLUSION

Human progress is a process that can be likened to the growing and tending of plants. This chapter argues that the progress of any society requires the ability of its people to gain and utilize knowledge, generate positive attitudinal changes and then discover how to solve pertinent problems in each phase of the economic development process--acquisition of the HF. Relevant policy recommendations have been made for the formulation of policies and implementation of economic development programs in sub-Saharan ACs.

Sub-Saharan ACs vying for economic development must realize that this process is a dynamically evolutionary one. After the process has been initiated, it must be sustained. As the process proceeds, it is important to develop the necessary HF and to create relevant and efficient institutions to support and facilitate the process. It is possible that economic growth without development may ensue if sub-Saharan ACs continually lack the ability to create a disciplined labor force. Systemic attitudinal changes in all areas of economic, political and social life must be effected in consonance with the evolutionary process. By critically evaluating, reforming and improving on existing norms and institutions, positive attitudinal changes may facilitate the discovery process for the attainment of progress. The success of the whole program will rest solely on the people's discipline in pursuing answers to the problems of the economic development process, in respecting humankind and in being committed to society's ideals.

NOTES

1. For a detailed discussion and analysis regarding learning by example and doing, refer to the following sources: Arrow, K. 1962. "The Economic Implications of Learning by Doing." *Review of Economic Studies*, 29 (June); Kennedy, C. and Thirlwall, A. P. 1972. "Technical Progress: A Survey." *Economic Journal*, 82 (March): 38-39; Argote, L. and Epple, D. 1990. "Learning Curves in Manufacturing." *Science*, February 13, 1990; Tolman, E. C., Richie, B. F. and Kalish, D. 1946. "Studies in Spatial Learning. Part II: Place Learning versus Response Learning." *Journal of Experimental Psychology*, 36: 221-229; Sells, S. B. *Psychology.* New York: The Ronald Press, 1962.

Boulding, K. E. 1966. "The Economics of Knowledge and the Knowledge of Economics." *American Economic Review,* 16 (2): 1-13; Siegel, A. W., Kirasic, K. C. and Kail, R. W. 1978. "Stalking the Elusive Cognitive Map. In I. Altman and J. F. Wohlwill, eds. *Children and the Environment.* New York: Plenum; Mansfield, E. 1993. *Managerial Economics.* New York: W. W. Norton and Company, pp. 268-271.

2. Some scholars do not believe that need and/or demand can call forth invention. Among these scholars are Veblen, T. 1964. *The Instinct of Workmanship.* New York: Augustus M. Kelley, p. 314; Jewkes, J., Sawers, D. and Stillerman, R. 1969. *The Sources of Innovation.* New York: Norton, p. 170; Kranzberg, M. and Pursell, C. W. 1967. *Technology in Western Civilization.* New York: Oxford University Press, p. 15.

3. See Milward, A. S. 1973. *The Economic Development of Continental Powers (1780-1870).* London: George Allen and Unwin, p. 179.

Part II

ACHIEVING A TURNAROUND
IN AFRICAN ECONOMIC
DEVELOPMENT

7

Recognizing and Harnessing the Universal Laws of Economic Development in Sub-Saharan African Countries

INTRODUCTION

For every living thing, the process of development is continuous from birth to death.[1] Development happens over a period of time and is patterned after the laws of nature. In particular, human growth proceeds through childhood, puberty, adolescence, adulthood, old age and death. The basic objective of this chapter is to examine the concept of the natural growth process in order to derive underlying laws of growth, and then to explain the economic growth and development process of nations by applying these laws. It is argued that unless sub-Saharan ACs know and fully understand these laws of nature, exploit and capitalize on the concepts and deliberately pursue the process of economic development in the direction of, and in agreement with these hidden laws of growth, they will continually find it difficult to achieve economic growth and development.

As a rule of nature, all living things grow, mature and die. Regardless of how long this growth and development process takes, the process is usually methodical, although fluctuations will occur. Both plants and animals grow, develop and die. For example, a little mustard seed placed into the soil and provided with required amounts of moisture, sunshine, nutrients, protection and care finally sprouts, develops primary roots, puts out leaves and thereafter continues to grow and develop, obeying the natural laws of growth and development. Similarly, human development proceeds through childhood, puberty, adolescence, adulthood, old age and death.

In this chapter, it is argued that although when left on its own the economy of every country will obey the universal laws of growth and development (either positive or negative), the processes of economic growth and development can either be directly or indirectly influenced (i.e., positively or negatively) by appropriate and timely human intervention (see Chapter 6). To be successful, the society must have adequate knowledge about how the hidden laws of economic growth operate. Where the requisite knowledge is lacking, very little may be achieved through sporadic trial-and-error responses to seasonal problems (see

Chapter 10). Those who do not know what their problems are cannot work toward solving them. In his book *War and Peace*, Tolstoy wrote that

> doctors came to see Natasha, both separately and in consultation. They said a great deal in French, German and in Latin. They criticised one another, and prescribed the most diverse remedies for all the diseases they were familiar with. But it never occurred to one of them to make the simple reflection that they could not understand the disease from which Natasha was suffering, as no single disease can be fully understood in a living person; for every living person has his complaints unknown to medicine-- not a disease of the lungs, of the kidneys, of the skin, of the heart, and so on, as described in medical books, but a disease that consists of one out of the innumerable combinations of ailments of those organs. (Quoted in Jameson and Wilber, 1979, p. 35)

This quote illustrates perfectly the conditions of economic development in sub-Saharan ACs. For many years development economists, armed with their varied ideologies, have developed theories and techniques for diagnosing, explaining and remedying problems of underdevelopment in sub-Saharan ACs (see a detailed presentation on these theories in Chapter 2). In these attempts, economic development theorists have made generalized diagnoses and have correspondingly prescribed economic policies for dealing with problems that throttle the process of economic progress. Although these theorists focus their attention on the same problems, their resulting diagnoses and policy prescriptions are usually at variance with each other.

Since most of these policies have not been successful, sub-Saharan ACs have remained like Natasha, who experienced the misfortune of not being healed simply because all her physicians were unable to agree on the causes and cures for her ailment--which they had no clues about anyway. When doctors act in ignorance and on guesses, the likelihood of their success is limited. Every doctor involved would have to acquire proper knowledge about what ails Natasha for her to be healed.

This observation reveals that if sub-Saharan ACs are to derive any concrete benefits from the activities of orthodox economic development theorists, they (sub-Saharan ACs) must identify and proclaim what they know and feel to be the main hindrances to the process of economic development. It is the patient who tells the physician what he or she feels like in the body, except when fully incapacitated, unconscious and unable to talk. This communication removes the necessity of trial-and-error diagnostic procedures, which may complicate the severity of the disease. However, when the patient describes symptoms that do not relate to the actual disease, doctors may be misled in misapplying their treatments. Similarly, when the patient's accurate description of symptoms are ignored, the wrong treatment will be the result. Sub-Saharan ACs seem to have suffered from both problems for many decades. This failure was a direct result of the inability to recognize and effectively exploit the underlying natural laws of growth and development (see Chapter 9 on the role of knowledge in economic development).

In attempts to understand and deal with problems of economic development, every sub-Saharan AC must first acquire an understanding of the laws which govern the processes of economic growth and development. After doing so, they can fashion their own economic model for achieving these goals. The goal of this model must be focused on how to deal with the root causes of every obstacle to economic advancement. To each of these countries, the best model of economic development is the one they craft from their own critical evaluation of existing social, economic and political conditions that prevail in the country (Goulet, 1978, p. 52). In this way, the diagnosis and policy prescriptions will be closer to reality than those based on the theoretical conceptualizations of armchair economic development experts.

PEOPLE MAKE ECONOMIC GROWTH AND DEVELOPMENT HAPPEN

As I discussed in Chapter 3, no economic development process can be initiated, maintained and sustained without the existence of the necessary HF. It is people who know what to do and how to do it that make things happen in society. Their role and relevance can neither be neglected nor bypassed in the economic development process. The HF forms the real foundation for economic growth and development (see the extended analysis of this principle in Chapter 5). This view about the crucial role of the HF forms the basis for the first law of economic growth and development.

First Law

The principal requirement for economic growth and development is the availability of a well-educated and disciplined labor force that has acquired positive human qualities and/or characteristics (i.e., the HF). That is, the people of a nation must possess the relevant components of the HF necessary for economic progress.

THE PROCESS OF ECONOMIC GROWTH AND DEVELOPMENT IS CUMULATIVE

The ultimate goal of every human economic and business activity is to satisfy the needs of humanity. For centuries, many countries have concentrated their efforts on developing technology for providing the basic necessities of life. In all countries, economic development plans are drawn up to facilitate these processes. Throughout the years, some countries have been more successful than others. Often, nations that have attained an advanced level of industrial progress think that although it took them many years to arrive at their current industrialized state, economic growth in sub-Saharan ACs can be accomplished through accelerated economic development planning and programs. This belief presupposes that economic growth and development can be accelerated[2] when desired. This belief has led many sub-Saharan ACs in the last several decades to pursue economic development plans and programs. Labels such as *the big push, unbalanced growth strategy, accelerated economic development planning, import-substitution industrialization, integrated rural development, human-centered development, Marshall plan* and many others have all been used to identify these programs.

These approaches have not produced the expected results, despite the total amount of resources poured into each strategy. The outcomes reveal that the process of economic growth and development is a continuously cumulative one, with occasional hindrances and fluctuations. It follows then that the process of economic growth and development must be viewed as a continuing phenomenon with occasional pauses to deal with prevailing setbacks.[3] This approach will consolidate the foundation structures and prepare for the arrival of subsequent phases of economic growth and development.

Writing about the development of the human child, Breckenridge and Lee (1955, pp. 143-144) observed that "severe neglect or abuse will seriously disrupt his [the child's] growth. . . . Because growth is continuous we must realize that what happens at one stage carries over into and influences the next and ensuing stages. . . . Even seemingly sudden spurts in the tempo of growth lead into and grow out of quieter, less dramatic periods. It may be possible that in the quieter periods the child is mobilizing his forces for ensuing spurts."

Through the application of the main principle underlying this view to the process of economic growth and development, it can be argued conclusively that unexpected interruptions of the economic development process in sub-Saharan ACs must be viewed as challenges rather than unsurmountable difficulties. Problems encountered must be studied in detail and suitable solutions found for them. Governments must not be too quick to respond to these problems when they do not know what their exact causes are.[4] Certain hindrances may act as stimulants for the people to develop more efficient alternative procedures for responding properly to the changing economic forces. Patience, in some circumstances, may even prove that nothing is wrong.

Newly developing African economies must not be forced into pursuing programs they are not ready for.[5] Instead, these economies must be left alone to grow and develop at their own pace. Problems that occur during the development process must not only be seen as being destructive but also as being challenges to be faced and dealt with successfully through the fashioning of new methods. Too many attempts to intervene without adequate knowledge of what the true hindrances are will create many more problems than they solve. It is, therefore, necessary to limit such attempts.[6] This view leads to the second governing law of the process of growth and development.

Second Law

Although the process of economic growth and development is continuously cumulative, *ceteris paribus,* it must necessarily be directed and supported indirectly through human factor development, which will in turn impact the relevant variables that may be known to be acting as hindrances and are, therefore, preventing the process from following its expected path. The goal of this action is to facilitate and maintain the process on its desired course rather than blindly pursuing interventionist policies, which are usually based on insufficient knowledge.[7]

Nature is full of examples of this law. For example, an eaglet cannot be forced to fly many kilometers while still a fledgling. Parent eagles, therefore, take their time and train young ones in a gentle, orderly and continuously cumulative fashion. During such trial and training flights, eaglets are educated and trained to develop the necessary skills and stamina for long flights and taught how to succeed even in bad weather. Without successfully developing the necessary flying characteristics, life would be full of misery and hopelessness. The education and training of lion cubs and baby tigers to hunt for food is another illustration of this law.

THE RATES OF ECONOMIC GROWTH AND DEVELOPMENT FLUCTUATE

A historical review of the economic growth patterns of industrially advanced countries (DCs) reveals that all aspects of growth proceed at different rates. The data in Table 7.1 show that although the DCs experienced high rates of economic growth at the initial stages of their economic development process, there were periods during which economic growth and development decelerated. It is clear from the data that in the infancy of their industrial development, the rates of growth of output and per capita income in each economy, although high, fluctuated. The time spans were great, supporting the view that economic growth and development occur over an extended period of time. This is made possible through persistency in pursuing growth-inducing policies and consistent program development and project implementation by the people.

In addition, as these economies moved toward higher average productivity, fluctuations in the growth rates persisted. These fluctuations did not necessarily imply disastrous conditions. In the midst of severe fluctuations, these economies continued to gather strength and momentum for further economic growth and development. The fluctuations may have been propelled by sectoral and institutional changes. This phenomenon illustrates the third important hidden law that underlies economic growth and development.

TABLE 7.1
ANNUAL GROWTH RATES OF OUTPUT
IN THE DEVELOPED COUNTRIES

Country	Year	Duration	Output	Per Capita Income
U.K.	1841-1881	40	2.54	1.33
	1881-1921	40	1.77	0.86
France	1841-1861	20	2.23	1.84
	1861-1901	30	2.00	1.77
	1901-1920	18.5	1.46	1.60
	1920-1958	38	1.55	1.18
Germany	1851-1871	20	1.63	0.89
	1871-1913	40	3.09	1.87
	1913-1935	23	0.57	0.04
Japan	1878-1918	40	4.14	3.05
	1918-1957	39	3.97	2.57
Sweden	1861-1881	20	2.88	2.15
	1881-1921	40	2.69	2.01
	1921-1957	36	3.77	3.16
U.S.S.R.	1913-1928	15	0.54	0.00
	1928-1958	30	4.40	3.71

Source: Kuznets, S., 1965. *Economic Growth and Structure: Selected Essays.*
New York: W. W. Norton and Company, p. 307.

Third Law

Successive phases of economic growth and development do not necessarily
proceed at a steady rate of growth through time. In the midst of a
seemingly chaotic situation, there is always an inherent underlying
orderliness that must be identified and exploited.

This law suggests that sub-Saharan ACs must not panic when they observe
decline in the growth rate of output (except when this decline persists for
decades). A short term decline in the economic growth rate, therefore, must not
necessarily call for immediate government intervention. Structural adjustment
policies and stabilization programs will not be appropriate in all cases. Policy

planners must be aware of the performance of each variable and closely monitor output growth rates. Those variables that do not grow at expected rates must be reexamined and dealt with accordingly. Planners could minimize fluctuations in the rate of growth of every variable by adhering to the observed laws of economic growth and development.

THE VARIABILITY OF SECTORAL ECONOMIC GROWTH AND DEVELOPMENT

Just as the growth rates of various economic variables fluctuate, so also do the sectoral growth rates vary. Although certain variables and/or changes may be more dominant in some sectors, they may be inactive in others. A careful study of advanced economies shows that their agricultural, manufacturing and tertiary sectors did not only grow at different rates but also served as leading sectors at different points in time. Tables 7.2 and 7.3 contain information on the gross domestic product by type of economic activity in selected countries. Observe from both tables that the percentage contribution of each sector differs from those of others. All sectors do not contribute equally to output. They grow at different rates. This phenomenon is the foundation for the fourth crucial law of economic growth and development.

Fourth Law

Different sectors (and regions) of the same economy grow and develop at varying rates. Since the sectoral (and regional) rates of economic growth and development also vary from one country to another in similar periods, each sector's (or region's) contributions to total product will vary from one country to another. As such, each requires its own unique plans, policies and programs for initiating, promoting and sustaining growth and development. Adequate resources must be channeled into supporting relevant sectors and/or regions in the initial stages of the development process. This, however, must be preceded by continuing HF development programs.

Based on this law, sub-Saharan ACs must determine the stronger and more productive sunrise sectors to which they must deliberately provide more incentives for growth to ensue. That is, sectors that command many forward and backward linkages and possess the potential to lead and direct others must be appropriately developed to be the main backbone for the entire economy. This calls for the availability of the necessary HF and the ability of the people to pursue successfully tactical and strategic planning. Sub-Saharan African planners must not arbitrarily select sectors for economic development assistance. The currently existing cash crop economies and the bogus international division of

TABLE 7.2
GROSS DOMESTIC PRODUCT BY KIND OF ECONOMIC
ACTIVITY (%) (DCs)

Country	Year	Agri.	Mfg.	Cons.	Wrt.	Transp.	Other
USA	1950	7	32	5	7	17	29
	1953	5	33	5	7	16	31
	1958	5	29	5	6	16	35
	1960	4	28	4	17	6	34
	1963	4	28	4	17	6	36
	1970	3	26	5	17	6	37
	1972	3	25	5	18	6	37
	1973	4	25	5	17	6	37
Germany	1950	10	39	5	7	13	20
	1953	9	40	6	6	13	20
	1958	7	40	6	7	13	21
	1960	6	42	7	15	6	19
	1963	5	41	8	15	6	20
	1970	3	43	8	14	6	24
	1973	3	41	8	13	6	27
	1974	3	40	7	12	6	30
Japan	1950	26	25	4	7	17	18
	1953	22	24	5	8	16	22
	1958	19	26	5	10	16	22
	1960	13	33	6	17	9	19
	1963	11	34	6	17	9	20
	1970	6	35	7	17	7	25
	1973	5	36	8	19	8	29
	1974	5	35	7	18	7	31
U.K.	1953	5	35	6	8	12	28
	1958	4	35	6	8	12	29
	1960	4	32	6	11	8	25
	1963	3	30	6	10	8	27
	1970	2	28	5	9	7	29
	1972	3	27	6	9	7	31
	1973	3	27	6	9	8	31

Source: *United Nations Statistical Yearbook*, various issues (1950-1974).

TABLE 7.3
GROSS DOMESTIC PRODUCT BY KIND
OF ECONOMIC ACTIVITY (%) (LDCs)

Nation	Year	Agric.	Mfg.	Cons.	Wrt.	Transp.	Other
Ghana	1968	43	13	4	12	4	19
	1970	48	11	4	12	4	15
	1971	45	11	5	13	5	16
	1972	48	10	4	12	4	16
Kenya	1954	47	9	4	7	14	18
	1958	42	10	4	8	13	21
	1960	40	10	4	9	13	23
	1964	38	10	4	9	7	23
	1970	31	11	5	8	7	26
	1972	31	12	5	8	7	27
	1973	28	12	5	8	7	27
	1974	26	12	4	9	7	27
Nigeria	1950	74	3	3	5	9	5
	1953	69	3	3	6	13	5
	1958	69	5	2	4	12	7
	1960	59	5	4	12	4	8
	1963	57	6	4	12	5	8
	1970	45	7	5	12	3	12
	1972	40	7	7	11	3	10
	1973	35	7	7	10	3	10

Source: *United Nations Statistical Yearbook*, various issues (1953-1974).

labor and/or specialization need an immediate and critical review and extensive examination in light of this law. The selection of the sunrise sectors must be based on the fourth hidden law of economic growth and development: Develop the more productive sunrise sectors and allow them to strengthen the weaker ones on a continuing basis.

Economic progress will ensue at different rates in different regions of the same country. Table 7.4 shows that as economic progress continued, regional incomes in the United States rose in every region. In the 1800s, there were huge differences in per capita incomes by region in the United States. Similar results for other industrialized countries have led me to conclude that when economic growth ensues, regions of the same country grow at different rates. These differences are, however, narrowed as regional interdependencies.

TABLE 7.4
U.S. REGIONAL REAL PER CAPITA INCOME (WEIGHTED
AVERAGE PER CAPITA INCOMES OF STATES IN 1959 DOLLARS)

Region	1880	1920	1940	1959
New England	833.3	1410.3	1744.2	2396
Middle Atlantic	829	1514.6	1820.2	2540
Great Lakes	602.7	1222.5	1536.8	2337
Southeast	295.3	639.6	790.3	1565
Plains	531.7	982.3	1112.9	1978
Southwest	358.2	914.1	963.1	1887
Mountain	983.3	1158.2	1223.5	1990
Far West	1251.3	1530.5	1808.7	2565

Source: Harvey, S. P. and Dodds, V. R., 1963. *How a Region Grows*, p. 18.

The different growth rates of regional incomes are usually due to varying factors, such as the availability of the relevant HF, taste changes, the nature of income distribution, technological development and its applications, government policy, transportation and telecommunications systems, location of economic activity, resource endowment, the size of the internal market, organization, adaptation to change and many others. Harvey and Dodds (1963, p. 22) observed that "since these national change-initiating forces operate differently for different commodities and since the regions differ widely in their patterns of production, some regions will be stimulated to rapid growth while others will be little differentiated. . . . The impact upon regions varies with the degree to which their industries are dependent upon transportation as a factor in production or marketing." (See also Denison, 1967.)

Kuznets (1965, p. 325), writing about the pattern of U.S. growth, noted that

the pattern of past growth leaves its impression in the institutions that the country develops to deal with the problems generated by past growth; that these institutions may persist beyond their useful time and constitute obstacles to further growth under changed conditions; and that sustained economic growth requires continuous adjustments of social and political institutions to changed conditions--adjustments that are in good part required because the institutions that proved useful earlier and were, in fact, required in earlier economic growth are now obsolete. The impressive record of economic growth in this country was not accomplished by the repetitive application of invariant rules of economic and social behavior; it had to be a creative adjustment to changed conditions; and the cost of some of the conflicts that had developed between old and new institutions (the most striking and costly example was the Civil War) was quite high. Minimization of such costs of adjustemeent is as desirable today as it ever was, and the general point that economic growth almost naturally produces obsolescence and thus requires attention and drive to remove the resulting obstacles could, I believe, be illustrated today.

In many developing countries, people have depended on institutions, techniques and cultural norms that have become obsolete because they do not have the required capability to solve new and more complicated problems of the modern society. It is, therefore, true that as long as any group of people is not willing to let go cf its archaic modes of life, techniques and procedures for solving pertinent social, economic and political problems, it will be extremely difficult for that society to achieve development. In view of this observation, it can be argued that any society whose culture is literally stagnant will be eluded by the winds of change and development. Changing social, economic and political conditions must be carefully responded to by developing new procedures, techniques and institutions to facilitate and direct the development process. The attainment of these objectives must be one of the major duties of the existing leadership that possesses the necessary HF.

THE BRITISH EXPERIENCE OF ECONOMIC GROWTH (1700s-1900s)

The British experience of economic growth and development in the initial era (see Table 7.5) included the following:

1 A doubling of per capita income in the take-off period (1783-1802).
2 The growth of the industrial production index at annual rates of 1% and 3% between 1700-1783 and 1783-1802, respectively.
3 An acceleration in the rates of growth of pig iron and cotton in these decades.
4 An acceleration of capital formation between 1830 and 1860. Railways were well developed. Between 1860 and 1914, gross capital formation fluctuated and experienced declines in the interwar years. Recovery began after the war. Investment rose thereafter. Gross capital formation in fixed assets, including net foreign investments, grew at 10.2% and 15.6% in the 1860s and 1950s, respectively.
5 An average annual real output growth rate of 1.2% between 1780 and 1972.
6 Decelerated growth for the periods of 1831-1841 and 1861-1871. These declines might be due to the depressions of the late 1830s and early 1840s and the negative effects of the American Civil War on the textile industry.

TABLE 7.5
APPROXIMATE TIMING OF LEADING
SECTORS: GREAT BRITAIN (1783-1972)

Sector	Maximum Rate of Expansion	Estimated Time Sector Became Leading Sector	Estimated Time Sector Ceased to Lead	Comments
Cotton textile	1780s	1780s	1860s	-
Pig iron	1790s	1780s	1880s	-
Railroads	1830s*	1830s	1870s	Market slowdown in railway construction in 1850s, some revival in 1860s
Steel	1870s@	1870s	1920s	-
Electricity	1900-1910	1900-1910	-	As in other advanced countries, the high energy prices of the 1970s may bring electricity's role as a leading sector to a close

TABLE 7.5 CONTINUED

Sector	Maximum Rate of Expansion	Estimated Time Sector Became Leading Sector	Estimated Time Sector Ceased to Lead	Comments
Motor vehicles	1900-1910	1920-1929	1960s	-
Sulphuric acid	1870s	$	1890s	From 1890s, sulphuric acid production fluctuated at rates approximating industry index
Nitrogen	1940s	$	-	-
Plastics & resins	1940s	$	-	-
Synthetic Fiber	1920s	$	-	-

Legend:
* = Figures for mileage added in each decade are as follows:
1825-1830, 71; 1830-1840, 1400; 1840-1850, 4586; 1850-1860, 2985; 1860-1870, 4493; 1870-1880, 2001; 1880-1890, 1718.
@ = Estimate begins in 1871 with 329,000 tons. Maximum growth rate may have come earlier, at very low levels of production.
$ = Industry not on sufficient scale to be regarded, in itself, as a leading sector.

Source: Rostow, W. W., 1978. *The World Economy*, p. 379.

7 Expanded per capita growth between 1861-1871 and 1891-1901 as a result of declining input prices and favorable terms of trade.

The British experience is indicative of the view that economic growth and development are not necessarily smooth processes. As real economic progress ensues, nations need to identify economic growth-inducing forces and encourage their continuing contribution to economic development in sub-Saharan ACs. Alternatively, all negative forces must be isolated, studied and prudently dealt with. Structural adjustment policies and stabilization programs alone will not necessarily create the long-lasting expected positive impact on human welfare.

THE AMERICAN EXPERIENCE OF ECONOMIC GROWTH (1790-1972)

The industrial development of the United States spanned almost two centuries. The highlights of the American economic growth and development experience (see Table 7.6) include the following:

1   The New England textile industry began to expand after 1816.
2   Railway development and expansion occurred in the 1840s (in the East) and the 1850s (in the Midwest).
3   The development of heavy industry took place during this era.
4   An export boom occurred in the 1790s.
5   The postwar boom lasted until 1817.
6   Expansion of cotton into the West took place in the 1830s.
7   Massive agricultural expansion was typical of the 1850s.
8   Cotton textile industry production expanded between 1816 and 1842.
9   American output grew in the 1790s due to rising agricultural prices and the expansion of foreign trade.
10 Per capita output expanded at the rate of 2% between 1789 and 1802.
11 The economy experienced relative stagnation of industrialization between 1839 and 1843.
12 Both agriculture and industry expanded in the 1850s.
13 A depression ensued in the 1890s. An economic boom occurred in the 1920s.
14 Gross investment increased from 9% to 14% from 1834-1843 to 1849-1858.

The American experience also substantiates the view that economic growth is neither stable nor constant. In the economic development process, every economy must experience the ebb and flow of business and economic activities. Although some of these may exert expansionary impacts on economic growth and development, others may contract productive activities. Sub-Saharan ACs must know that the way and manner in which these forces are harnessed and/or dealt with is crucial. Moreover, it is important to develop the necessary HF, infrastructure and efficient institutions that are required for continuous economic progress. It will be helpful for sub-Saharan ACs to study the experiences of advanced nations and apply the knowledge gained to their unique circumstances. They must avoid direct adoption and application of economic development procedures, policies and programs used in the past by the DCs.

TABLE 7.6
APPROXIMATE TIMING OF LEADING
SECTORS: UNITED STATES (1790-1972)

Sector	Maximum Rate of Expansion	Estimated Time Sector Became Leading Sector	Estimated Time Sector Ceased to Lead	Comments
Cotton textiles	1805-1815	1820s	1870s	-
Pig iron	1840s	1840s	1910-1920	-
Railroads	1830s	1830s	1890s	-
Steel	1870s	1870s	1920s	-
Electricity	1880s	1900-1910	-	-
Motor vehicles	1900-1910	1910-1920	1950s	Production set back severely in 1930s, even relative to industrial index
Sulphuric acid	1870s	$	1920s	-
Nitrogen	1940s	$	1920	-
Plastics	1940-1945	$	-	-
Synthetic fiber	1950-1955	$	-	-

$ = industry not on sufficient scale to be regarded, in itself, as a leading sector.

Source: Rostow, W. W., 1978. *The World Economy*, p. 393.

LESSONS FROM THE EXPERIENCES OF THE
DEVELOPED COUNTRIES

The most common features of the industrial development of the DCs throughout the years include the following:

1 Leading sectors such as cotton textiles, railways, chemicals, electricity and the automobile industries all expanded at different times and rates. Each experienced times of acceleration and deceleration. In many cases, the rates of growth of key sectors lagged behind that of industrial production, especially in Britain (Rostow, 1978, p. 107).

2 Before the First World War, governments of industrialized countries articipated in the economic development process by preparing the needed HF and building the basic infrastructure--railways, roads, bridges and many structures to facilitate economic growth and development.

3 Effective financial systems were developed on a continuing basis to support investment programs and economic development efforts. Central banks controlled the currency both to influence the level of inflation and to make investment funds easily available to investors.

4 The various fluctuations in the growth rates of different industries and sectors reveal that growth rates are never equal. Cyclical fluctuations can be said to be the direct results of such growth rate imbalances.

5 An occasional slowdown in the growth rate does not necessarily imply a permanent stagnation. Consequently, governments should not always respond to such fluctuations with sudden, harsh and draconian interventionist economic policies. Natural economic forces must be given room to solve some of these problems.

INFLUENCING THE RATES AND PATTERNS OF ECONOMIC GROWTH AND DEVELOPMENT

It is critical to remember that there are hindrances to the process of economic growth and development. It is, therefore, relevant to maintain a growth-inducing environment and be aware that the rates and patterns of economic growth and development can be influenced by the appropriate manipulation of the existing environmental conditions. Economic growth and development will proceed smoothly in environments in which other cooperating factors are available and well employed. Economic environments that are devoid of the required HF, as well as social, political and intellectual stability, will curb economic growth rates and dismantle the patterns of economic growth and development. Many sub-Saharan ACs have been unable to provide fertile environments within which economic progress will occur. It is, however, encouraging to know that when such deficiencies are corrected (especially those relating to HF decay), the rates of economic growth and development in sub-Saharan African economies will be positively affected.

The existence of order in the economic development process has many implications for attempts to achieve economic progress in sub-Saharan ACs. It implies that the pursuit of productive economic development policies must go beyond mere timely responses to recurring disaster and/or temporarily fulfilling basic needs. For example, although for many years specific international aid programs have been designed to alleviate the suffering of those who have been struck by epidemics, floods, hurricanes, earthquakes, drought, etc., these programs do not necessarily contribute to continuing output growth and long-run economic development. They are stop-gap measures that temporarily minimize pain but fail to overcome permanently the real causes and problems of economic underdevelopment. They are usually concentrated on current consumption rather than investment in perpetually productive ventures. Such assistance will never produce economic progress because it ignores existing laws of economic growth and development. Worst of all, these policies and programs fail to deal with the glaring HF decay and/or underdevelopment.

Food, flood and health aid programs for Ethiopia, Somalia, the Sudan and many other sub-Saharan ACs are examples of foreign assistance that have contributed little to continuing economic progress in these areas. Rather than grow and develop economically, these nations have continued to suffer from recurrent problems, and they temporarily survive on international assistance. The proverbial adage, "give a man fish today and he will return for more fish tomorrow, but teach a man how to fish today and he will continue to fish for his own use forever" is in line with the laws of economic growth and development. Sub-Saharan ACs that depend on aid and other forms of economic development assistance may continue to depend on these forever if they are not helped to produce and provide for themselves. To overcome this, economic development assistance and other kinds of aid must be designed on the basis of the laws of economic growth and development. Rather than addressing temporal needs, they must be used to develop the foundation for an extensive and long-lasting economic development program. This initial program must place a higher priority on HF development.

Having determined what their national needs and problems are, every sub-Saharan AC must be encouraged and allowed to decide how to use all aid packages and forms of economic development assistance to overcome recurring problems permanently. Foreign aid is less effective when donor countries stipulate how the assistance must be used. However, when sub-Saharan ACs cannot manage their local resources effectively, they may not successfully allocate foreign financial assistance. Much of it may end up in personal Swiss bank accounts due to poorly developed HF. Myint (1970, p. 75) is correct to say that

> a country which cannot use its already available resources efficiently is not likely to be able to absorb additional resources from aid programs and use them efficiently. That is to say, a country's absorptive capacity for aid must to a large extent depend on its ability to avoid serious misallocation of resources. A similar conclusion can be drawn about an underdeveloped country's ability to make effective use of its opportunities for international trade. If we find that a country is not making effective use of its already available trading opportunities, because of domestic policies discouraging its export production or raising the costs in the export sector, then we should not expect it to benefit in a dramatic way from the new trading opportunities to be obtained through international negotiations.

Although Myint's observation is perfectly true for all sub-Saharan ACs, very little has been done in the past to address this problem effectively. The DCs continue to prescribe and implement aid and other loan programs and lofty economic development plans, policies and programs. They have failed to recognize that sub-Saharan ACs lack the relevant HF and that unless these are developed, none of these plans, policies and programs aimed at economic development will be successful.

The laws of economic growth reveal that sustainable economic growth and development cannot be birthed through sporadic and disorderly interventionist economic plans, policies, programs, revolutions and intermittent infusion of international development aid and/or loan schemes. Although these may be of temporary help at certain points in time, they do not necessarily prepare the ground for permanent economic progress. Well-planned and effectively organized economic development policies and programs are necessary for the attainment of economic emancipation. These, of course, may not be successful without the availability of the required HF.

Economic development and industrial expansion require the availability of the positive HF, a better government, improvement in public vision, resourcefulness, intelligence, thoughtfulness and introduction and application of both indigenous and adapted foreign technologies and capital. John Stuart Mill, writing on improvement in industry, pointed out that these are critical to industrialization.

CONCLUSION

Our human endeavors are geared toward satisfying the needs of humanity. In every attempt to fend for their people, it is necessary that sub-Saharan ACs recognize and use the concepts of the hidden laws of development that influence the actual process of economic growth and development. Using the analogy of the growth process of living things, this chapter has shown that economic development is a continuously cumulative process. Every sub-Saharan AC that desires to achieve economic development must be aware that the economic development process cannot be successfully attained through ad hoc responses to natural disasters and/or wars in affected areas. Economic development programs which come about as responses to needs and catastrophic events may temporarily alleviate pain and suffering but will not lead to long-term productivity growth and economic development in sub-Saharan Africa.

Deliberate planning and effectively articulated programs must be put in place to achieve economic growth and development. The execution of these programs requires a well-prepared labor force that possesses the necessary HF and is capable of altering existing social, economic, intellectual and political environments that are not conducive to rapid economic growth and development. By successfully changing the existing unproductive environmental conditions in sub-Saharan ACs, the hidden laws of economic growth and development may be unleashed for economic progress. When this process begins, it is also necessary to sustain it. The sub-Saharan African economic condition will then begin to change for the better.

NOTES

1. Human development is a life-long process and has many dimensions. Although the physical growth of the body ceases at some point in time, other forms of growth (i.e., intellectual, emotional and spiritual) may continue until death.

2. From the perspective of the human factor approach to economic growth and development, a society may be successful in accelerating its rate of economic progress through stabilization policies as long as it possesses the HF necessary to do so. Without a well-prepared HF, however, very little progress will be made regardless of the magnitude of resources injected into the economy through demand and supply management policies.

3. The HF appproach to economic development is slightly different from the balanced growth strategy advocated by Lewis (1955), Nurkse (1952, 1958), Rosenstein-Rodan (1957) and Scitovsky (1954) and the unbalanced growth strategy of Hirschman (1958). The HF approach maintains that the process of economic development must be pursued on the principle by which homes and other buildings are built. When building a house or apartment complex, it is crucial that the contractors dig deep and pour adequate concrete to lay a solid foundation before building. As the building process continues, proper cementing is required for a stable building.

The HF approach requires that the proper foundation be laid first for the development of the HF necessary to initiate and sustain the development process. Since the HF is the main cement that holds the whole process together, other programs will fall in their proper place in due course. This approach does not necessarily subscribe to the selection of a particular sector or group of sectors that can generate both strong forward and backward linkages. This selection, as discussed in the chapter, can be done if and only if the relevant HF is available. The HF approach, therefore, is not necessarily concerned about whether the balanced growth strategy is better than the unbalanced strategy. Its main concern is that regardless of which development strategy is being pursued by a sub-Saharan AC, it must have available the required HF.

4. Some orthodox economic development theorists will argue that immediate government intervention through demand and supply management policies to deal with emerging economic problems must be in place immediately. To be successful, this policy requires adequate knowledge of what is wrong and that the people possess the ability (i.e., the necessary HF) to develop new and more efficient techniques for dealing successfully with the root causes of economic underdevelopment. Since this is usually not the case in the sub-Saharan African situation, the HF approach to economic growth and development does not hold this view. In the past, sub-Saharan African governments responded continuously by instituting mere make-shift economic measures that helped them in the short

run to achieve temporary reliefs, but caused permanent damage to the economic development process. This was due to the continuing lack of the required HF (see also note 2).

5. Whether or not the current comparative advantage theories have been fair and useful to sub-Saharan ACs is an issue for further research and analysis. Sub-Saharan ACs have, however, been dragged along to participate in the existing international division of labor and/or specialization through the production of tradeable cash crops. In recent years, feminism, environmentalism and many other movements have been added to the list.

6. Since Law 1 is concerned with the availability of the HF necessary for economic development, appropriate measures must be taken immediately to deal with HF decay and/or underdevelopment when it is diagnosed to be the pertinent problem.

7. This law is not advocating direct and continuing demand and supply management policies per se. It holds that programs aimed at facilitating economic growth and development must first and foremost develop the HF necessary for economic progress. It does not, however, rule out totally the use of demand and supply management policies. These policies can be pursued as long as the required HF and appropriate knowledge about the existing problems are available. Otherwise, such policies and programs will not have any significant and permanent impact on the economic development process.

8

Investment in Preventive Maintenance Management Programs in Sub-Saharan African Countries

INTRODUCTION

You only have to take a brief tour of a few sub-Saharan African countries (ACs) to realize the existing state of the social infrastructure and property. Public transportation facilities and telecommunications systems are not able to perform at their optimum levels because vehicles and communications equipment are broken down and there are few or no resources with which to import spare parts for proper maintenance. Highways, city streets, city lights, government bungalows, hospitals, schools, telephone lines and many other structures are in a state of perpetual shambles and disrepair because authorities have not aggressively pursued preventive maintenance management programs on a continuing basis. This chapter discusses the impacts of either the absence or the existence of preventive maintenance management programs in sub-Saharan ACs. A few policy recommendations for improvement are made.

My belief that international economic development assistance offered to sub-Saharan ACs in the past has wrongly placed emphasis on irrelevant concerns leads me to begin to search for and identify the true pertinent, nontraditionally recognized problems of economic underdevelopment in sub-Saharan Africa. Elsewhere I have suggested that one such never-before-recognized major hindrance to economic growth and development in sub-Saharan Africa is the lack of relevant human characteristics--the HF (see Chapters 3, 4 and 5). In this chapter, I discuss another pertinent, nontraditionally noted problem of economic underdevelopment in sub-Saharan Africa: the lack of continuing preventive maintenance management programs in all sub-Saharan ACs. If economic growth and development are viewed as cumulative processes, then what has already been achieved or attained must be consolidated, facilitated and maintained in an ongoing manner through relevant and efficient preventive maintenance management programs.

In view of these developments, the goal of this chapter is to investigate the impacts of preventive maintenance management programs (i.e., the maintenance budget) and capital expenditures on the level of infrastructure development in sub-Saharan ACs. Adequate data do not exist with which to determine the proportion of funds committed to each of these in sub-Saharan African budgets. The analysis presented is based on the information derived from interviews. Based on results from these interviews and other existing secondary information, policy suggestions are made in regard to how sub-Saharan ACs can develop efficient and progressive preventive maintenance management programs and effectively manage the capital expenditure budget in order to provide a long-lasting basis for successful economic development.

When initial capital expenditures are made to put up bridges, highways, schools, hospitals and many other structures, these infrastructure projects must neither be left to deteriorate nor become nonfunctional before frantic steps are taken to provide new replacements (or rehabilitation) through the allocation of new capital expenditure funds. Unfortunately, however, this has not been the case in sub-Saharan ACs. For example, in Nigeria, Ghana, Kenya, Zaire, Burkina Faso, Cameroon, Agola, Malawi, Tanzania and the rest of sub-Saharan ACs, infrastructure is usually not properly maintained on a continuing basis.

THE STATE OF PREVENTIVE MAINTENANCE MANGEMEMENT

In what follows, I present in detail a description of the existing state of preventive maintenance management in sub-Saharan ACs. This presentation is based on data and information collected through personal interviews and conversations with citizens of many sub-Saharan ACs. The impressions of a few tourists, travelers, diplomats, students and many others are also drawn on to describe the state of infrastructure in sub-Saharan ACs. Since independence, sub-Saharan African governments have not accomplished much in the area of preventive maintenance management. Many existing structures are currently bowing to dilapidation. Often, a visitor to meteorological stations will observe that weather instruments and other related equipment are broken down and are, therefore, unable to function as desired. In certain cases, due to frequent breakdowns, relevant statistics on the weather are not readily available. When they do exist, one realizes immediately that there are gaps and missing data and/or information.

Since maintenance management has not been accorded its proper place in the development program of sub-Saharan ACs, repair work is usually done sporadically. In many cases, money alloted for such maintenance programs is either misappropriated or diverted into other areas. Every year, when new inputs are imported for the construction of new projects, very little is assigned to preventive maintenance management programs. This is one of the main reasons why physical capital stock has not been effectively maintained.

One important area that has been severely neglected is rural water supply. Many years ago, sub-Saharan African governments spearheaded programs that brought clean water to some rural areas through the construction of water pipelines and taps. Today, many of these initial pipelines and taps are not useable due to lack of proper maintenance. In certain areas, water taps have been closed or turned off to prevent the waste of water through continuing dripping and/or leaking.[1] Roads and highways suffer from the same problems of poor and inefficient maintenance. Roads and highways, therefore, develop cracks, pot holes and irregular bumps. In some cases, first-class roads revert into third-class roads or are no better than feeder roads because the macadamized surfacing has worn away over many years of over use. The wear and tear occur because regulations restricting the classes of vehicles that are authorized to travel on certain roads and highways are usually ignored. The inability to enforce rules lead to abuse and misuse of social facilities. Freight vehicles carrying different kinds of heavier materials travel on roads that are neither designed nor built to support their full weight.

Vehicles imported to be used as public transport are usually parked in transportation depots because there are no spare parts either to repair or maintain them. They are usually left to the mercies of the weather. In some countries, broken-down vehicles are auctioned to private citizens, who repair them and use them as a means of private transportation. Tractors on state farms are not usually exempted from this plight. Other items that fall into this category are public restrooms, trains, state buildings and so on. In the cities, gutters (i.e., drainage systems) are usually not given the attention and care they deserve. They are usually clogged up with garbage, paper wrappers, used cans, twigs and many other items that render them nonfunctional and therefore useless, thus creating problems for the city. In some sub-Saharan African universities and other institutions of learning, one sees broken furniture packed tightly either inside or outside corners of classrooms, left to the mercy of the tropical weather. Many items suffer from complete disrepair and are, therefore, not functional. In many of these institutions of higher learning, glass louvers are now being replaced with wooden louvers and/or windows, which usually have a low life expectancy because of weather conditions. Saint (1992, p. xix) notes that "maintenance of university buildings and equipment is a little recognized problem which has a direct bearing on educational policy. Where classrooms are poorly lit, bathrooms do not function, and laboratory equipment is broken, student learning becomes more difficult. These problems are compounded where institutionalized maintenance programs--and budgets for them--do not exist."

In the area of water transportation in Zaire, Caputo (1991, p. 20-21) observes

we had left Kinshasa on a Thursday afternoon--a week late, but that was not unusual. The city, home to three to five million people (nobody knows for sure), marks the beginning of the river's long navigable curve into the interior. In the old days, I was told, boats sailed from both Kinshasa and Kisangani every Monday, passing each other in mid-river. But the voyages have become less and less frequent. Built in the mid-fifties, the fleet of pushers has suffered greatly from lack of maintenance. One by one the boats have fallen to ruin and joined the hundreds of rusting wrecks litering the riverbanks. By the time I left Zaire, only two boats still functioned. Public transportation between the capital of Zaire and its fourth largest city had been reduced to one voyage about every six weeks. The only other way to get from Kinshasa to Kisangani is by plane, but the fare is far beyond the reach of all but a tiny fraction of Zairians, so competition for passage on the boat is intense.

Caputo notes further that the street leading to the docks is badly damaged and contains numerous potholes. The boat was in terrible shape due to lack of continuing preventive maintenance management.

In general terms, schools, clinics, hospitals, harbors, electriticity poles and wires, water pumps, drainage systems, highway public telephones and many other structures are neglected and left to break down beyond repair. As will be noted later, this is one of the major reasons why rehabilitation programs are common in sub-Saharan ACs. My interview results suggest that effective preventive maintenance management programs do not necessarily come as integral parts of social infrastructure development in sub-Saharan ACs. Governments in these countries seem to respond to programs that deal with crises when a whole structure is either no longer functioning or when the country cannot do without it. Social infrastructure is usually overused until it needs new capital funds for a new face lift or full rehabilitation. Although the annual total value of replacement investment in sub-Saharan ACs is not necessarily zero, its magnitude is negligble. There exist little data on how much funding is committed to an ongoing infrastructure maintenance in sub-Saharan ACs.

In most sub-Saharan ACs, although funds are annually committed to capital expenditure, very little is made available for effective preventive maintenance management budgets (recurrent capital expenditure). When funds are annually made available for such expenditures, they are misapplied, mismanaged or misappropriated. Items, machinery and other structures quickly degenerate into a severely pathetic state of dilapidation in sub-Saharan ACs. One of my interviewees from Zimbabwe noted the following:

1 The state of machines is not properly maintained and managed because most of the workers lack the technical know-how to do so.
2 Trains and other public transport systems are currently failing to provide the services they are required to because the people managing the affairs lack managerial skills. Many are usually appointed to these positions based on political considerations.
3 The health department is being managed effectively. This is the case because of the inputs of expatriates from Canada, Pakistan, China and other foreign countries.
4 The infrastructure (i.e., roads and highways) as a whole is one of the best in Southern Africa, and many neighboring countries utilize the Zimbabwe transportation system as an entry point to other southern ACs, such as Malawi, Mozambique, Zambia and Zaire.
5 In general, the total social infrastructure is somewhat maintained.

When asked to describe the state of social infrastructure in Kenya, the respondent said that "the Kenyan infrastructure is poorly maintained in many regards. Many roads are falling apart--especially the older ones. Garbage is left to get rotten in certain areas. The telecommunications system is in its best form in Kenya." The interviewee from Ethiopia pointed out that

the state of roads is badly maintained. It gets worse during the rainy season. Rest rooms are poorly cared for. School buildings are not usually maintained as they should be. You can see cracks, holes and other evidence of lack of proper maintenance. School desks, tables and chairs suffer a similar plight. Although many vehicles are not road worthy, they still ply the streets. The mere sight of these vehicles makes one wonder sometimes why such vehicles are allowed on the roads and why nobody complains about their use. Sewage and garbage disposal systems are usually in a bad state. Evidence regarding effective maintenance management programs is either scanty or non-existent. In Ethiopia, the whole national infrastructure is poorly maintained and is in pretty bad shape.

Interviewees from Nigeria, Cameroon, Malawi, Tanzania, Egypt, Zambia and Zaire have all expressed similar views and sentiments. Thus, the interview results point out clearly that the plight of the social infrastructure in sub-Saharan ACs is almost identical. My own travel to Togo, the Ivory Coast and Ghana in 1989 was a great eye-opener in relation to why the state of the sub-Saharan African infrastructure is in the form it currently assumes. Note, however, that since 1989, Ghana has made continuing efforts to save its social infrastructure from a total collapse due to the commitment of the Rawlings government to overcome the destruction of both rural and urban infrastructure. New roads are being built and old ones are being rehabilitated. It is, however, the case that when both the new and rehabilitated infrastructure are also neglected continually due to the lack of the appropriate HF to maintain them, other costly future rehabilitation programs have to be undertaken to salvage the decaying social infrastructure.

Major factors that have contributed to the plight of the infrastructure in sub-Saharan ACs include the following:

1 Programs designed and aimed at monitoring and assessing the life of items and/or machines are lacking.
2 Relevant equipment and structure repair records are not usually available. There are hardly any existing records on repairs. Expert analysis of how these items perform is also non-existent. This makes it difficult to track the performance record of equipment and infrastructure in sub-Saharan Africa. If there were systematically kept records concerning successes and failures, it might be easier to set up efficient and effective preventive maintenance management programs in sub-Saharan ACs.
3 Existing inventories of spare parts and relevant materials for maintenance are usually misapplied, mismanaged or misappropriated.

4 Poor planning and overuse of public property is common. For example, state automobiles for public transportation are used intensively for private gains without frequent and methodical preventive maintenance management programs. This has been the plight of farm equipment, school accessories, government vehicles and many other items.
5 In many cases, since sub-Saharan Africans do not possess all the necessary knowledge about certain imported technologies and/or machines in use, there is a lack of efficient and appropriate diagnostic check testing and meaningful repair procedures.
6 Preventive maintenance management seems to be a low priority in economic development planning in sub-Saharan ACs. As such, managers of public property do not consider it crucial to the economic development process. They therefore fail to build into contracts--awarded to both domestic and foreign firms--effective follow-up preventive maintenance management programs.

These observations suggest that there is a dire need for immediate diagnosis and identification of the actual problems of economic underdevelopment in sub-Saharan African economies.

THE THEORY AND ROLE OF PREVENTIVE MAINTENANCE MANAGEMENT

For longer life spans and efficient operation of the social infrastructure, continuing and sufficient preventive maintenance management programs are necessary. Although rehabilitation programs may be useful, they will not help achieve the greatest benefits from a decaying social infrastructure. To achieve this, it is critical to develop a relevant maintenance management technology concept (MTC). The MTC is a scientific approach to failure prevention and maintenance improvements as currently applied in the DCs. It emphasizes the continuous application of technological procedures to track and deal with problems immediately.[2] It is mainly concerned with structures, materials, corrosion, oxidation, preservation, fracture, mechanics, diagnostic checks, life predictions, repair processes, quality assurance and the life cycle phases of machinery. Its main objective is either to prevent or maintain and ensure effective functioning of all machines. It is the systematic and scientific approach to preserving a plant's physical facilities and equipment in optimum working order. According to Rolka (1982, pp. 8-11), this concept emphasizes the following:

1 Focusing research and development on maintenance objectives;
2 Being able to retrieve information easily from existing databases for making design-and management-related decisions;
3 Implementing new technology to upgrade performance and durability;
4 Monitoring the state and performance of every structure and/or

machine;

5 Conducting frequent inspections that are carefully designed and articulately implemented to avoid the destruction of machinery;

6 Assessing how failure occurs and how to prevent it effectively; and

7 Assessing the repair process and verifying that it has been done as required.

The primary objective of maintenance technology is, therefore, to accomplish an extended time period of operating machines and/or infrastructure and reduce the frequency of unexpected breakdowns (Rolka, 1982). This allows for continuous maintenance management programs whose objective is to achieve trouble-free operations of machines and other social infrastructure. The relationship between the frequency of maintenance management programs and the probability of breakdown is illustrated in Figure 8.1. There exists an inverse relationship between the two variables, implying that to maintain a high value of trouble-free operations, sub-Saharan ACs need to step up the frequency of their maintenance management programs.

Figure 8.1 also illustrates the trade-off relationship between the probability of infrastructure breakdown and the frequency of its maintenance. The 45-degree line is the locus of all combinations, where the probability of breakdown is equal to the frequency of infrastructure maintenance. On this locus, either every breakdown is immediately maintained or every expected breakdown is dealt with in principle through preventive maintenance management programs. When the preventive maintenance management authority is on top of maintenance, the society's position will be below the 45-degree line (say, point T). In this case, infrastructure growth and development will proceed smoothly. Alternatively, if society finds itself at a point above the 45-degree line (i.e., D), there will be many more breakdowns than the maintenance management board is able to cope with. This situation may not only lead to a total collapse of social infrastructure in the not-too-distant future but will also require huge sums of financial resources for rehabilitation. The sub-Saharan ACs' situation is like that shown by point D.

Since neither 100% infrastructure maintenance nor 100% breakdown is permissible, the point of equality, B, seems appropriate. Sub-Saharan ACs' governments need to establish programs and institutional structures which will ensure that preventive maintenance management programs effectively prevent breakdowns or maintain infrastructure as soon as a breakdown occurs. If there are many breakdowns in one jurisdiction of the country with fewer resources to maintain them and yet there are fewer break-downs in another jurisdiction with a surplus of funds and if these funds are not easily transferable across jurisdictions, the overall impact will be an upward shift in the maintenance breakdown trade-off curve. Since this can lead to severe infrastructure breakdown in the future, procedures must be created to deal with this type of problem when it occurs.

FIGURE 8.1
THE FREQUENCY OF MAINTENANCE MANAGEMENT
PROGRAMS AND THE PROBABILITY OF BREAKDOWN

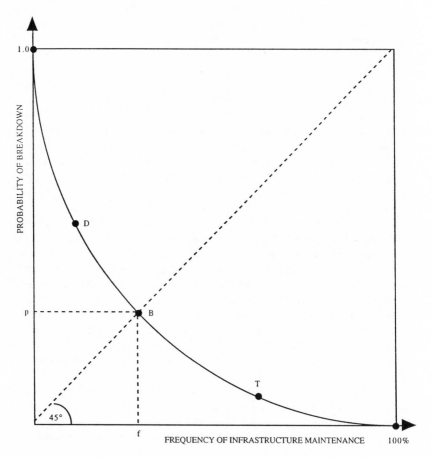

In the sub-Saharan African environment, in which weather changes in terms of dry/hot and wet/cold conditions lead to corrosion, rusting, oxidation and many other negative results, severe damage occurs frequently to many structures through the destruction of metal (i.e., steel) components. In other cases, cracks and seasonal peeling off of concrete coatings usually lead to huge destruction of existing infrastructure.

ELEMENT OF PREVENTIVE MAINTENANCE MANAGEMENT IN SUB-SAHARAN ACs

In the case of sub-Saharan ACs, the preventive maintenance management program must be aimed at the development and institution of relevant action programs to overcome or prevent the deterioration or destruction of equipment and the social infrastructure. Acquired experience must lead to the development of appropriate technology for the efficient management of the social infrastructure and equipment. A successful preventive maintenance management program in sub-Saharan Africa requires that impulsive actions and activities be avoided. The whole program requires detailed planning, organization, and proper scheduling. People who are involved in this vital program must know what to do, how to do it and when to do it.

The program requires the proper documentation of relevant materials to be used, the various estimated costs and how the work must be done and monitored. This calls for effective leadership responsibility and accountability. Those who are to accomplish the tasks must make sure that the work is done as expected, and the inspecting team must see to it that those who execute the maintenance management program do not get away with shoddy work. The inspecting officers must be properly educated and trained to check work thoroughly and ensure that work has been done according to all stipulated guidelines. What is done should not be treated as another repair work; rather, it should be viewed as effective work done to improve the efficiency of the structure in question and to prolong its life span.

Sub-Saharan African governments must know that economic development requires not only new investment in the creation of new structures and projects but also in maintaining those structures and projects that are already in existence. The Ewe proverb, *Hafleho mehia o, hanyihoe hia*, is intuitive. The proverb maintains that it is not the funds one uses to purchase a hog that matter but the financial resources to maintain the hog after it has been bought and paid for. The inability to set aside sufficient financial resources or the misappropriation and misapplication of the funds made available for frequent preventive maintenance management programs in sub-Saharan ACs have caused many difficulties for development programs. Merely building social infrastructure without any carefully premeditated program to keep it functional over the years is almost equivalent to not building it in the first place. One crucial element of a development program is effective protection against damage and acts that have the potential to cause significant losses.

TYPES OF PREVENTIVE MAINTENANCE
MANAGEMENT PROGRAMS

The life span of social infrastructure in sub-Saharan ACs can be prolonged through condition maintenance management programs. Relevant moves must be made without delay to repair existing social infrastructure when the inspection department reveals that some repair work must be done. The repair must be viewed as an emergency case to be dealt with immediately. When this task is accomplished to the satisfaction of the inspection team, the complete destruction of structures and/or the frequent failure of machines, public transportation systems, electricity, running water taps and so on will be successfully circumvented. Therefore, a monitoring team must act as an effective watchdog, overseeing the nature and state of the social infrastruture, ascertaining the existing conditions of national property and insisting that work is done immediately and accurately to avoid further damage.

The continuing development of appropriate technology may, in the long run, replace human effort in trying to locate problems and difficulties. Strives and Willard (1982, p. 5), writing on condition monitoring, noted that the major goal is to develop relevant artificial intelligence sensors that have the capability to blow the whistle regarding a possible malfunction or breakdown of a piece of equipment, social infrastructure or property.

Modularization, a design approach to maintenance, can also be useful in the sub-Saharan African maintenance management program. It involves the design of machines that operate using replaceable modules. When a piece of equipment develops problems, interchangeable modules can be easily replaced and repaired. The repaired module can be used in future operations. (See Shives and Willard, 1982, p. 6, for a detailed discussion of this issue.)

Another maintenance management procedure is referred to as reliability-centered maintenance (RCM). It was initially developed by United Airlines in 1965 for aircraft maintenance programs. This procedure can be used in the sub-Saharan African maintenance management program to keep tools, machines, structures and so on in continuous functioning order.

Preventive maintenance management programs designed for sub-Saharan ACs will assist in reducing the magnitude of malfunction as well as future rehabilitation costs. This can be achieved by properly educating and training sub-Saharan Africans to acquire and use the relevant HF to prevent future failures and/or destruction rather than to wait until little problems balloon into disasters. In terms of aviation maintenance management, King (1986, p. 1) observed that

Aviation maintenance activities are the backbone of all successful aviation enterprises. Good maintenance provides safer and more reliable aircraft, increases aircraft usage, and provides confidence of air travel to the approximately 300 million passengers that want to enjoy the freedom, timeliness, and safety of modern aircraft. Good maintenance management is that tangible asset that provides for the aviation industry the essentials necessary to the establishment of flying confidence by the public. Without good maintenance management, the aviation enterprise is adversely affected.

Normally, we would not need to belabor the crucial role preventive maintenance management programs play in the success of every human endeavor. The mere building of structures without adequate programs to maintain and sustain them is obviously not sufficient for sustained economic progress. But in the past, sub-Saharan ACs have made huge capital expenditures without setting aside sufficient resources to maintain them. This failure has led to the destruction of the basic infrastructure that was built during the colonial and early postcolonial eras. My personal interviews with several sub-Saharan African diplomats, ambassadors, high commissioners and students have confirmed that preventive maintenance management has not been accorded top priority in the sub-Saharan African economic development program. This is one of the main reasons why many programs have failed and, after several years of attempting to develop, sub-Saharan ACs still go abroad to procure foreign assistance for rehabilitating decaying social infrastructure, declining cash crop production, dying mineral mines and so forth. It is important for sub-Saharan ACs to concentrate on preventive maintenance management programs rather than rehabilitation projects. Preventive maintenance management programs must be viewed and treated as integral components of the economic development program rather than a tack on--an appendage that can be ignored forever, as has been the case in sub-Saharan ACs. Although preventive maintenance management programs have the potential to minimize productivity losses and sustain the economic development program, rehabilitation projects are usually costly and involve much time and significant financial resources because the whole program must begin again, almost from scratch. However, this is not the best way for sub-Saharan ACs. Edwards (1991, p. 54) observed that "design problems represent by far the most important single reason for the unsatisfactory performance of agricultural projects. If planners are to avoid repeating past errors and to reduce the need for rehabilitation measures, it is important to understand the nature of such problems and to explore means of improving project design."

Unlike rehabilitation programs, preventive maintenance management programs sustain and improve the value of property and the social infrastructure at minimal costs on a continuing basis. They also can lead to the development of appropriate indigenous technology for sustaining the useability of the social infrastructure and equipment. In some cases, they can serve as the basis for developing proper safety procedures and attitudes. Project rehabilitation programs can be likened to closing the stable gates after the horse has bolted away--one will have to purchase a new horse and start all over again. This has been a common experience in sub-Saharan Africa from the economic development perspective. Cracknell (1991, pp. 42-43) pointed out that

> poor original project design is also an important factor leading to
> subsequent deterioration and premature need for rehabilitation. Some
> roads, particularly in Africa, have been built to accommodate vehicles with
> limited axle loads, and as the heavier lorries came into use, they caused
> serious damage (the main spine road through eastern Botswana is an
> example of a major road built to inadequate axle loading standards). . . .
> It follows of course that if roads are not built according to proper quality
> standards, pavement failure can occur earlier than it would otherwise do.

This implies that infrastructure projects for sub-Saharan ACs must be properly
designed to avoid spending huge amounts of money on them for rehabilitation
purposes in the future. Similarly, roads, highways, streets, bridges and many
other structures must be used only by the classes of vehicles they have been
constructed for. The rules must be rigidly enforced. The local maintenance
management board must be given the powers to enforce all established
regulations. This must be the case because, according to Cracknell (1991, p.
48), "evaluators have found that the quality of maintenance tends to decline the
more the responsibility for it is switched from the local level to the government
level. The main reason is that the Public Works Department [PWD] is often
chronically starved of the necessary funds since governments often fail to attach
adequate funding to maintenance work." Although the PWD usually is allotted
a meager maintenance budget, it is the only organization that has the sole
authority for developing, implementing and overseeing almost all maintenance
management programs in many sub-Saharan ACs. In most cases, personnel and
employees of the PWD have little education and training and work with
inappropriate tools and technology (Cracknell, 1991, p. 46). Supervision is often
lapsed, and that which is carried out is usually poorly done.

It is necessary to overhaul the PWD in all sub-Saharan ACs. This review
exercise must involve personnel hiring, education and training. People who are
employed by all PWDs must possess the relevant HF so that they can be
effective on the job. This requires the development of effective education and
training programs by the PWD to groom employees for the tasks they have been
hired to do. Similarly, the purchasing personnel in this department must learn
the art of shopping and purchasing the relevant resources for the maintenance
management program. As I have discussed elsewhere in this book, the success
of this program will depend heavily on the availability of sub-Saharan Africans
who possess the necessary HF. When the required HF is lacking, very little will
be achieved in the area of preventive maintenance management. If, however, the
people who work at the PWD bring integrity, dedication, devotion,
accountability, responsibility, resourcefulness, commitment and the like to the
job, much will be achieved in sub-Saharan Africa. These people must be
educated, trained and equipped to deal with all institutional, conceptual,
technical, financial, social, political, environmental and similar problems. The

availability and use of these individuals will improve significantly the life span of the social infrastructure in sub-Saharan Africa.

CRITICAL ISSUES IN MAINTAINING INFRASTRUCTURE AND EQUIPMENT

To develop, maintain and sustain the social infrastructure and equipment, both the maintenance management budget (MB) and capital expenditure (CE) must be accorded a position of preeminence. Assume that the actual level of infrastructure development (LID) in any sub-Saharan AC is determined by the magnitudes of MB and CE. This relationship can be specified mathematically as $LID = f(MB, CE)$. In analyzing the level of infrastructure development in any sub-Saharan AC, three possible relationships between MB and CE are apparent. First, MB and CE can be viewed as perfect complements. In this case, growth in the level of infrastructure development is possible if both types of expenditure grow at some fixed proportions. There is no substitutability in this case. Second, some scholars may argue that there is some degree of substitutability between MB and CE. Third, MB and CE may be considered perfect substitutes. In this case, once the initial capital expenditure is made, a nation may continue to provide most resources for developing new infrastructure and equipment. Once the basic expenditure has been made to develop social infrastructure, a small maintenance budget is readily available. After several years, when the structures begin to fall apart, a new dose of funding can be made available for rehabilitation purposes. Although the third scenario is the worst of the three, it has been the main choice made of sub-Saharan ACs. This is one of the primary reasons why the sub-Saharan African social infrastructure is in a deplorable state of disrepair.

To deal effectively with this problem, sub-Saharan African leaders need to reevaluate their economic development programs and then start to treat MB and CE as compliments rather than substitutes. This will lead them to develop appropriate programs to build new social infrastructure and at the same time sustain existing ones. The relationship between the level of infrastructure development and the total value of the capital expenditure and maintenance budget is a fixed proportion (i.e., Leontief technology). This implies that developing and sustaining the infrastructure in sub-Saharan Africa require that both inputs be used in fixed proportions.

To achieve the maximum level of infrastructure development per period of time in each sub-Saharan AC, the magnitudes of the preventive maintenance budget and capital expenditure must be selected to maximize the magnitude of the level of infrastructure development (LID). That is, in their attempts to achieve a high level of infrastructure development, the critical minimum amount of contribution to be made by each type of expenditure toward this goal must be determined and maintained.

The *Isoinfras*

An *isoinfra* represents the level of infrastructure development in any sub-Saharan AC as it relates to the various combinations of maintenance budget and capital expenditure to maintain a given level of infrastructure development. As shown in Figure 8.2, there is no substitutability between MB and CE. To maintain a particular level of LID, MB and CE must be available in fixed proportions. To increase LID, however, both MB and CE must be increased in proprotional magnitudes. Any significant decline in value of either MB or CE will affect the level of LID. The problem faced by sub-Saharan ACs in the past is that while they focused on CE, MB was severely neglected. Since MB and CE need to be combined in fixed proportions to achieve high expected levels of LID (i.e., from LID_0 to LID_3) and yet sub-Saharan ACs could not do so, their economic development planning and programs have not been successful. Figure 8.2 is a representation of an *isoinfra* map that illustrates the relationship between LID, MB and CE.

Sub-Saharan ACs must know about the actual impact of increases in either MB or CE on the marginal productivity of the other and vice versa. This knowledge will help determine how to allocate existing scarce financial resources toward MB and CE. If sub-Saharan ACs begin to assign more resources to preventive maintenance management programs in order to meet the fixed proportions requirement, the value of funds committed to CE will be more productive than if they do not. The reverse is also true for CE. It is, therefore, crucial to investigate the marginal impacts of changes in CE on MB and vice versa. The responses of LID to either proprotional or disproportional changes in CE and MB must also be thoroughly investigated.

If we assume that funds from foreign sources are to be committed solely to capital expenditure and funds for the maintenance budget originate from domestic sources, then the magnitude of each of these components will depend on the availability of funds from its supporting sources. Traditionally, however, many sub-Saharan ACs pay more attention to capital budgeting than they do to the preventive maintenance management budget. When attention is paid to the aforementioned budget, funds from local sources or from foreign exchange earnings may be used to secure resources for implementing and sustaining the successful development of the social infrastructure and other capital stock. Regardless of the sources of funds for supporting the total values of MB and CE, sub-Saharan African goverments must keep the balance between the dollar values assigned to each expenditure category. If these amounts fail to meet the fixed proportions requirement, problems will be created for the development and sustainability of the magnitude of LID.

FIGURE 8.2
AN *ISOINFRA* MAP OF INFRASTRUCTURE DEVELOPMENT

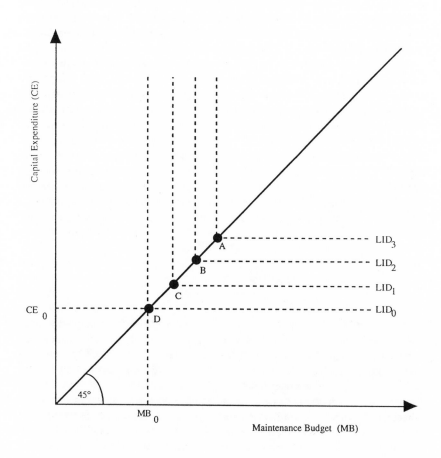

RECOMMENDATIONS FOR PREVENTIVE
MAINTENANCE MANGEMENT POLICY

Each sub-Saharan AC must be in the habit of describing and/or defining all infrastructure failures, causes and consequencess. Since each of these problems has the potential to diminish human productivity, programs of action must be readily available for dealing with each problem category. Recommendations for effective and efficient preventive maintenance management policy must be based on sound principles. In what follows, some of these principles are presented and briefly discussed.

The success of the sub-Saharan African preventive maintenance management program requires a proper stipulation of repair requirements and practices. Repair requirements and practices necessitate (1) a group of people who identify what needs to be done in terms of repairs; (2) inspectors of the work and how it performs; (3) reporters, whose duty is to document in detail what has and has not yet been done; and (4) service repair managers, whose sole duty is to instruct others regarding what must be done (McKinley and Bert, 1967). A good workable preventive maintenance management program requires the creation of national, regional and district maintenance management boards, whose major duties must be to see to it that maintenance teams fulfill rigidly set standards and adhere to all stipulated maintenance management principles. These are discussed next.

The Principle of Total Separation

McKinley and Bert (1967) observed that an effective and efficient maintenance management program must be based on the principle of total separation of the inspection function from the operating division. This, in my view, is necessary for overcoming all conflict of interest problems. When the same group of individuals operates both departments, this may spell disaster for the country because the necessary checks and balances will be absent. In sub-Saharan ACs, in which conflict of interest guidelines are usually not properly defined and/or stipulated, the violation of this principle will render ineffective the preventive maintenance management program. When they exist but are not enforced, the same problems may arise.

The Principle of Progressive Inspection

To keep machines, structures and the social infrastructure functioning properly, it is necessary to inspect these items and projects on a continuing basis. If the various local maintenance management boards fail to achieve this principle, the program will not succeed. This principle suggests that one of the best ways to know what is happening to social property is to inspect it continually to identify any imminent problems. This will lead to early detection and prevention of greater damage in the future. To operate on this principle, each locality's maintenance management board must establish continuous maintenance management schedules and enforce them rigidly. McKinley and Bert (1967, pp. 342-350) suggested that in the case of certain instruments, the repair program must involve disassembling, inspecting, repairing and reassembling. By diligently pursuing this procedure frequently, future disasters will be avoided. It may be necessary to invest huge sums of money in the development of procedures for detecting when a structure may need additional work either to improve its current standard and efficiency or to sustain its contribution to the economy.

The Principle of Maintenance Record Keeping

As noted earlier, there must be knowledge about what needs to be done. After the work has been done, it must also be documented. Thus, it is necessary to keep maintenance records regarding whether or not the repairs done were minor or major (McKinley and Bert, 1967). Analytical maintenance management programs must be used to record the work done, when it was accomplished and how it was completed. This record will be of assistance to the various maintenance management boards regarding what plan of action to pursue in the future.

It is also necessary to create and/or encourage the development of private business organizations whose duty must be the continuous survey of the whole country to locate, document and describe all cracks, damage, or wear and tear regarding all existing social infrastructure and other property in need of maintenance. These organizations and/or businesses must be certified and their activities carefully monitored (McKinley and Bert, 1967). The specific locations and types of damage with full estimated repair costs must be documented and presented to the appropriate authorities.

The Principle of Contracts and Maintenence Clauses

In the past, many contracts for the building of highways, hospitals, schools, roads, dams, telephone lines, electric cables and many other structures were signed with mostly foreign building companies. Although these companies did their best to fulfill the initial building contracts, sub-Saharan African leaders failed to have enshrined in these contracts preventive maintenance management clauses. Thus, as soon as the contracting firm completed its initial building obligations, that was it. If there occurred any damage in the future, these countries usually went through a painfully costly process again, looking for someone else to provide the finance for rehabilitating the crumbling or dilapidated infrastructure in question. This way of doing business with foreign building companies has caused many difficulties and problems for sub-Saharan

ACs. In modern sub-Saharan ACs, this error can easily be corrected in regard to building new infrastructure or rehabilitating old and dilapidated structures--by including clauses on preventive maintenance management in every contract. Companies that win these contracts must also know that they will engage in continuing preventive maintenance management programs for a number of subsequent years.

Other private contracting and building companies and organizations must be allowed to bid on the repair and preventive maintenance mangement projects. The winning bidder must be a company that has built a good reputation for itself and has demonstrated a good track record in relation to the quality of its work and preventive maintenance management programs. Regardless of who wins the bid, the contracts must stipulate clearly the building projects and must include preventive maintenenace management clauses. The goal of these clauses is to elicit from the contractors effective and efficient long-lasting repair work.

The Principle of Failure Prevention

There are many important variables that determine how to prevent mechanical failures and the destruction of the principal structural foundation of the social infrastructure and equipment. These include the following:

1 The ability of a nation to identify and assess how the processes of wear, tear, corrosion, and the like occur in the environment in question.
2 The need for national engineers to know and be aware of how existing levels of humidity, earth movement (i.e., soil creep), continuing temperature changes, oxidation and hence rusting and many other factors affect the life span of the social infrastructure and facilitate the process of destruction.
3 The need for proper treatment of all building materials used in the construction of the social infrastructure so that they withstand harsh environmental conditions. This may relate to treatments against insects, oxidation, vibrations and so on. Whatever is done in this direction will affect significantly the life span of existing social infrastructure and machinery.
4 The crucial importance of a labor force that possesses the relevant HF in designing, building and operating the social infrastructure in sub-Saharan ACs.

The Principle of Contracting Out

In every sub-Saharan AC, the central government is responsible for building and maintaining the social infrastructure. Private businesses and organizations have not been given the opportunity to be actively involved in the development of the local social infrastructure. To correct this oversight, government social infrastructure development could be contracted out to reputable local companies that have the necessary tools and personnel to do the job effectively and efficiently. Again, as noted earlier, when projects are contracted out, care must be taken to articulate contracts that will make it the sole responsibility of the company to assume the role of preventive maintenance management. In this way, much pressure will be taken off the central government. The success of the contracting-out program will depend on how effectively the other principles are implemented.

CONCLUSION

As has been discussed elsewhere in this book, economic development is a continuous process. As such, instead of focusing on project rehabilitation programs, sub-Saharan ACs must begin to put significant financial resources into preventive maintance management programs. It is important that all levels of government involved with this program be properly and adequately prepared to manage it. The PWDs in sub-Saharan ACs need reorganization and redirection. The success of this vital department in sub-Saharan ACs will depend mostly on people who have been educated and trained to acquire the necessary HF. In this way, sub-Saharan ACs stand a greater chance of prolonging the life of their social infrastructure and hence paving the way for a continuing economic development process.

NOTES

1. The Malawi Rural Pipe Water Program is, however, one of the most successful ones in Africa because the program has been supported, managed and maintained by the communities involved. This program has been carefully designed and stipulates clearly the roles of the community and government. Committees are usually created to identify problems, see to continuing repairs and enforce rules regarding the use of water.

2. Since sub-Saharan ACs may not have the required technology for implementing the MTC, they need to develop a substitute procedure for accomplishing this process. The principles discussed later in this chapter can be used to develop viable substitute programs.

9

Knowledge Acquisition, Technology Transfer and the Process of Economic Development in Sub-Saharan African Countries

INTRODUCTION

The desire to be self-reliant, the hope of attaining good living standards, the dream of conquering the natural environment and the expectation of gaining appropriate technology for economic development require an unrelenting search for appropriate wisdom--a necessary requirement for progress. Based on these facts, this chapter[1] argues that effective economic development programs can be successfully initiated, properly executed and continuously sustained after a society has acquired basic abilities in planning, organizing, directing and controlling a creative economic development process. This chapter contends that to be successful, sub-Saharan Africa's economic development programs must first create the environment within which the practical acumen that makes progress happen is acquired for dealing with everyday social, political, intellectual, business and economic problems. The chapter concludes with the view that solutions for sub-Saharan Africa's problems of economic underdevelopment exist and that these solutions can be discovered through the acquisition and application of relevant knowledge.

For many decades, orthodox economic development theorists have been unable to devise appropriate theories to help sub-Saharan African countries (ACs) achieve progress. Consequently, these countries have not only been unable to provide the basic necessities of life for their citizens but have also failed to develop appropriate economic policies and programs that can create congenial environments within which technological change and economic progress can take place. The proper pursuits of and the desire for economic development in sub-Saharan ACs call for wise leadership that is sympathetic toward change. This is necessary for national economic progress. To be successful, economic development programs for sub-Saharan Africa must be based on knowledge of the problems of economic underdevelopment and how to use this knowledge base properly for effective, efficient and creative management of human and natural resources--the necessary ingredients of economic progress.

From the corporate perspective, culture is often considered to be a set of shared beliefs (i.e., corporate culture) that propels the behavior of top managers and employees in the company (Lorsch, 1989). Although these rules and principles may be effectively used in one environment, they may be of little use in others (see Chapter 6). Yet the saturation of home markets, the intensification of competition, increasing innovation, escalating inventiveness and the growing desire to maintain global competitiveness require that sub-Saharan ACs manage their human and material resources efficiently if they hope to develop and compete successfully in the global marketplace.

In sponsoring students to go abroad to acquire relevant knowledge, sub-Saharan ACs expect that each student will acquire the wisdom and experience needed for the formulation and implementation of national economic development plans and policies. It is too often the case, however, that some of these students, on their return, are unable to accomplish assigned organizational, leadership, production and managerial tasks because their acquired knowledge and technical skills cannot be easily applied to their countries' needs. This failure in the application of acquired knowledge leaves many returnees physically, emotionally and psychologically disillusioned. The acquired Western knowledge, which has been effective in Western-type cultures, fails to achieve similar expected results in sub-Saharan ACs. This is also often the case with knowledge gained from socialist countries, and it results in an intellectual culture shock.

This phenomenon is one of the contributing factors to the observed intellectual capital drain being experienced by sub-Saharan ACs. Overseas graduating students, knowing and believing that they may not have the true opportunities to use their acquired knowledge successfully in their own countries of origin, usually prefer to take employment in other countries. Some scholars who return to their countries, sooner or later discover that there are either too many hindrances and frustrations in trying to apply acquired knowledge or conclude that what they have learned cannot be easily applied to solving social, economic and political problems in their countries. These attitudes and intellectual capital drain are also refueled by the feeling that knowledge gained from abroad may be more relevant elsewhere. This feeling must be dealt with by providing both the opportunity and the relevant enivironment for scholars to readily apply what has been learned constructively.

To overcome the problem of intellectual culture, however, students must be retrained and re-educated in the ability to use the knowledge acquired. Newcomb (1885, pp. 72-75) observed that

knowledge is a product of labor, since, omitting exceptional cases, no one can acquire it without that exertion of the faculties called labor. The acquisition of knowledge may therefore be regarded as an act of production. . . . Some kinds of knowledge have been applied so as to increase the production of wealth, while other kinds have not. The former may be called useful, and the latter, so far as the production of wealth is concerned, may be called useless. . . . What we are to remember is that all the benefits now or hereafter to be obtained from electricity would never have been known had not several generations of philosophers, out of pure curiosity, devoted themselves to the investigation of the laws of that agent.

In the knowledge literature, many scholars in the past seemed to be aware that knowledge becomes useful when men and women have developed the ability to use it to solve the problems of humanity. Those who gain knowledge and yet are unable to employ it in problem solving may not achieve economic progress. Dewey (1965, pp. 143-144), for example, noted that

a quantum of knowledge usually has little or no economic payoff until it is "incorporated" or "embedded" in a set of specialized men and machines. One might say that income is increased by growth of knowledge which makes possible the creation of better men and machines. Alternatively, one might say that income is increased by investment in men and machines who are specialized and make use of the growth of knowledge. One statement is as true as the other; taken together they suggest the logical impossibility of isolating the contribution of investment and technical progress to income growth.

It follows that economic development programs must either create or encourage the acquisition of wisdom that can articulate, analyze and creatively solve everyday business, economic, social, intellectual and political problems if they are to be successful. To initiate and sustain the economic development process, the labor force that possesses the relevant HF^2 in sub-Saharan ACs must achieve and maintain a knowledge base that is necessary and sufficient for dealing with prevailing circumstances. Since successful economic development programs require an appropriate knowledge base, the existing labor force in sub-Saharan ACs must, prior to undertaking economic development planning, policies and programs, first acquire the pertinent wisdom before any long-lasting economic progress can be attained. The conclusions of this chapter are used as the basis for recommending procedures that must be followed to achieve economic development in sub-Saharan Africa.

The rest of the chapter is organized as follows: The following section explains the shock of economic underdevelopment, and the subsequent section discusses the role of knowledge in technology transfer and economic development. Then there is a discussion of how sub-Saharan ACs can use acquired knowledge to overcome problems of economic underdevelopment and to enhance their economic performance in the global environment. The final section contains some conclusions and recommendations for economic policy and programs.

THE SHOCK OF UNDERDEVELOPMENT: A CONCEPTUALIZATION

The term *development* means different things to different people. In this chapter, the term refers to the state in which the basic necessities of life (i.e., food, shelter, clothing and belongingness) are readily available for all people at all times (see Chapter 1 for an extended eclectic definition). Orthodox economic development theory has not been successful in mapping out a clear-cut route whereby sub-Saharan Africans can attain economic development. The frustrations, confusion, discouragement and bewilderment that originate from the inability of sub-Saharan ACs to attain economic progress by successfully handling problems perpetuate the feeling of failure. Sub-Saharan ACs therefore become disoriented toward the applications of existing orthodox economic thinking and its policy prescriptions because they often realize that all previously proven economic development theories in developed countries (DCs) are unsuccessful in helping sub-Saharan Africans manage and solve their development-related problems (see Chapters 2 and 3 for further discussions of this issue).

Since confidence in existing economic development theory drives the behavior of policy planners in sub-Saharan ACs, a call for constructive democratic modifications necessary for economic progress in sub-Saharan Africa is usually unheeded. This behavior on the part of sub-Saharan Africa's economic development planners and consultants does not only produce economic development policies and programs that are myopic in focus but also forces them to respond negatively to new ideas regardless of changing circumstances and the availability of new information. This leads many sub-Saharan ACs' governments to formulate and implement policies as though economic, social and political conditions in Africa are identical to those of the DCs.

Ineffective economic policies and programs are the results of a lack of relevant knowledge about what actually ails sub-Saharan ACs and how one should go about dealing with these ailments. Failure has, therefore, characterized sub-Saharan African economic development planning, policies and programs for three main reasons. First, sub-Saharan African policy makers, economic development planners and international consultants do not possess the appropriate knowledge about what actually ails sub-Saharan African economies. Second, the sub-Saharan African people are neither well prepared nor possess the necessary HF for the economic development program--a problem of HF deficiency (see Chapters 3 and 4). Third, sub-Saharan Africans lack the relevant technological know-how required for economic progress. Although the acquisition of this knowledge is a necessary condition for sub-Saharan African economic development, the sufficient condition is that the sub-Saharan African people must develop the ability to use acquired knowledge to overcome the problems of economic underdevelopment.

THE ROLE OF KNOWLEDGE IN THE PROCESS OF
ECONOMIC DEVELOPMENT

The existence of economic underdevelopment perpetuates low productivity and poor living conditions in sub-Saharan ACs. If sub-Saharan ACs congregate, learn and acquire new knowledge about their existing circumstances and environments, they may together pull themselves out of the trap of economic underdevelopment. Unfortunately, since sub-Saharan Africans have been crushed by the forces of economic underdevelopment for many decades, they often remain in this state, continuously failing to recognize the relevant knowledge upon which progress depends. It is time that sub-Saharan ACs rise to the task, adopt and maintain a more constructive, positive outlook on things and work more effectively to acquire and develop the relevant knowledge base necessary for economic development. The ability to utilize this knowledge (wisdom) is relevant to the development of appropriate technology, effective economic planning and policy formulation and efficient program development and management.

Sub-Saharan ACs may not develop by merely pursuing economic policies devised and.imposed on them from outside the continent. Such policies often require sub-Saharan ACs to meet certain conditions that do not necessarily address the real problems of sub-Saharan African economic underdevelopment. It is a fruitless venture to try to create in sub-Saharan ACs conditions for economic development that are mainly relevant to the DCs yet are unproductive in sub-Saharan Africa. For example, for many decades economic development policies for sub-Saharan Africa have been based on known rules and/or procedures that once worked in the DCs. These rules and procedures usually disregard existing differences among domestic conditions in the DCs and sub-Saharan ACs. Thus, policy makers sweep under the rug the main problems to be solved and the actual tasks to be performed. A major result is that sub-Saharan Africa's problems of economic underdevelopment have been left largely unsolved regardless of efforts directed at them in the past. Hayek (1945, pp. 88-91) could not have been more accurate when he noted that

we make constant use of formulas, symbols, and rules whose meaning we do not understand and through the use of which we avail ourselves of the assistance of knowledge which individually we do not possess. We have developed these practices and institutions by building upon habits and situations which have proved successful in their own sphere and which have in turn become the foundation of the civilization we have built up. . . . Any approach, such as that of much mathematical economics with its simultaneous equations, which in effect starts from the assumption that people's knowledge corresponds with the objective facts of the situation, systematically leaves out what is our main task to explain.

Sub-Saharan Africans need to articulate precisely what is necessary for economic progress. For many years, the DCs have concentrated their efforts on activities that create the relevant data, understanding, knowledge and wisdom (all embodiments of the HF) necessary for economic progress. Although for centuries resources have been channeled into research and development, scientific discoveries, experimentations, the development of technology, etc. in the DCs, sub-Saharan ACs have failed to do likewise on an ongoing and intensively productive scale. Sagasti (1987, p. 174) has observed that

the developing countries of the "Second Civilization" have not managed to acquire a research base of their own to generate scientific knowledge in a systematic, large scale and continuous fashion, to transform this knowledge into production techniques, and to incorporate these new science-based techniques into production. In these countries, science, technology and production have grown in an imitative, fragmented and disjointed way, each being almost totally dependent on the evolution of their counterparts in the highly industrialized countries of the "First Civilization."

This observation is true for sub-Saharan ACs. As long as the situation remains as is, there will be little change in sub-Saharan Africa's condition. A way out will be the development of programs aimed at the creation and use of information and knowledge. "A techno-economic intelligence group deeply involved in the process of [economic] development would have to undertake the seemingly improbable task of acting as the main focus for the gathering, transfer and processing of critical information for the process of [economic] development" (Sagasti, 1987, p. 175).

The search for knowledge and the ability to use it can be viewed together as a process of wisdom acquisition. My conceptualization of the process of economic development consists of four intertwining phases whereby wisdom is acquired for economic progress (see Figure 9.1). When any of these phases is ignored, the economic development program may stagger and drift, unable to arrive and dock in the harbor of economic development. In phase I, the key variables for which an intensive search is mounted are relevant data. This implies that at the bottom of the knowledge pyramid are data (Dedijer and Jequier, 1987, p. 13). The individual is usually confronted with data from which much information can be gathered. The available data or information to be collected are used as the basis for scientific inquiry. This data usually must contain information about human behavior as well as existing beliefs about society and the universe (Lane, 1966, p. 650). Through continuous analysis, more valuable information is gleaned from the available and/or acquired data.

In phase II, further studies, experience, experimentation, scientific research, estimation, hypotheses testing, etc. will generate more evidence and information that must be digested and understood. After gaining understanding through more detailed and specific investigations, theorizing, interpretation, synthesizing, reformulation, evaluation and inference, people may be led to acquire knowledge in phase III. This knowledge may be organized and classified into various categories, as suggested by Machlup (1962) (see Table 9.1 for details). From

TABLE 9.1
MACHLUP'S FIVE CLASSIFICATIONS OF KNOWLEDGE

I. Practical Knowledge: disaggregated as

1 Business knowledge
2 Household knowledge
3 Political knowledge
4 Professional knowledge
5 Working people's knowledge
6 Other practical knowledge

II. Intellectual Knowledge: classified as an
   integral part of

1 Liberal education
2 Humanistic and scientific learning
3 General culture

III. Small Talk and Pastime Knowledge: for
   recreation and emotional fulfillment.
   Examples include

1 Local gossip
2 News of crime
3 Novels, stories and jokes
4 Games, etc.

IV. Spiritual Knowledge: about God,
   the soul and the human spirit

V. Unwanted Knowledge: not consciously
   desired

Source: Adapted from Machlup (1962, p. 21) and Bell (1973, p. 175).

this classification, inferences about natural laws of economic growth and universal principles of life, work and development may be made and/or discovered (see Chapter 7). Inferences may include the meaning and relevance of acquired knowledge to human-centered economic development, human performance, human factor development, organization and management of institutions, social progress and so on.

Phase IV involves efficient application of acquired knowledge to enlighten society about the operation of natural laws of economic development in specific environments. When successfully applied, acquired knowledge should lead society to deal effectively with hindrances to its plans, policies and programs for economic progress. At this phase, the process of economic development will be put in motion because wisdom is the true genie for human creativity and economic development. It is one of the most important components of the HF and produces instruction, prudence, leadership, etc. (see Figure 9.1).

Societies that lack the ability to apply acquired knowledge may not overcome their many problems of economic underdevelopment. This wisdom must be created from within the environment or be a modification of imported wisdom-- adapted to deal with pertinent problems in society. Wisdom does not only lead a society in problem-solving ventures but also provides the necessary instruments with which a nation can break the vicious cycle of economic underdevelopment. As illustrated in Figure 9.1, wisdom alone has the power to create a snow-balling effect on the process of economic development. Its lack will mount hindrances to economic progress in sub-Saharan Africa, which is in fact the case currently.[3]

In what follows, I present some axioms of knowledge that are relevant to the economic development process and may be useful to sub-Saharan African economic development planners, policy makers and program developers.

AXIOMS OF KNOWLEDGE FOR AFRICAN
ECONOMIC DEVELOPMENT

A general survey of existing economic development literature reveals that problems of economic underdevelopment in sub-Saharan Africa have been attributed to symptoms rather than actual causes. In an attempt to put the real causes of sub-Saharan Africa's economic underdevelopment in perspective, the following three axioms about the role of knowledge in the process of economic development are proposed and deemed to encompass the totality of the causes of and remedies for economic underdevelopment in sub-Saharan Africa.

Axiom 1: Knowledge of What Actually Ails African Economies

Although many attempts have been made to prescribe solutions to problems of economic underdevelopment in sub-Saharan Africa, many of these programs and policies fail because the planners neither possess first-hand knowledge nor understand fully what actually ails sub-Saharan African economies. Such policies and programs are therefore usually directed toward redressing symptons rather than actual causes of pertinent problems of sub-Saharan African economic underdevelopment. The experience of economic underdevelopment in sub-Saharan ACs is therefore partly due to lack of knowledge and the ability to use that knowledge base to salvage disintegrating sub-Saharan African economies.

FIGURE 9.1
FROM DATA TO DEVELOPMENT THROUGH WISDOM

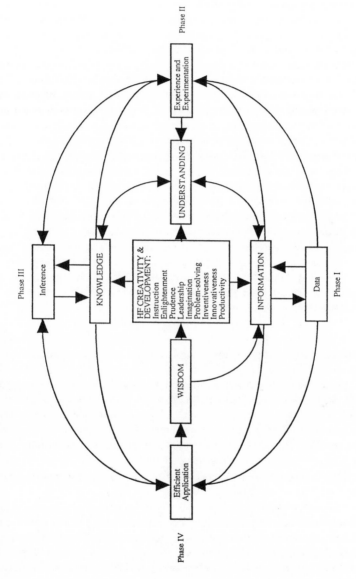

An example that supports the validity of this axiom is an inadequate appreciation of the strength of intratribal solidarity and/or loyalty and its conflict with the economic development of multi-tribal national loyalties in ACs by policy planners and program developers.[4]

Axiom 2: Harness and Articulately Use Available Knowledge and HF

The necessary requirement and sufficient condition for successful management of economic development programs (i.e., long-range economic development as opposed to dealing with an immediate crisis, such as starvation, drought, flood, epidemics, etc.) in sub-Saharan Africa are the acquisition of the appropriate knowledge and HF by sub-Saharan Africans and their ability to use it. Once the sub-Saharan African people acquire this knowledge and transform it into the necessary wisdom for economic policy and programs, economic underdevelopment will become an issue of the past in sub-Saharan Africa. The acquisition of knowledge that cannot be used for problem solving may be of little assistance in combating problems of economic underdevelopment. In dealing with sub-Saharan Africa's problems, governments, economic development theorists, policy planners and international consultants fail to apply the relevant knowledge to sub-Saharan Africa's real problems. Existing knowledge has not been successfully transformed into the necessary wisdom that makes economic development happen.

Axiom 3: Knowledge of Blueprints and Existing Opportunities

Economic development planners and policy makers for sub-Saharan ACs lack the appropriate know-how about how to employ available resources and indigenous sub-Saharan African technology to accomplish desired objectives of economic development plans and policies. They therefore look elsewhere for the so-called appropriate technology with which to solve sub-Saharan Africa's problems of economic underdevelopment.

Two basic conclusions are derived from these axioms of knowledge for sub-Saharan African economic development:

1 Sub-Saharan African economic development planners and policy makers who pursue economic policies and programs indiscriminately may be likened to hunters who shoot randomly into a flock of birds. Just as these hunters may return home empty-handed (although such random shots may by chance hit some birds sometimes as well), such policy makers may also fail to achieve their goals in sub-Saharan Africa. It is therefore necessary to aim at an individual bird before pulling the trigger.
2 Policies aimed at sub-Saharan African economic development must scratch

where sub-Saharan Africa itches, heal where it hurts and nurse where it ails.

These axioms point out that the origin of economic underdevelopment in sub-Saharan ACs is a lack of knowledge and/or an inability (i.e., lack of the positive HF) of the sub-Saharan African people to apply existing knowledge. This situation has led to the use of inefficient management techniques and/or styles, ineffective policies and weak economic development programs in sub-Saharan Africa.

In my view, the ability to translate and adapt well-proven techniques and knowledge from one cultural environment to another has the power to enhance and maintain what has been shown to work in other cultures. Parallel and/or literal importation and use of such knowledge and/or techniques often leads to ineffective and/or negative results in the new environment. However, sub-Saharan ACs that gain the necessary wisdom to solve their own economic problems will have a greater chance of succeeding in their economic development efforts.

Sub-Saharan Africans do not necessarily have to look elsewhere for this wisdom. Sub-Saharan Africans before slavery and colonization had already developed indigenous technologies for solving problems of their time (i.e., of their own cultures). Although slavery and colonialism have destroyed the continuity and further development of such knowledge, a careful and informed intellectual journey into the past may lead to the re-discovery of technological knowledge that can be modified, improved and developed for dealing with problems (see details in Chapters 4 and 6).

The preceding analysis therefore casts doubt on the view that the problems of sub-Saharan African economic underdevelopment exist because sub-Saharan Africans lack political stability, financial resources, physical capital and many other requirements for economic development. Although these deficiencies are evident in sub-Saharan Africa, their existence is symptomatic of the sub-Saharan African people's inability to develop the relevant HF and to utilize relevant knowledge. That is, these lacks are consequences rather than causes. They must be addressed indirectly through programs aimed at grooming the sub-Saharan African people to acquire the HF necessary for leadership, productivity increases and progress (see an extended discussion of this issue in Chapter 4).

It follows, therefore, that the severity of economic underdevelopment in sub-Saharan Africa must be viewed as representative of an absence of relevant knowledge and the ability to apply it to real problems, techniques, managerial styles, policies and technology. It can be argued conclusively, therefore, that the degree of severity of economic underdevelopment in sub-Saharan Africa must be viewed as a measure of the absence of indigenous knowledge and wisdom required to identify and conquer the forces of economic underdevelopment. The lower the degree of severity of underdevelopment, the more successful a sub-Saharan AC will be in attempts to achieve economic progress. Wisdom, rather than knowledge is power. Sub-Saharan Africa's problem is a result of a severe deficiency of the necessary HF rather than an inavailability of resources.

A basic conclusion is that the ingenuity of a country's people in adapting and using acquired knowledge determines the degree of success at controlling and solving the problems of economic underdevelopment. In this case, the availability of required wisdom regarding proper development of the HF, management styles, organizational skills, economic policies and programs to enhance productivity will alleviate the severity of economic underdevelopment in sub-Saharan ACs. Appropriate technology transfer programs are necessary but not sufficient for overcoming the problems of economic underdevelopment in sub-Saharan ACs.

PROMOTING APPROPRIATE TECHNOLOGY TRANSFER

The late 1950s and early 1960s marked the beginning of an era in which many sub-Saharan ACs began to experience political freedom. The postcolonial era ushered in a period of growing hopes and aspirations regarding economic development and economic freedom. During this era, development planning became the major policy vehicle which all independent sub-Saharan ACs utilized in their attempts to achieve structural changes and economic development. One specific program used intensively was import-substitution industrialization.

After achieving self-government, sub-Saharan ACs realized that political freedom was meaningless without economic success. The import-substitution industrialization program was aimed at setting up manufacturing outlets to produce goods that were previously imported. At this point in time, sub-Saharan African economic development planning programs were more concerned with raw materials processing than technology transfer. Sub-Saharan African leaders, therefore, pursued policies that favored setting up product assembling plants. Such factories mushroomed in Ghana, Nigeria, Kenya, Tanzania, Uganda and many other countries.

During this epoch, sub-Saharan African leaders failed to perceive that the import-substitution industrialization program could not successfully achieve technology transfer (acquisition) from developed countries (DCs). Sub-Saharan African governments sponsored their nationals to Western European countries and the Americas to study and acquire Western know-how. Those countries that believed in socialism sought similar assistance from Eastern European nations. From the earliest years of sub-Saharan African independence to the present, many sub-Saharan Africans have acquired education and training abroad. Technical assistance has also poured in from abroad. International organizations, foreign nongovernmental organizations (NGOs), private companies, individuals and many others have contributed much to the program.

Regardless of the intensity of these efforts and the colossal amounts of financial resources poured into sub-Saharan African economic development programs, little has happened by way of technology transfer. Foreign technical assistance and returning nationals who have acquired Western philosophy-based education and training have been unable to crack open the appropriate technology box to draw out relevant wisdom for sub-Saharan African economic development. At present, technology transfer programs have failed in sub-

Saharan Africa.

My view of technology transfer agrees with that of Steele, Rosenberg and Frischtak. Steele (1979, p. 112) noted that "technology is taken to mean the body of knowledge, skills, and lore that provides the capability to produce goods and services, to design and develop new ones when appropriate, to apply them to the specialized needs of the customer, and to install and service them." Rosenberg and Frischtak (1985) also observed that "technology might be more usefully conceptualized as a quantum knowledge retained by individual teams of specialized personnels. This knowledge, resulting from their accumulated experience in design, production, and investment activities, is mostly tacit, that is, not made explicit in any collection of blueprints and manuals. It is acquired in problem-solving and trouble-shooting activities within the firm, remaining there in a substantially uncodified state."

Appropriate technology for sub-Saharan African development must therefore be viewed as the acquisition of information and/or knowledge required for designing and producing the essential goods and services. Sub-Saharan African technology transfer programs must therefore be aimed at obtaining the blueprints or know-how of required production processes and/or procedures--both from home and abroad.

Areas of concern for sub-Saharan African technology transfer programs must include the following:

1 Species preservation (plants, animals, landscapes, etc.)
2 Environmental concerns
3 Disease (epidemics) control through scientific knowlege
4 Production process improvement and technological development
5 Management and organizational procedures
6 Efficient and democratic running of countries
7 Human factor engineering for economic development
8 Curriculum development
9 Infrastructure development and maintenance management

CREATING THE REQUIRED INFRASTRUCTURE FOR TECHNOLOGY TRANSFER

Baranson and Roark (1985) classify technology transfer into three broad groupings: technology transfers that impart (1) operational, (2) duplicative and (3) innovative capabilities. Although all three are useful, category (3) is what sub-Saharan Africa actually needs--the ability to invent and innovate techniques and/or procedures for dealing with sub-Saharan African underdevelopment problems.

To achieve success in technology transfer programs, sub-Saharan ACs must not only put in place the required infrastructure but must also have people who possess the appropriate HF to organize, manage, maintain and control the technology transfer program. The sub-Saharan African people must be able to identify technologies that can deal effectively with sub-Saharan Africa's economic problems.

The model proposed in this chapter for developing sub-Saharan African technology transfer programs assumes the following:

1 Sub-Saharan ACs have a well-disciplined labor force that possesses the positive HF necessary for the acquisition and utilization of foreign technology. Failure to make this caliber of people available for the technology transfer program will also doom it.
2 Sub-Saharan ACs finalize agreements about the required technology and the rights to use and transfer them. ACs have the permission to modify and adapt purchased technology (i.e., very few barriers exist to hinder smooth technology transfer in this sense).
3 Sub-Saharan ACs have well-developed and -equipped local institutions and social infrastructure both for receiving technology from elsewhere and for developing and improving domestic technology.
4 There is understanding of international technology transfer laws, codes of ethics and conduct in relation to technology transfer.
5 Sufficient financial resources exist for the acquisition, assimilation, adoption and improvement of appropriate technology.
6 Developers and owners of technology are willing to facilitate the transfer of their technology to sub-Saharan ACs.

A PROCEDURE FOR TECHNOLOGY TRANSFER TO SUB-SAHARAN AFRICA

Successful strategic and tactical planning demands that planners have a firm grasp of the objectives to be pursued. When planners do not grasp why they plan, success will elude them as specifics are either ignored or glossed over. In my view, technology transfer programs for sub-Saharan ACs must involve continuous planning and pursuit of specific technologies that have the potential to deal with sub-Saharan Africa's problems of economic underdevelopment. The aim is to avoid sporadic, situational and/or piecemeal programs that lack vision, consistency, potency and relevance. The whole sub-Saharan African technology program must be a premeditated venture, the long-term goals of which must be to equip sub-Saharan Africans with the technological know-how to deal with problems of economic underdevelopment. As noted elsewhere, the search for this know-how must not only be conducted in foreign lands. The relevant know-how can also be developed at home without having to look for it elsewhere.

My suggested procedure for achieving this goal in sub-Saharan Africa is illustrated in the flow chart presented in Figure 9.2. At stage I, each sub-Saharan AC must identify and pool the available technology that can be used to satisfy human needs. The choice of appropriate technology may be hindered if sub-Saharan Africans are not aware of the different types of existing technology. Stage I is therefore a significant link in the technology transfer program chain.

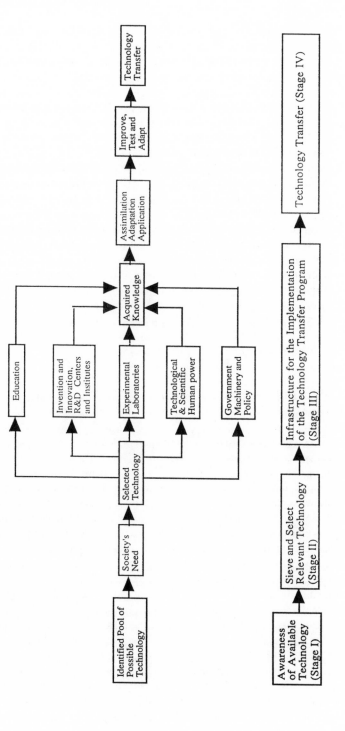

FIGURE 9.2
A PROCEDURE FOR TECHNOLOGY TRANSFER TO AFRICA FOR DEVELOPMENT

Having sampled existing technology at stage I, the identified needs of society must be used as the basis for the selection of appropriate technology.

At stage II, sub-Saharan Africans must critically reevaluate their immediate needs, focusing attention on the primary ones. This list can be extended to include Herzberg's classification of higher needs. At this stage, crucial steps must be taken to select relevant foreign technologies or to develop indigenous ones. The needs of the typical sub-Saharan AC must lead the way--shedding light on the more appropriate technologies.

The selected technologies must be passed through the available social infrastructure and/or institutional structures to help sub-Saharan Africans acquire the relevant knowledge or develop skills necessary to tap the wisdom embedded in them. Thus, stage II is the main hub of the technology transfer program. The success or failure of the sub-Saharan African technology transfer program will be determined at this stage. It is, therefore, important that each sub-Saharan AC see to it that the required infrastructure is made available for the program. Some of the major requirements include educational facilities and relevant programs, invention and innovation centers, experimental laboratories, initial technological and scientific humanpower (this involves effective leadership and the required HF), research and development (R&D) programs and efficient government machinery and pertinent policy. Each of these is discussed briefly next.

Education and Training

The education and training infrastructure must provide relevant curricula for the technology transfer program. The existing sub-Saharan African education structure, which encourages mere rote learning, must be revamped and reconstructed to encourage critical thinking and the acquisition of analytical, inventive and innovative skills. It must educate and train students to explore the principles and mechanics of the technology being borrowed. The education system and training programs must encourage understanding and provide the freedom to explore relevant ideas which can be used to modify the available technology to meet sub-Saharan Africa's needs. The curricula must be designed to view students as individuals who have a quest for practical knowledge and productive skills, in contrast to the view perpetuated by the existing curricula--that sub-Saharan African students have minds that are *tabula rasa* and need to be filled. This kind of education has not been productive in sub-Saharan Africa. All levels of education (i.e., primary, secondary and university) must be aimed at the acquisition of relevant knowledge and skills. Many sub-Saharan ACs have neglected the development of universal primary education. This situation must be reversed. Many more resources must be channeled into primary education to increase the literacy rate. The value of education to the develpment process is discussed in Hanson and Brembeck (1966).

Invention and Innovation Centers

These centers can either be attached to educational institutions or be established as independent institutions. They must have the required facilities, tools, machines and skilled technological and scientific humanpower to provide the necessary assistance to students at different levels in their academic career. These must be places where students can freely share and discuss novel ideas that hold prospects for technology transfer to sub-Saharan ACs. The centers must also encourage the modification and/or development of new technologies for sub-Saharan Africa through relevant application of acquired knowledge.

Experimental Laboratories

Laboratories cannot be omitted. Not only must they exist as physical structures, but they must also be equipped to promote extensive experimentation with acquired knowledge. If possible, depending on the nature and the stipulations of the contracts signed for technology transfer, the experimental laboratories must encourage the dismantling and reassembling of imported machinery for purposes of detailed study and scrutiny (see assumptions 2, 4 and 6 discussed in the previous section). These laboratories must also be equipped with modern equipment to facilitate scientific exploration of ideas and observed natural phenomena. They may stand on their own or be attached to educational and training institutions and invention and innovation centers.

Technological and Scientific Humanpower

People with knowledge, skills and the ability to make things happen are needed for technology transfer to sub-Saharan Africa. Until now, sub-Saharan African people have not been well-prepared to deal with problems of economic underdevelopment. The required HF must be developed in sub-Saharan Africans to help them to organize, implement and manage the sub-Saharan African technology transfer program. Visionary leadership with technological acumen to lead and direct the program must be readily available for successful technology transfer programs. At the inception of the program, sub-Saharan ACs may draw on technological and scientific humanpower from abroad. This, however, must be done on a temporary basis. The goal is to have these foreign experts and/or scholars train the sub-Saharan Africans to take eventual control of this area.

As is obvious today, the role of the necessary HF in economic development and technology transfer programs is too important to be continually neglected in Africa (see Chapter 5). Richta et al. (1969, p. 202) observed that

since the advances of science and technology are to a large extent dependent on the level of human powers of creation, in this context expenditures on welfare, education, work adjustments, services and transport, increasing free time, improving working and living conditions, and lessening worries about winning a livelihood can give better returns for society than expansion of the actual production process alone; conversely, neglect of these aspects is increasingly felt to be irrational economic wastefulness.

Continuing success at technology transfer programs requires the HF. Sub-Saharan ACs need to pay attention to this issue in their development policies and programs.

R&D Centers and/or Institutes

Very little technology transfer can take place when there is a lack of research and development (R&D). In view of this, it is necessary to institute research centers and/or institutes to support the whole technology transfer enterprise. These centers and/or institutes will also serve as invention and innovation think-tanks for indigenous technology development.

Incentives and Indigenous Technology Centers

Sub-Saharan Africans possess a massive technological base that has been stagnant since colonization. The decay in the development of indigenous technology can be attributed to slavery and colonialism (refer to Chapter 4 for an extended discussion of this issue). These two events have terminated the developmental process of sub-Saharan African technology and have clearly destroyed the natural sequential evolution of existing technology in sub-Saharan Africa. However, after independence, many sub-Saharan ACs did not have the desire, devotion, determination and willingness to take a second look at traditional technology to determine if it could be salvaged. In addition, existing foreign technology seemed at that time to be more appealing to the sub-Saharan African leadership. Over three decades since independence, many ACs have failed to take the necessary steps to encourage indigenous engineers, technologists and those who have been formally schooled to help in the salvaging process.

I believe that one route to attaining economic development in sub-Saharan ACs is to see how traditional technology can be improved and used to enhance the production process. To achieve this goal, sub-Saharan African governments must pursue premeditated policies whose objective must be to help individuals who have the knowledge improve on it. For example, blacksmiths, herbalists, medicine men and women and other indigenous engineers who possess the know-how must be offered incentives to think about ways whereby they can improve the skills they have and enhance their efficiency. It may be useful to create funds for local craftspeople and/or engineers that will help them experiment on an ongoing basis to evolve and improve their know-how.

In addition, annual competition programs involving talent demonstration with attractive prizes will go a long way toward challenging these people to use their creative abilities. Annual fairs for inventors and innovators must be organized and supported by governments and local businesses. Prospective inventors and innovators should not only be encouraged to develop new machinery and tools but must also be provided with funds and the necessary materials to do so. This program also requires the promotion of citizens' interests in science and technology. Those who participate in these annual events must be encouraged to gear their inventions and innovations to the environment, health, manufacturing, recreation, production, computers, automobiles, robotics, transportation, preservation, furniture, medicine and so on. National seminars and conferences must also be organized so that those individuals who have the technological acumen can meet each other to discuss and exchange ideas about how to develop and improve on the acquired technological know-how.

These indigenous technologists and/or engineers must be used to give talks, lectures and demonstration classes in schools that will help open the minds of the youth about existing traditional technology--how it functions and how it can be enhanced for future use. Traditional technological know-how such as kente weaving, automobile repairs, wooden/clay stove manufacture, ceramics, pottery, house building, cotton spinning, boat building, irrigation, carpentry, cooking and much more can be supported and improved by both government and private business grants.

In the same way, elementary school science teaching must be based on an inquisitive curriculum. That is, pupils must be provided with science teachers who have the ingenuity to lead and guide their students to explore how things work and how this knowledge can be harnessed for household chores and other human activities. The search for and the discovery of how nature works must be an integral part of this curriculum. These pupils must also be encouraged to use their acquired knowledge and skills to practice inventions and/or innovations. This kind of curriculum must form the basis for both the secondary school and university science curricula. Science laboratory assignments given out to students must not be aimed at mere reproduction and/or replication of scientific experiments designed in Europe and North America. Sub-Saharan African science teachers must develop their own experiments--carefully constructed and tailored to lead students gently toward developing inventive and/or innovative abilities. The whole science education and training program must have integrated into it meaningful procedures for developing the positive HF in every student.

While these activities occur, these local engineers can be furnished with relevant information and, where possible, samples of foreign technologies that perform similar functions. The goal must be to encourage critical thinking and study, evaluation and careful analysis of how to adapt these technologies to the traditional setting.

The success of these programs requires a carefully articulated vision about what sub-Saharan Africans desire, how they want to achieve it and by what time. The development of appropriate technology requires a master plan that specifies what the society's needs are and furnishes those who are involved with the relevant and sufficient resources and/or inputs.

OPPORTUNITIES FOR ONGOING CROSS-FERTILIZATION

Discoveries must be disseminated throughout the country and, if possible, the whole sub-Saharan African region. This can be done through African-based journals, scientific communications, letters, conferences, books of proceedings, lectures and such. These will create a forum for the exchange and cross-fertilization of ideas.

Government Machinery and Policy

Sub-Saharan Africans need government leaders who possess the ability and resources to provide the necessary infrastructure for the technology transfer program. Government bureaucracy must not only be streamlined but also designed to facilitate the program (see Figure 9.2). Policies must be carefully tailored to encourage everyone to participate in the economic development program. Policies must aim to provide the financial resources, equipment and technical expertise required by both the public and private sectors as well as educational institutions. Instead of being paternalistic, governments must give leadership to all other institutions and steer the program in the required direction.

The goal of stage III (see Figure 9.2) is to foster the acquisition of the technological knowledge that sub-Saharan Africans need. Activities in stage III must provide sub-Saharan Africans with the practice and confidence to try newly acquired ideas. At this stage, the process of assimilation, adaptation and application of knowledge gained must occur. This stage blends smoothly into stage IV by encouraging the improvement, testing and adoption of acquired appropriate technology. Sub-Saharan ACs will acquire relevant technology and employ the knowledge gained at stage III to develop technologies capable of dealing with their problems of economic underdevelopment.

It is only when sub-Saharan Africans are able to apply the acquired technological knowledge to solve their present problems that technology transfer has occurred in sub-Saharan Africa. Otherwise, we must reenact the process from stage III (see Figure 9.2), and carry it through to the end. This unrelenting endeavor will lead to mission accomplishment.

Some relevant nagging questions are as follows: What role can transnational companies (TNCs) play in this process? Do they stand to benefit from the whole process? If so, then how? If true technology transfer is to occur, those who own and manage the technology must be willing to cooperate and share it with sub-Saharan Africans. In the real world, this willingness and cooperation will be forthcoming when the owners perceive that the imminent gains will far outweigh the costs. In Adjibolosoo (1992, pp. 346-356), I discussed some of the major net benefits to be derived by TNCs and their home countries when they participate fully in technology transfer to sub-Saharan ACs.

POLICY RECOMMENDATIONS

Although sub-Saharan African economies have been bombarded with all kinds of problems of economic underdevelopment, sub-Saharan Africans need to sift through the rubble to achieve success in the economic development effort. Although this is not as easy as it sounds, it is my conviction that wisdom is wisdom, no matter where it is being applied, provided it is used properly (Adjibolosoo and Mestre, 1992). To attain economic progress, sub-Saharan ACs must achieve success in developing technology based on relevant knowledge. Only acquired wisdom has the power to overcome ignorance and economic underdevelopment in sub-Saharan ACs.

Absence of wisdom will create misunderstanding about the process of economic development and how it occurs. Although sub-Saharan ACs do not currently have readily available answers to the problems and difficulties of economic underdevelopment, if they learn and achieve the ability to acquire and utilize existing knowledge they will develop new techniques with which to overcome recalcitrant problems of economic underdevelopment.

Using economic policies and planning programs that ignore relevant conditions in sub-Saharan Africa to deal with economic underdevelopment may not produce expected results. The best way to deal with economic underdevelopment is to understand thoroughly the reasons for it in sub-Saharan African terms and try to do something about it. In the absence of this, all other mechanisms used will be artificial and may not produce desired results. By using quick-fix methods (i.e., structural adjustment programs, stabilization policies, *coups d'etat*, revolutions, etc.) and relying on intermittent international aid packages, sub-Saharan ACs may not successfully deal with, control and overcome the problems of economic underdevelopment. Sub-Saharan African leaders and their domestic and foreign economic policy consultants must go beyond this level of thinking if they really want to succeed in their nation-building efforts.

Economic policy makers and economic development planners in sub-Saharan ACs require appropriate wisdom, management and organizational skills, policies and programs to deal with economic underdevelopment. Even though artificial techniques may produce initial successes and relief from frustration and confusion, these may not be permanent outcomes. Once the impacts of these artificial solutions to hindrances of economic underdevelopment dissipate, old problems will reappear. Only earnest desire to gain and the power to use sound knowledge will deal with economic underdevelopment on a permanent basis in sub-Saharan ACs. This is what will create economic, social and political prosperity for sub-Saharan ACs. Marshall (1930, pp. 779-780) observed that

> for mental faculties, like manual dexterity, die with those who possess
> them: but the improvement which each generation contributes to the
> machinery of manufacture or to the organon of science is handed down to
> the next. There may be no abler sculptors now than those who worked on
> the Parthenon, no thinker with more mother-wit than Aristotle. But the
> appliances of thought develop cumulatively as do those of material
> production. Ideas, whether those of art and science, or those embodied in
> practical appliances, are the most "real" of the gifts that each generation
> receives from its predecessors. The world's material wealth would quickly
> be replaced if it were destroyed, but the ideas by which it was made were
> retained. If however the ideas were lost, but not the material wealth, then
> that would dwindle and the world would go back to poverty. And most of
> our knowledge of mere facts could quickly be recovered if it were lost, but
> the constructive ideas of thought remained; while if the ideas perished, the
> world would enter again on the Dark Ages.

Marshall's observation illustrates the sub-Saharan African condition today. Due
to slavery and colonization, sub-Saharan Africans have not only lost most of
their ancestral wisdom but have also been unable to piece together all the broken
fragments of knowledge passed on from one generation to another through oral
tradition. If sub-Saharan Africans could rediscover how to weave together their
ancient ideas and those borrowed from abroad, they might use them to re-create
wealth and enhance the human condition in sub-Saharan ACs. This, however,
will not happen without having developed the HF in the people.

CONCLUSIONS

This chapter has shown that what has usually been labeled as economic
underdevelopment is actually a lack of relevant wisdom that has bred short-
sighted and sporadic structural adjustment programs and stabilization policies,
poor management practices by economic policy makers and economic
development planners and improperly developed HF in sub-Saharan Africa. It
is therefore clear that any AC which desires to develop must ensure development
and/or transfer of appropriate technology through well-trained and educated
people who possess the ability to use available knowledge by applying it
meaningfully in the sub-Saharan African context. When this deficiency is
overcome, instances of economic underdevelopment in sub-Saharan Africa will
diminish drastically. This will mean that sub-Saharan ACs which are successful
in preparing their people to acquire the necessary HF and an astute labor force
that is able to apply knowledge to achieve technological development and/or
transfer will increase their chances of success in development programs.

Although independence was achieved over three decades ago, many sub-
Saharan African economies are still struggling to develop economically. One

basic reason for the inability to develop is the fact that sub-saharan Africans lack the appropriate HF and the necessary institutional structures for successful technology transfer. To overcome the main problems of economic underdevelopment and the inability to transfer technology, sub-Saharan ACs must develop a solid social infrastructure and other institutional structures to facilitate the transfer of appropriate technology. I hope that this can be achieved through the procedure developed and presented in this chapter. If sub-Saharan Africans fail to erect the required infrastructure for technology transfer, economic development programs are not likely to succeed. Putting the cart before the horse may complicate technology transfer problems. Sub-Saharan Africans must develop the necessary infrastructure and institutional structures before instituting and operating technology transfer programs.

NOTES

1. The original version of this chapter was presented at the ninth Annual Conference of the Canadian Association for the Study of International Development at Carleton University, Ottawa, Ontario in June 1993. I am grateful to the participants in the session in which this chapter was presented. The section on technology transfer was also prepared for the Fourth International Conference on Management of Technology, Miami, Florida in February/March, 1994. For the contents of the complete paper for the Miami conference, see Adjibolosoo, S. B-S. K. 1994e. "Promoting Technology Transfer for African Development." In T. M. Khalil and B. A. Bayrakter, eds., *Management of Technology IV: The Creation of Wealth.* Vol. 2: 1556-1564. The permission from the Industrial Engineering and Management Press, Norcross, Georgia, to reprint relevant sections of that paper in this chapter is highly acknowledged.

2. The HF is viewed as the unique human qualities and/or characteristics that create a disciplined and loyal national labor force. A more detailed definition of the HF can be found in Chapter 3.

3. The analysis, however, should be viewed as a multicausal one rather than a mono-causal one. Although it recognizes that there are many intervening variables that affect the process of economic development, the view in this chapter is that knowledge about all these variables must be translated into wisdom, which can be used to pursue economic development in sub-Saharan ACs.

4. I am deeply indebted to professor Deane Downey, Trinity Western University, for this example. See also Adu-Febiri, 1995, for a detailed discussion of this issue.

10

A Program of Action for Economic Development in Sub-Saharan African Countries

INTRODUCTION

It is clear from the discussion in Chapter 2 that there are hundreds of policy prescriptions for dealing with the sub-Saharan African economic development predicament. These policy suggestions have had permanent negative impacts on the economies of sub-Saharan ACs. Asante (1991, p. 40) noted that current economic development strategies and policies in Africa have had three distinct effects on African economic development: There has been (1) little evaluation of available resources and their distribution on the continent, (2) neglect of the role and importance of domestic African markets, and (3) hindered economic cooperation among African nations.

These policies have encouraged and perpetuated a strong dependency of sub-Saharan African economies on what happens in advanced economies. They have also encouraged an emphasis on the role of international trade in sub-Saharan African economic development. Sub-Saharan ACs have therefore been rendered vulnerable to all fluctuations occurring in advanced countries' economies. The sub-Saharan African economic development program is therefore at the mercy of these fluctuations.

In recent years, many African economists have begun to question and critically reevaluate the validity and effectiveness of orthodox economic development policies and plans that have been designed for sub-Saharan ACs since independence. In view of these failures, Adedeji (1989, pp. 91-92) suggested that ACs need not continue to copy economic policies and strategies of the developed countries--each African country must evolve its own unique policies to solve existing problems.

When Adedeji assumed the leadership of the United Nations Economic Commission for Africa (ECA) in 1975, he had his own agenda for an African economic development program. Adedeji's development strategies for Africa's progress have as their pillars (1) national and collective self-reliance and self-sustaining development, (2) regional cooperation and integration, and (3) human-centered development. What most sub-Saharan ACs are realizing today is that the traditional economic development theory-based policies have been inadequate in dealing with their problems of economic underdevelopment. Sub-Saharan ACs therefore need to put in place a new program of action that can deal effectively with these problems. In what follows, I present some fundamental principles necessary for a new program of action as well as some specific recommendations for positive action.

UNDERLYING PRINCIPLES OF THE NEW PROGRAM OF ACTION

Policies directed at dealing with economic underdevelopment must be chosen carefully and implemented with caution and must be ready to change in the face of new and more relevant information. The goal must not only be to put the economic development process into motion temporarily but to sustain its continuing progress. It is appropriate to point out that some of these policies may create short-term hardships. In this case, the temptation for policy makers will be to discontinue them. Instead of doing so, policy makers must review and project the long-term costs and benefits. Policies deemed to generate more wealth and benefits must be maintained, and they must have a human face. Such policies must be based on foundational principles that may not be easily evaded or brushed aside. Some of these principles include the following:

1 Sub-Saharan AC leaders must willingly cooperate to integrate and exploit comparative advantages existing in sub-Saharan African economies. Underlying this principle is the recognition by sub-Saharan Africans that economic development is a process that occurs over a period of time.
2 Sub-Saharan Africans must always look within themselves for answers, harnessing domestic resources (saving, labor, technology, etc.) and putting them to use to solve problems of economic underdevelopment. Although the role of external assistance and environment is crucial, it should neither be made to play a major role nor be looked up to.
3 Made-in-Africa policies and strategies for agriculture and industry must be formulated. It is imperative either to discontinue or minimize cash cropping[1] and turn relevant land to food cropping and raw materials production for domestic use.
4 Sub-Saharan Africa must fashion carefully articulated, unified and effectively coordinated intracontinental science, technology and industrial policies.
5 National programs must be pursued and practiced democratically. Sub-Saharan ACs must institute and uphold freedom of speech, press freedom and the chance for everyone capable to contribute to the dialoguing process aimed at economic development.
6 Regional educational institutions must be created for training sub-Saharan Africans to acquire the required HF for the economic development

program. The African economic development program will fail if it does not have a disciplined labor force (i.e., the relevant HF) to manage the whole program (see Chapter 5).

SOME RELEVANT RECOMMENDATIONS

Sub-Saharan African governments must do the following:

1 Establish an all-encompassing intra-African economic development financing institution, better organized and equipped than the African Development Bank (ADB).
2 Perceive and stick to the traditional roles of the state as suggested by Adam Smith in his *Wealth of Nations*. Each country's government must be committed to people-centered economic development and the building and sustaining of the social infrastructure.
3 Avoid the policy attitude of "if it ain't broke don't fix it" and relinquish quick-fix procedures and/or programs (see Chapter 9 for further discussion). For example, they must discontinue structural adjustment policies and stabilization programs and move away from IMF and World Bank-initiated and -directed economic development plans and policies. The IMF and World Bank must be invited in on terms determined by sub-Saharan African governments. Otherwise, there is a need for great caution.
4 Develop institutions and institutional structures to initiate and maintain the effectiveness of political, economic, social and press freedom.
5 Develop programs to groom selfless and visionary African leadership that will create and manage the sub-Saharan African economic development program. These leaders must acquire abilities to undertake teamwork and uphold the team spirit necessary for progress. The development of the HF must be the top priority in this process
6 Develop other sources of foreign exchange acquisition. Foreign exchange can be obtained from many other sources, such as increased tourist activities, dual citizenship obligations, remittances of emigrants, official operation of *Bureaux de Change* and so on. These will minimize the initial temporary pain of discontinuing cash crop production in sub-Saharan ACs.

DEALING WITH MISSING LINKS: SOME RELEVANT PROPOSITIONS

Problem-solving procedures require that one knows what the real problem is. People cannot successfully deal with difficulties if they cannot identify what they are. Those who try to solve problems without knowing what they are will end up creating more problems. In some cases, more severe problems arise. This has been the plight of sub-Saharan ACs.

The Ewes' view[2] about the results of failing to address the right problems by refusing to acknowledge their existence, *a denial syndrome,* is clearly illustrated in the following fable:

> A young man once went through a forest across rugged terrain with great difficulty. It was not until he came back home that he noticed he had sustained severe injuries on the right leg. When the relatives heard about his malaise, they decided to seek someone who was knowledgeable in medicine to nurse the wound with appropriate herbs. Since the victim knew how painful these kinds of treatments were, he requested that the treatment sessions be held in the evenings. Every time the medicine person came, the young man would present the left foot for nursing. As treatment continued for many evenings, he would twist and writhe with moaning and groaning, thus faking pains. This behavior continued until the time his trick was discovered, the wound had become worse and life threatening. At this point in time, nothing else could be done to save his life except amputation. By not allowing the medicine person to nurse and dress the wound on the right leg, the young man lost this leg. Although the medicine person applied the right treatment using the necessary herbs, it was misapplied treatment.[3]

Many sub-Saharan ACs seem to have fallen into the *denial syndrome* illustrated by this Ewe fable. Attempts to solve problems of economic underdevelopment must first identify precisely the true factors that militate against industrial progress. To overcome the problems of economic underdevelopment, sub-Saharan ACs need to know and effectively deal with the real hindrances to progress. Otherwise, they will continue to be like a hunter who shoots randomly into a flock of birds, hoping to kill some. The fact is, such hunters usually end up with no game at all. Any continuing long-term refusal to acknowledge the actual pertinent problems will plunge sub-Saharan ACs into economic disaster. Table 10.1 lists some major missing variables and links that sub-Saharan ACs must put in place if they expect to achieve economic success. If these key variables are not properly dealt with in economic development planning and policy making, no amount of foreign assistance, policy and resource availability can help reverse the direction of sub-Saharan Africa's economic decline and underdevelopment.

Although orthodox economic development theory is intuitively sensible as postulated, its assumed premises are usually not relevant to Africa; therefore, very little will be achieved regardless of the magnitude of external assistance and advice. Existing policies and programs need to be reviewed and, if possible, current economic development approaches that are based on orthodox economic theories whose premises and foundational presuppositions have little relevance to the existing sub-Saharan African condition must be altered. In what follows, I suggest five propositions in addition to several policy recommendations regarding how sub-Saharan ACs can break the vicious cycle of economic underdevelopment.

TABLE 10.1
SOME KEY PRIMARY AND SECONDARY TARGET FACTORS

KEY PRIMARY TARGET FACTORS

I. Relevant Education and Training Must:
1 Foster critical thinking
2 Produce problem solvers
3 Be relevant to current problems and issues
4 Develop creativity (i.e., inventiveness and innovativeness)
5 Be liberally broad-based (i.e., interdisciplinary)
II. Developed HF (its characteristics):
1 Integrity
2 Responsibility [also resourcefulness and resilience]
3 Accountability
4 Dedication [and commitment]
5 Vision and a sense of mission
6 Entrepreneurial spirit
III. Work Ethic and Social Ethos:
1 Principled living
2 Commitment to work life [and general human welfare]
IV. Institutions (social, economic and political):
1 Proper organization
2 Efficient management
3 Constantly monitoring performance
4 Frequently evaluating performance
V. Preventive Maintenance Management:
1 Build productive capacity
2 Foster program continuities
3 Maintain existing infrastructure

ADJOINING SECONDARY TARGET FACTORS

1 Political Stability
2 Free competitive markets (i.e., less government intervention)
3 Efficient capital and financial markets
4 Capital accumulation
5 Natural and human resources
6 The rule of law and press freedom

Source: Ezeala-Harrison, F. and Adjibolosoo, S. B-S. K. 1994. *Perspectives on Economic Development in Africa*. New York: Praeger.

Proposition 1

If the premises of conventional economic development theories are modified to incorporate and/or reflect the social, economic and political conditions that actually exist in sub-Saharan ACs, reformulated policies will be effective. To achieve successful reformulation, attention must be focused on the identification and inclusion of variable(s) that orthodox and heterodox economic development theorists and sub-Saharan African leaders frequently overlook. Since the sub-Saharan African economic development effort has not fully benefited from previous economic development programs based on these theories, one is led to the view that alternative theorizing rather than continuing and maintaining existing orthodox policy direction is in order. Usually, the inability to isolate the real economic problem variables and deal with them effectively results from a lack of shared vision and long-term perspectives. This observation is the basis for proposition 2.

Proposition 2

The absence of a shared vision, a long-term perspective, coupled with the pursuit of sporadic disaster-driven policies and programs, whose underlying principles are found in orthodox and heterodox economic development thinking, have forced sub-Saharan African economies into a terribly inescapable trap of economic underdevelopment. In many sub-Saharan ACs, policies and programs are usually crisis driven. It is normally during problem situations (i.e., earthquakes, droughts, famine, epidemics and so on) that other foreign governments and international organizations put up temporarily ad hoc relief programs to mitigate the impacts of the problems of economic underdevelopment. Although these programs achieve temporary relief, they rarely ever produce sustained economic development. To achieve economic progress, sub-Saharan African leaders must act on accurate foresight and deliberately target specific projects and then develop and sustain them. If this is not done, a state of perpetual poverty will be maintained. The sub-Saharan African economic development process must therefore be based on a well-developed and feasible plan. This view leads to the third proposition.

Proposition 3

It is crucial to develop national mission statements that articulate a vision for each sub-Saharan African country. This vision must possess long-term perspectives of hopes and aspirations. Based on this, economic development plans, policies and programs must not only focus on present needs and problems but must also perceive their implications for the future and develop the required HF to co-ordinate all policies and projects in order to reach the society's vision, and although that direction may be modified, it must not lead to tampering with the national vision.

Research has shown that the successes of many Asian Pacific Rim countries are not only due to the availability of resources but are also because they deliberately pursued programs to develop in their available labor force the relevant HF. They correctly viewed the development of the HF to be crucial and of high priority in their economic development process. Oman and Wignaraja (1991, p. 81), for example, noted that

> the rapid industrial take-off and export success of the East Asian NIEs [newly industrializing economies] was fuelled by heavy investments in human skills and technological capital aimed at creating (1) a literate workforce responsive to intensive on-and-off-the-job training, (2) a pool of highly skilled middle-level technical manpower able to absorb and build on imported technologies, and (3) adequately staffed R&D [research and development] departments in firm and government-funded institutes closely related to industry.

Sub-Saharan African economic development plans, policies and projects must focus on programs that foster the development of the positive HF. To achieve this goal, sub-Saharan ACs must identify the various primary and secondary factors that make economic development happen. Although the primary factors are requirements that cannot be compromised in the process of economic progress and must therefore be developed at all costs, the secondary factors are necessary but not sufficient in themselves (Adjibolosoo, 1994c, p. 215). This view forms the basis for proposition 4.

Proposition 4

In the development process, the necessary requirements are the HF, institutions, raw materials and infrastructure. However, no nation can attain economic development without having properly developed and prepared its people, through education, training and mentoring, to acquire the HF necessary for organizing, directing and managing its resources, and programs. To develop economically, every sub-Saharan African state must, therefore, make HF development a prime target. Programs aimed at HF development must be the foundation stone for the economic development process. HF development programs must concentrate on relevant education and training programs to produce pathfinders--people with vision, analytical minds, communication abilities, management acumen, leadership skills, problem-solving abilities, creativity and the like. They must be honest and reliable, willing to take risks and able to make well-informed and carefully balanced decisions. The groomed labor force and leadership that possess the necessary HF will direct and lead the people to uphold the law and human rights, establish press freedom and so on.

I view the HF and its effectiveness in developing and implementing excellent preventive maintenance management programs; relevant education, training and mentoring procedures; efficient social, economic and political institutions; universal work ethic and social ethos and such as the major primary target factors. Alternatively, I classify political stability, competitive markets, efficient capital and financial markets, continuing respect for the rule of law and press freedom and so on as the secondary target factors (see Table 10.1). Since the availability of the secondary target factors is dependent on the existence of the primary target factors, when the primary target factors are nonexistent, the secondary target factors will not be forthcoming. The availability of the primary target factors is, therefore, a necessary and sufficient condition for economic progress (Adjibolosoo, 1994c, pp. 213-215). Sub-Saharan ACs and any other nations that lack the primary target factors will not attain continuing economic development.

The development of these factors requires many years of programs, whose initial goal must be the production of the primary factors. This may be a slow process, but when sub-Saharan ACs finally acquire the primary factors, they will produce the kind of people and institutions required to attain economic progress. Trebilcock (1990, p. 3) observed that

> modern research insists that individual growth was gradualistic, evolutionary, achieved not in the violent spontaneous outbursts of revolution, but in the plodding long run. Illumination for the industrial pathway was provided not by the thunderbolt from a clear blue sky but by decades of candle-ends. . . . Stock must be taken not only of the physical resources, or the lack of them, but also of social endowment which will supply, or fail to supply, an entrepreneurial shockforce which may be able to innovate a way past the obstacles imposed by the allocation of resources.

Education and training, in their current forms in many sub-Saharan ACs, will not produce the caliber of people required for the economic development process. Existing education systems and training programs need restructuring to turn out a well-rounded people who possess the necessary HF. Relevant knowledge acquisition is necessary for achieving this goal (see Chapter 9 and Hayek, 1945, pp. 519-530).

One of the greatest threats to the economic development process is program/policy discontinuity. Sub-Saharan ACs must guard against this malaise, which has plagued them for many decades. Every program and structure requires continuous and frequent revisions and maintenance to endure (see Chapter 8 for details). To be continually productive, the development process must be sustained. This view is the basis for proposition 5.

Proposition 5

Economic development is a cumulative process. That is, nations that have attained industrialization have learned to sustain and prolong the lives of their infrastructure and other capital stock through continuous rehabilitation and/or programs. ACs must create preventive maintenance management programs to rehabilitate and sustain their infrastructure. Roads, highways, railway lines, schools, hospitals, telecommunications systems and so on must not be left to degenerate beyond repairs. Otherwise, Africans will continue to spin the wheels of economic development fruitlessly (i.e., try to lift themselves up by their bootstraps).

In this way, many sub-Saharan ACs will maintain, improve and build on what has already been attained. Huge sums of financial resources must be spent on fixing and sustaining existing social infrastructure and capital stock. Structures such as bridges, highways, schools, hospitals, dams, irrigation canals, fishing grounds, forests and so on must not be neglected to dilapidate and/or collapse, as is the case in sub-Saharan Africa today. By religiously adhering to a program of this nature, sub-Saharan Africans will not only sustain achievements but will also have existing solid superstructures on which to continue to build. Economic development planning and economic policies based on these five propositions will have positive impacts on economic progress in sub-Saharan ACs.

IMPLEMENTING THE HF MODEL OF ECONOMIC DEVELOPMENT

Acknowledgment of the aforementioned issues must lead sub-Saharan ACs to institute appropriate procedures for facilitating the effective operation of the economic development program. This view suggests that the pursuit of economic progress in sub-Saharan Africa must be based on a model of HF development. A schematic presentation of this model is shown in Figure 10.1. By effectively implementing this model, sub-Saharan ACs will experience sustained economic growth and development. A successful application of the model can be achieved in the following manner:

1 First, know that the roles of the rulers and the ruled are crucial to the economic development process. Second, identify and agree on goals, plans and projects. This involves the isolation and assessment of existing resources--social, economic and political. Third, create education and training programs to achieve the required HF. Outline the basic superstructure and plan how to build it. Do the necessary groundwork-- basic infrastructure and relevant institutions. These become the foundation pillars for the envisioned economic development program.
2 Identify and deal with bottlenecks. This involves (1) continuing strategic and tactical planning and (2) building the required superstructure and the necessary basic infrastructure. At this stage, social, economic and political institutions must be revamped for effectiveness. Plan how to accomplish the program. Specify clearly the strategic and tactical aspects of the plan. In the plan, stipulate all requirements, functions, resources, execution procedures, time duration, etc.
3 Attack the problems by concentrating on variables with stronger backward

FIGURE 10.1
A HUMAN FACTOR MODEL OF SUSTAINED DEVELOPMENT

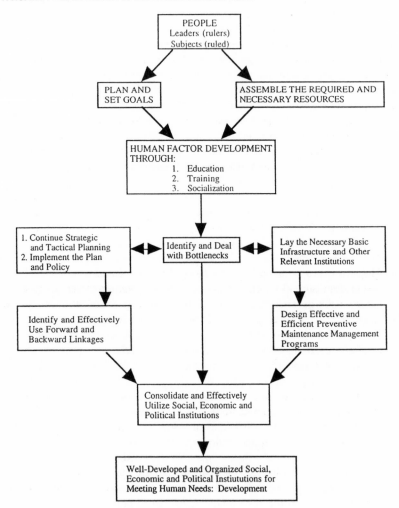

and forward linkages (i.e., exploit all interdependencies and complementarities).

4 Consolidate the development of social, economic and political institutions. Utilize the properly developed HF to manage and direct them.

5 Constantly review the overall goal of the program so that its aims are consonant with each of the following crucial issues:

a Preventive maintenance management programs must be instituted and effectively employed continuously. Problems must be diagnosed and effective policy solutions must be prescribed (see chapter 8).

b Relevant knowledge must be acquired and applied (see Chapter 9).

c Appropriate institutional structures must be developed and utilized (i.e., social, economic and political rent-seeking activities that hinder economic growth and development must be addressed through education and training programs). Education policies, training and/or mentoring programs and the curricula must be constantly revised to develop the appropriate HF necessary for productivity growth.

d People's minds must be developed to settle for nothing less than that which is excellent and productive. Successes in Asian countries like Singapore, Hong Kong, Taiwan, South Korea, Thailand, Malaysia and many others are due to their affordable and well-educated work force (Kraar, 1989, p. 43).

e The process of economic development must be continuously refueled. Inject financial and other material resources as sectoral fluctuations and growth patterns determine (see Chapter 7). Keep government intervention at a minimum. But every sub-Saharan AC's government must strive for excellent foresight to determine what is desired and productive and then carefully create the environment which leads entrepreneurs into those areas; promote job creation and business opportunities; and encourage and reward entrepreneurship.

f Existing social, economic and political practices must be utilized efficiently. Existing administrative, political and institutional hindrances must be identified and procedures to deal with them effectively must be developed within the limits of the law.

The programs must provide the necessary environment for economic growth and development in sub-Saharan ACs. When they are successfully implemented, new technologies will evolve and be used to sustain and further economic progress. The history of growth reveals that cotton spinning machines, steam engines, steam boats, railways, steel, the internal combustion engine, electricity, the telegraph, the telephone, radio, television, computers, and so on were all breakthroughs at different points in time (Rostow, 1978, p. 367). Each of these developments was improved on over a long period of time, with many modifications. The result was economic growth and development. Economic progress can occur in sub-Saharan ACs when these countries begin to formulate programs and policies managed by people endowed with appropriately cultivated HF.

THE HUMAN FACTOR AND CONSTITUTIONAL DEMOCRACY

The constitution of a nation usually specifies the rules and principles for the organization and governance of that country. For this reason, the basic assumption is that for any economic development to occur, there must be a carefully thought out constitution. Very little can be achieved in terms of progress if a country does not craft a constitution that can foster constitutional democracy. Viewed from the human factor perspective, it is the cultivation of productive attitudes and the development of positive HF in people rather than the creation of a perfect constitutional blueprint that have the power to mobilize internal and external resources for economic development.

In a recent report presented to the chairman of the Provisional National Defence Council (PNDC), the National Committee for Democracy (NCD) in Ghana observed that "the constitution of any nation, as a document in itself does not confer a good government. It is essentially a guide to those who direct the affairs of the nation. Above all, it must be the ultimate repository of the people's will, and their expression of faith in themselves as the main factor in determining the affairs and its destiny."[4] The NCD is aware that the constitution of any nation is nothing more than a document that stipulates the rules for governing a nation. It is therefore necessary for every sub-Saharan African country to recognize that successful implementation of its constitution rests in the will of the people. People must not only be part of the process that produces the constitution but must also be prepared to implement it successfully. This task calls for proper preparation of all sub-Saharan Africans.

That is, education for democracy must go hand in hand with education for social, economic and political development. Sub-Saharan Africans must not only be taught how the democratic process works and what their individual rights and privileges are but must also be educated to understand that successful democracy requires individual dedication, integrity, responsibility, devotion and accountability to uphold the relevant principles on which the constitution is built. Institutions designed for achieving democracy and human-centered development in sub-Saharan ACs will be directed and controlled by human beings. The success or failure of these institutions will, therefore, depend on the will and the universal principles held by those who administer them. It is, therefore, critical to realize that the workability and success of the constitution depend on people's loyalty and willingness to conduct themselves appropriately in upholding all stipulations of the constitution.

By merely stipulating in the constitution how people must react to unpopular governments, sub-Saharan ACs may only be preparing the necessary but not sufficient conditions for effective democracy and economic development. This was the case for the Third Ghanaian Republic headed by Dr. Hilla Limann. When the constitution for the Third Republic was being drafted, much time and effort were expended to find appropriate clauses to enshrine in the constitution to discourage military takeovers. Although such a clause was successfully developed and woven into that constitution, it was suspended through a military takeover in 1981. This example points out that an excellent constitutional blueprint is only necessary but not sufficient for practicing successful democracy and freedom of speech in a nation. Democratically elected governments in Benin, Burkina Faso, Gambia, Liberia, Nigeria, Togo and many other ACs have suffered similar plights.

Leaders must be committed to nation building and use their acquired HF to promote national welfare. Authorized power must neither be abused nor compromised. If authority is to be obeyed, leadership must faithfully model the way. However, "lack of integrity and exemplary standards of personal conduct by those in positions of trust also undermines the very structure of authority in which such persons function. As such, maintenance of the trust of the people in the structures of authority, especially when there is failure to deliver the promises of leadership, requires that the substance and style of leadership manifest a transparent integrity."[5]

A necessary but not sufficient condition is teaching citizens how to get rid of inefficient governments by availing themselves of the democratic process. The ability to do so rests in the people's will. The sufficient condition for successful implementation of the constitution is, therefore, the availability of the productive HF. Every citizen's attitudes toward work and life must be sharpened by his or her willingness to hold the constitution in high esteem and be prepared to defend it. People's attitudes and values are important for successful application of the constitution in achieving justice, fairness, equity and human-centered development.

ROLE MODELING AND ECONOMIC POLICY EFFECTIVENESS

A widely accepted and generally practiced way of life may go unchallenged if it is indulged in by respectable people. In sub-Saharan ACs, illegal rent-seeking activities usually go unchallenged because officials in high places and respectable positions indulge in them (see Chapter 3). Since they fail to recognize that their behavior encourages their immediate subordinates to follow in their footsteps, this behavior indirectly urges others to do likewise.

A police superintendent who sends his subordinates to the streets and highways to extort money from drivers, merchants, traders and many others is suggesting to subordinates that extortion, bribery and corruption are acceptable. A public bus/transit driver who tells his conductors not to issue tickets to passengers while collecting bus fares is not only teaching conductors how to be dishonest but also how to misappropriate public funds. Role models who indulge in corrupt behavior stifle progress. It is time to encourage integrity, selflessness, dedication, devotion to duty and the willingness to participate in the democratic process responsibly and with accountability. Leaders must not only be role models but must also teach subordinates that genuine wealth comes from hard work. For many years, public ministers, headteachers, headmasters, principals, school matrons, domestic bursars, national produce buyers/sellers and so on have acted selfishly and wrongfully in positions of trust.

To achieve a successful constitutional democracy and human-centered development, it is necessary to initiate a positive inward attitudinal revolution in sub-Saharan Africa. The inception of this revolution must not be imposed on citizens. It must be achieved through effective education and training programs which sensitize people's conscience for nation building. Responsible self-interested behavior must be pursued to produce private wealth and public welfare with integrity.

While this revolution progresses, it is necessary to institute appropriate rewards and punishment systems to serve as monitors. Effective role models must be rewarded for their achievements. The corrupt must be brought before the law, properly tried and treated accordingly (Adjibolosoo, 1994b, pp. 130-132). Self-aggrandizement must be scorned, and embezzlement and public fund mismanagement must be eschewed. Individuals must respect and care for public property and resources. If the new constitution fails to evolve institutions that can successfully prepare the required HF, sub-Saharan Africans may not realize their social, economic and political aspirations.

THE NEED FOR A CHANGE IN CULTURAL MIND-SETS

Inquiry and dialoguing must occur in many areas of each society's life. This is necessary for proper evaluation of a people's mind-sets. James and James (1991, p. 97) viewed mind-sets as "firmly held beliefs, opinions, and expectations that govern the way we view ourselves, other people, and the world. They are built up through experience and become habitual ways of thinking and feeling that affect our actions." Mind-sets can therefore be deemed to be attitudes. Since these affect the economic development process, they must be under constant review. Although positive mind-sets may productively lubricate the economic development process, negative ones may either thwart or destroy it subliminally. A transformed mind-set is, therefore, a necessary prerequisite for a renewed character and life. These are crucial for human progress. As everyone knows, when an individual buys and wears new clothes for a period of time, that individual becomes attached to the clothing and will usually not wear any others as long as the preferred clothing is still useable.[6] This phenomenon is a strong attestation to the fact that people often prefer to stick to what they already know and have become familiar with through frequent use rather than change to something else that they either do not know or do not trust to serve their needs. This reveals that change is usually difficult to accomplish, and some will oppose it. Examples of this phenomenon abound. Two illustrative cases are ancient Israel and the dismantled Soviet Union. In the case of the Jews, when Moses led them out of Egypt into the wilderness on their way to the promised land, some among them wanted to return to Egypt and continue to be slaves rather than suffer in the wilderness and die. In the case of the former Soviet Union, when the winds of change began to blow, many opposed the expected changes. They prefer the old wine to the expected new one. It is now obvious to the rest of humanity that many Soviets are not ready and willing to go through what it takes to make the necessary changes that 'vill improve Soviet welfare in the future.

The irony, however, is that the process of economic development requires continuing changes and adjustments in life styles and problem-solving techniques. Although some initial changes may not be desirable in the short run, they may be useful in the long run. This is the main reason, in my view, that change must be allowed to happen in every society in the desired direction.

Truly, change does not just happen. It requires a people to take calculated risks and involves a willingness to continue with the program designed for achieving it. It is also a process that must be allowed to proceed with continuity. The main requirements for change are stipulated in Table 10.2. Until a society is ready and willing to allow the forces of change to have their way in the expected direction, very little will be achieved toward economic development.

REFORMING SOCIAL PRACTICES AND SELFISH OPPORTUNISM

Negative rent-seeking behavior, which is common in many societies (including sub-Saharan Africa), usually creates severe problems for economic development planning and policy. For example, in sub-Saharan ACs, inflation is not always a result of irresponsible monetary expansion, as people are sometimes made to believe. Usually, both domestic and foreign economists alike fail to recognize that continuous pressure on prices in the sub-Saharan African economy is also caused by unacceptable social practices and attitudes.

Many business men and women artificially inflate the prices of goods and services to cover operating costs. Embedded in these variable costs are the sums of money illegally paid to government officials to acquire import licences. In other circumstances, airport, harbor and border officials receive bribes before imported items are successfully cleared. Thus, after illegal fees are paid for clearing the goods, the value of these payments is usually treated by merchants as part of their variable operating costs. These payments are, therefore, passed on to consumers in the form of higher prices. This suggests that the faster the rate of growth of the magnitude of the extorted funds, the greater the inflationary pressure on prices. Similarly, when the police continue to extort money from drivers and merchants, these drivers pass the exact value of these unauthorized payments to merchants in the form of higher transportation fares and luggage charges. Merchants, in turn, pass these charges on to consumers at higher prices.

When people's attitudes begin to change against these practices, inflationary pressures in the economy will begin to taper off. Contractionary monetary policy may not be required to curb inflation. Successful education policies and training programs will increase both internal and external confidence in the economy. As international confidence in the economy begins to grow, sub-Saharan ACs will

TABLE 10.2
REQUIREMENTS FOR CHANGE

---

1 Readiness and willingness to accept the challenges of change and the drive and resilience to pursue it relentlessly.
2 Clearly perceived and defined alternatives (i.e., a vision and/or a sense of direction).
3 Openness to rethink and reevaluate the existing status quo and established cultural norms.
4 Leadership that has acquired the HF necessary for directing and assisting the people to accomplish relevant tasks.
5 Risk taking to translate thoughts (i.e., philosophies, ideas, etc.) into action.
6 A detailed plan and the will to implement it.
7 Periodic but continuing evaluation of positive gains, failures and pertinent problems.
8 Institution and maintenance of open communication systems to foster productive interpersonal relationships, teamwork and the cross-fertilization of ideas.
9 Rewards for outstanding performance and procedures for dealing with poor performance.
10 Establishment of other formal procedures for educating, training and mentoring all people involved in the process of change.

---

be prepared for the process of economic development.

Problems such as smuggling, hoarding, lack of properly managed preventive maintenance management programs, tax evasion and refusal to pay for public utility services (i.e., hydroelectric, telephone and water bills, etc.) will also decline. Changes in individual attitudes and willingness to see to it that everyone does the best for the country will pave the way for continuous resuscitation of an ailing sub-Saharan African economy.

For many years, successive sub-Saharan African governments have spent huge sums of money attempting to curb smuggling of cocoa beans, coffee, gold, diamonds and other essential (imported) commodities; hoarding; tax-evasion, etc. No sub-Saharan African governments have, however, been successful in solving any of these problems because they (the problems) have become culturally acceptable to those who practice and condone them. Since people have not only married themselves to these practices, but have also come to consider them as wealth-generating practices, they may not easily relent their holds on these practices, especially when they are forced against their wills and self-interest to do so. However, when informal social and attitudinal change revolutions ensue, the awareness they create through their accompanying education and training programs will have the power to break the relentless hold that these practices have on people. Until sub-Saharan Africans who practice these social rent-seeking activities begin to recognize and realize their detrimental effects on constitutional democracy and economic development, very little can be achieved in terms of progressive human-centered development.

Sound economic policy, development planning and programs will not spearhead sub-Saharan African economic development. What is required to start the program is education and training for the acquisition of positive HF and attitude change. In many developed and developing countries today, being sworn into a political or other type of office is usually nothing more than a mere traditional routine. Many civil servants take the oath to be dedicated, devoted, responsible and accountable; yet they usually fail to keep their oath. The only reason why many of these people do the opposite is that they lack the relevant HF, the necessary requirement for adhering to and executing one's oath.

In effect, the endogenous social and attitudinal revolution advocated in this chapter does not only have the power to develop the necessary HF but will also reduce total monitoring costs and hence free scarce resources and funds (which were previously used to deal with individuals involved) for more fruitful social, economic and political programs. As excessive tax evasion declines and sub-Saharan Africans become more willing to pay freely for their use of public utilities, funds will be made available for the maintenance of these services and the creation of social programs required for economic growth and improvements in human welfare. We now consider nine critical areas that need to be reviewed and studied in detail by sub-Saharan Africans.

Inter-Tribal Relationships

Humanness is neither established nor created by tribal/racial feelings and/or sentiments. For many centuries, different tribal/racial groups have viewed others with jaundiced eyes. The treatments meted out to one group of people by another are usually based on attitudes and stereotyping rather than on universal principles that value life and human relationships. The impacts of these principles should translate into productivity, employment opportunities and other benefits. Although existing intertribal/racial relationships have been entrenched for many years, people in sub-Saharan ACs need to begin to perceive that negative intertribal relationships will constitute barriers to national productivity growth and improvements in social welfare. Positive attitudinal changes will create fertile economic, social and political environments. These observations also hold true for international analyses and comparisons as well.

Foreign Aid and Technology

In this case, the starting point must be a critical reevaluation of how most sub-Saharan Africans view the role of foreign aid and technology in their economic development program. What are they? What is their value? What role have they played in sub-Saharan African economic development to date? What can sub-Saharan Africans do in the absence of these? If technology is viewed as the various procedures whereby societies create or generate material things for themselves, do sub-Saharan ACs possess any basic domestic technological base? It is my belief that by answering these pertinent questions sincerely, sub-Saharan African mentality may be affected in the positive direction about foreign aid and technology.

Thinking Clearly, Looking Ahead and Seeing Through the Veil

Attitudinal change requires the ability and desire to think clearly, look ahead and see through the veil. In the life of a society, minds can be locked up; thinking processes can be stymied; problem-solving abilities can reach plateaus; and motivation to achieve may be in an exponential descent. In these circumstances, a society must reach out into the depths and regain the golden keys of wisdom that unlock the gates of economic development (see Chapter 9). This requires relevant attitudinal changes in every important area and acquisition of the necessary HF.

The Perception of Hope versus Hopelessness

Many scholars today perceive the sub-Saharan African condition as being filled with crisis situations.[7] By reading such descriptions, one is engulfed in the feeling of hopelessness. Sub-Saharan Africa's problems are said to be extremely complex and therefore virtually unsolvable. Those who have poured resources into sub-Saharan ACs for many years are now ready to give up.[8] The dismantling of socialism has already begun to create processes for the marginalization of Africa.[9]

In addition to these, many events (both natural and artificial) continue to paint a dismal picture of the sub-Saharan African condition. Many are asking, "Can anything good come out of sub-Saharan Africa?" I ask, "Must sub-Saharan Africans lose heart and have their hopes dashed?" Not at all! These conditions and observations must rather serve as stimulants for sub-Saharan Africans to find relevant solutions to their problems. In my view, the current marginalization of sub-Saharan Africa is probably a blessing in disguise if and only if sub-Saharan Africans can capitalize on it and use its impacts to induce positive changes in their economies. It is not yet time either to order the requiem mass for sub-Saharan ACs or to sing their eulogy. There is hope as long as planet earth maintains its course and remains in orbit. The hope that creates the desire to gain knowledge, acquire meaning and retain the will to live must be nurtured and promoted. James and James (1991, p. 68) suggested that the urge to live and its motivating power to search for meaning increases when a person feels hopeful. Hope is a belief that certain wishes are attainable. With hope, the thirsty person sees the glass of water as being half full instead of half empty. In fact, hope includes seeing the possibility of a full glass. Yet hope is not the same as optimism. Optimism is waiting for things to turn out well without putting in the effort that is necessary for making changes. Hope is intrinsically active, not passive. Hope continually motivates us to do something to achieve our important and even our not-so-important goals. . . . Hope pervades our lives and sustains us through thick and thin. Hope is looking to the future with confidence.

It is necessary to go beyond mere optimism and reach out for the hope that creates the passion to conquer sub-Saharan Africa's problems of economic underdevelopment. This task in itself requires changes in attitudes and/or existing cultural mind-sets in sub-Saharan ACs. However, as Durkheim (1975, p. 352) pointed out, "the whole cannot change, unless its parts change, and in the same proportion."

Professionalism

Regard for humanity and the readiness to perform one's vocation with precision and integrity must lead to the establishment of generally accepted new professional ethical principles that must be adhered to in all circumstances. These principles must act as attitudinal and action compasses for everyone who participates in that profession. An individual's professional effectiveness will be strongly affected by his or her acquired HF. Such principles include responsibility, accountability, integrity, honesty and so on.

Growing Desire to Learn, Know and Improve

A general positive social desire must be present to study existing circumstances, know details about them and be ready to make changes that may be required for lasting improvements. These require continuous willingness to reevaluate old norms and traditional ways of accomplishing tasks as well as frequent and continuous reexamination of existing institutionalized behavior (that is, the status quo). It is neither necessary nor productive for a society to be locked up in the status quo. It is important, however, to aim at making continuous improvements. The myths surrounding the saying that "this is not how we did it in the past"[10] must be surrendered for critical dissection. Open-mindedness is one of the principal vehicles for initiating attitudinal change in society. Gordon (1980, p. 24) observed that "the society that is flexibly, continually, objectively, and intelligently re-evaluating its rules and norms is going to assimilate technology more readily, offer a higher standard of living to its members, and be a more pleasant place in which to live than is the society which is rigidly frozen in its ways." It requires the commitment to finding the facts, data, information and relevant knowledge required for informed decision making. Experience and learning may be productive teachers in this regard (see Chapter 9).

National Pride and Public Property

Allegiance to the nation-state must be based on the principle of national pride rather than individual self-interest or the feelings of tribal/racial superiority. Public property needs to be viewed as social wealth that must be protected with enthusiasm by all and used to profit all. When non-conformity to the behavior prescriptions of a society's institutions becomes endemic, that society may find it extremely difficult to achieve progress. Although it can be argued that no society is more moral than any others, what affects the economic development process is whether or not the breakdown of a society's moral fiber is either localized or systemwide--the state of HF decline.

Excuses and/or Rationalizations

Excuses and rationalizations are inimical to creative thinking, problem solving and the discovery process. A mistake is a mistake. Such excuses and/or rationalizations do not necessarily reveal the true causes of problems and/or mistakes. They are nothing more than plausible explanations for unjustifiable actions--empty reasoning. Those who are committed to problem solving through hard work need to quickly admit errors they commit and seek true solutions rather than hide in castles built with excuses and fortified with thick metal sheets of rationalizations. In a sense, problem solvers must refrain from projecting their blunders onto others and cease from burying their heads in deceit, as the proverbial ostrich does in the sand. Problems and difficulties can neither be excused nor rationalized away through nonchalant negative (sometimes unsuspecting) attitudes. Faulty ideas, techniques, character and systems (including culture) that lead to suboptimal human performance are usually nothing more than perfect mirrors of human deficiencies, intellectual finiteness and technological inadequacy. The accuracy and effectiveness of technology cannot be divorced from human character, insight and intellect. It is, therefore, crucial to recognize that the success of the human enterprise in attaining the good life is dependent on the ability of people to crack open the intricacies of the natural laws that govern economic progress. This ability is, however, limited in many regards. Humanity should, therefore, not blame technology and systems for its (humanity's) ineffectiveness and inefficiency. Instead, it will be more rewarding to locate the true sources of the problems and hindrances in itself and deal with them appropriately.

It is important to take the bull by the horns, as it were. This can be accomplished by defining standards that can guide individuals in recognizing and easily admitting their mistakes. In the absense of a well-disciplined labor force, effective monitoring programs may temporarily hedge against excuses and/or rationalizations. These may, however, have their own unpleasant consequencies (i.e., the use of hidden cameras).

Office, Authority, Power and Relationships

The filling of an office and/or position, the wielding of power and authority and the relationships these invoke in societies must be reviewed and studied more closely. Cultural practices that are the results of these relationships must be measured against their individual contributions to output growth and human welfare--human-centered development. Attitudes that exert negative impacts on these variables need to be reconsidered and dealt with appropriately. Positive attitudinal changes must be based on principled authority relationships that provide guidance for strengthening positive attitudes and for weakening those that destroy output and human welfare.

A UTILITARIAN APPROACH TO CHANGING CULTURAL MIND-SETS AND ATTITUDES

A utilitarian approach to attitudinal change requires that people be made to visualize the expected marginal utility that will be received or lost when specific societal activities are either discarded or maintained. Educational and training activities may be used to encourage and facilitate attitudinal changes in society. It must be noted, however, that since attitudes are in general the repositories for a person's values and a reflection of his or her character, lifestyle and outlook, attempts directed at fostering attitudinal changes for the purposes of human progress must be directed at universal principles, values, lifestyles, outlook and the acquisition of the HF. Relevant education and training programs must be used to project adequately the expected gains to all people in the society. This requires proper and effective communication at all levels of society.

Beach (1993, pp. 22-23) gave an interesting example of the utilitarian approach to achieving attitudinal change in organizations and society. He noted that changes that occur in society usually lead to corresponding changes in organizational culture and activities. Beach pointed out that many companies responded to the increasingly prevalent antismoking attitudes of the 1980s by making extensive efforts to eradicate smoking at work. As soon as these programs were started, the companies began to realize that they could make signifiant monetary gains in terms of reductions in insurance payments and sick leaves. This observation led the firms to intensify every program aimed at helping employees quit smoking. The interest taken by firms in the health of their employees, therefore, led to the institution of employee health-promoting programs. In the words of Beach (1993, pp. 22-23),

> soon the entire culture changed to favor health and fitness, and employees could be seen out jogging during their lunch breaks. In another case, promoted by the social change in attitudes about smoking, the firm's culture (not the management alone) first only made smoking illegitimate and then evolved to make health and fitness obligatory. This new culture ended up pressuring management into turning smoking areas into exercise areas, complete with sit-up boards and barbells, and converting part of the parking lot into a par-course. The firm now sponsors treatment programs to help the few holdouts quit smoking; many smokers find it far more attractive to quit than to be social outcasts who are exiled to the rain and cold when they crave a cigarette.

Embedded in this quote is utilitarianism at three levels regarding attitudinal change. At the first level, society in general began to abhor smoking and its ensuing general and specific health consequences. At the second level, in response to this antismoking sentiment, companies began to respond reluctantly at first. However, after perceiving that their positive responses would bring about monetary gains, companies capitalized on these sentiments and put extensive programs in place to help their employees quit smoking. Further, the menu at the company cafeteria was changed gradually to meet the new ideals and lifestyles. Fitness programs began to replace smoking lounges in the organization. At the third and final level, workers who realized the benefits of these programs tapped into them and participated fully in them.

In these examples, positive attitudinal change occurred because of the perceived utility at each of the three levels by every participant. Thus, expected potential gain to be derived from an action and/or activity has the power to generate positive attitudinal change in individuals in particular and society in general. It leads to the permanent development of the HF--a necessary requirement for economic development.

Although this may seem to be too difficult to accomplish initially, the availability of relevant knowledge that is properly studied and applied may trigger the required individual attitudinal change. Schumpeter (1942, pp. 202-203) observed that "human nature is certainly malleable to some extent, particularly in groups whose composition may be changed. How far this malleability goes is a question for serious research and not one that can be usefully dealt with in the platform style and reckless assertion or equally reckless denial."

Attitudinal change may be triggered by different forms of discipline (Schumpeter, 1942, p. 211). Examples include (1) authoritarian discipline, which refers to habits inculcated by official authority and other social agents and/or institutions; (2) individual discipline, which implies assisting people to obey rules and regulations through correction, admonition, and monitoring; (3) self-discipline, which implies habits that come naturally out of the individual's own free will; and (4) group discipline, which refers to being obedient and respectful to group norms, principles and social ethos.

These must never be neglected. Desired attitudinal changes may be induced through the use of any of these. It is necessary to keep in mind that both individual liberty and freedom of speech must not be violated when any of these procedures is employed to effect attitudinal changes in society. The basic objective must be the development of positive HF in the labor force. The whole process requires a deliberate shaping of character (see Holmes, 1991 for a detailed discussion of this issue).

These developments have great potentials for creating popular enthusiasm and willingness to participate in the economic development process. Once the enthusiasm and the willingness to participate come freely from a large proportion of the population, a strong unwavering foundation will have been laid for social, economic and political changes in every sector. In this way, the highway to social, economic and constitutional democracy will have been constructed, and economic progress then becomes inevitable.

ACHIEVING A COOPERATIVE INTEGRATION

Although the late 1950s and early 1960s brought political independence to many ACs, almost every attempt made since then seems to have failed to establish either a meaningful integration or regional cooperation in Africa. The Organization of African Unity was achieved in the first half of the 1960s. During this period and beyond, many regional and small group attempts have been made to foster unity and integration among several ACs. The outcomes of these efforts throughout the decades suggest that ACs may neither unite nor cooperate successfully.

The economic development literature is full of pronouncements regarding the impossibilities of African integration and/or political unity. These conclusions are based on incomplete examination of historical stylized facts and perfunctory philosophical theorizing and/or reasoning regarding past attempts at integration and/or cooperation in Africa for no less than thirty years (see Adjibolosoo, 1994f). I must, therefore, point out that the formation of the United States spanned an approximate period of 170 years (i.e., from January 7, 1789, when the Republic was founded, to August 21, 1959, when the fifthtieth state, Hawaii, joined). Similarly, the creation of the European Common Market has taken no less than forty years to accomplish--and is still not without its pertinent problems and hindrances. The Common Market has yet to attain every goal stipulated in its Charter of Association. The Canadian story is no different. The agreement for the Canadian Confederation was signed in 1876 by four provinces in accordance with the goals and objectives of Confederation. It then took a little over 100 years for all the other provinces to join. Even today, Quebec has not yet ratified the Charter of Confederation (i.e., the Canadian Constitution). In view of these historical data, one may ask, "Is economic integration possible in Africa?" In what follows, I argue that true economic integration and/or cooperation can be achieved when it is pursued on a piecemeal basis with individual country commitment rather than as it was done in the past (a more detailed analysis is presented in Adjibolosoo, 1994f).

Is Piecemeal Integration Possible?

Sages have always maintained that a journey of a thousand or more miles begins with a single step. Similarly, it has always been maintained by the ancients that little drops of water make a mighty ocean. As these sayings indicate, many of humanity's achievements were attained over long periods of time with many hindrances to overcome. Men and women, all through the ages, have had their dreams and visions and in many cases have had to rise above extenuating circumstances and difficulties to attain their cherished ideals. Those who see problems, become discouraged and rarely ever think of possible solutions never become problem solvers. At best, they become dependent on others, from whom they expect help in dealing with their difficulties. Unfortunately, this has been the plight of ACs since independence.

STARTING THE NUCLEUS: A FOUNDATION PRINCIPLE

Although the idea of cooperation through a piecemeal process is an interesting one, the basic problem with putting this philosophy into practice concerns how to build from scratch the initial nucleus or kernel on which subsequent additions can be made. A careful study of the problem and an extensive analysis of historical records reveal that the process can be put into motion by adhering to a basic workable structure that is built on solid principles.

The proposed principle for determining the size and magnitude of the initial nucleus takes into account existing patterns of informal (unofficial) movement of goods, services and people across the borders of ACs. Thus, faced with the problem of which countries to cooperate with in an attempt to start a kernel foundation for cooperative integration in Africa, the leading or initiating country must first study the patterns of unofficial migration to identify correctly how people and freight move from one AC to another. In so doing, that country will gain more revealing insights into how its citizens move.

When the direction of flow of people can be established, that nation, armed with the available data on unofficial migration, can approach the governments of countries to which their citizens have the tendency to travel in large numbers. An official agreement can, therefore, be signed to give credence and recognition to the flow. Other relevant policies may be put in place subsequently to facilitate the relationship. This kind of program could be extended to dances, art, crafts and many other areas relating to African cultural programs and life. An All-African Countries' Center may be developed and commissioned to coordinate these activities. Relevant action programs could be developed subsequently to facilitate the continuing integration process.[11]

Whatever program is pursued to attain the intended goals of the founding members, it must be borne in mind that without well-developed HF to help sub-Saharan Africans initiate and oversee every plan and project, the whole program may be doomed to failure. This is one reason that at the initial stages it is essential for member states to develop efficient joint education and training programs and thus prepare people to develop the necessary HF.

CONCLUSION

One cannot be successful without taking frequent stock of one's available resources and carefully planning how best to employ them. In the planning process, it is crucial to identify the most important issues and concentrate one's efforts and resources on them. If sub-Saharan ACs hope to achieve progress, it is time to reevaluate what has been done in the past and reconsider every theory on which ACs have based their economic policies and programs. Although orthodox and heterodox economic development theories are not necessarily wrong, their premises do not seem to reflect objectively the social, economic and political conditions in sub-Saharan Africa. This chapter has shown that when sub-Saharan ACs identify the real factors that are necessary and sufficient for economic development, they will attain progress by concentrating their resources on developing these factors. The five propositions discussed in this chapter are conjectures aimed at providing step-by-step foundational principles for a program of action for sub-Saharan African economic development.

It cannot be denied that sub-Saharan ACs have suffered a terrible plight of economic underdevelopment due to the pursuit of misguided policies and programs. In all of these policies, very little attention has been paid to HF development. Since it is true that only a well-prepared people have the power to initiate, direct, manage and control the sub-Saharan African program of economic development, every sub-Saharan African nation must develop a disciplined labor force that can be used to achieve national objectives. Sub-Saharan Africans must wean themselves of structural adjustment and stabilization policies and begin to hatch their own made-in-Africa policy solutions to their problems of economic underdevelopment.

ACs have struggled for the last four decades to achieve development and welfare improvement for their citizens. To date, very little has been achieved. Past attempts at regional and/or continental integration seem to be failing. Many ACs seem to be losing hope in their ability to achieve viable cooperation.

The success of the piecemeal economic integration program, however, will require a properly carved vision to which an unflinching commitment is necessary. Above all, every other vision, plan and program is bound to fail in the absence of people who possess the required human qualities and/or characteristics. It is, therefore, of primary importance for core members to establish institutional structures that can prepare the African people to acquire the necessary HF, which is crucial for a piecemeal integrative and co-operative program.

NOTES

1. My own recommendation is to phase out the production of cash crops over a period of time. This will free resources to be used to boost the production of staples for domestic use. Other sources of foreign exchange will be developed during the phasing-out period. Some of these are discussed later in this chapter.

2. The Ewes are an ethnic group in Ghana.

3. One of the favorite stories that my late maternal grandmother, Mrs. Egbo Badohu Blemewu Adjibolosoo, told us in our fishing village, Dudu, when we were children.

4. The National Commission for Democracy (NCD), 1991.

5. Ibid.

6. Note, however, that in the United States and other developed countries, some people want to have new clothes almost every day!

7. See, for example, Adedeji, A. 1989. *Towards a Dynamic African Economy: Selected Speeches and Lectures (1975-1986).* London: Frank Cass, pp. 15-57; Onimode, B. 1988. *A Political Economy of the African Crisis.* London: Zed Books (with the Institute of African Alternatives), pp. 1-23; Davidson, B. 1974. *Can Africa Survive? Arguments Against Growth Without Development.* Toronto: Little, Brown and Co.

8. At an international conference held in Miami in February 1992, I happened to engage myself in conversation with a successful global businessman about the sub-Saharan African condition. In his view, the African situation is so bad that it is beyond any possible repairs. For this reason, he has no plans to invest his financial resources in sub-Saharan Africa. The only thing that will encourage him to do so is when sub-Saharan Africans begin to put their own acts together--that is, create a conducive environment for global business. Advanced countries are begining to reduce the size of their foreign aid and international development budget (Canada is an example).

9. Some information on this issue can be found in G. A. Cornia et al., eds. 1992. *Africa's Recovery in the 1990s: From Stagnation and Adjustment to Human Development.* New York: St. Martin's Press, Inc., pp. 1-6.

10. In some cases, old methods and/or procedures may still be better than newly developed ones.

11. See Adjibolosoo, S. B-S. K. 1994f. "Achieving a Cooperative Integration in Sub-Saharan Africa: A Voluntary Piecemeal Harminization Process." Unpublished paper.

Bibliography

Adedeji, A. 1989. *Towards a Dynamic African Economy: Selected Speeches and Lectures (1975-1986)*. London: Frank Cass and Company Limited (Compiled and arranged by Senghor, G. C.).

Adedeji, A., Teriba, O. and P. Bugembe, eds., 1991. *The Challenge of African Economic recovery and Development*. London, England: Frank Cass.

Adelman, I. 1974. "South Korea." In H. B. Chenery et al., eds., *Redistribution with Growth*. London: Oxford University Press.

Adjibolosoo, S. B-S. K. 1992. "Investment in Lives Abroad: Technology Transfer and the Role of Transnational Companies." In T. M. Khalil and B. A. Bayracktar, eds., *Management of Technology III: The Key to Global Competitiveness*. Norcross, Georgia: Industrial Engineering and Management Press.

Adjibolosoo, S. B-S. K. 1993a. "The Human Factor in Development." *The candinavian Journal of Development Alternatives*, XII (4): 139-149.

Adjibolosoo, S. B-S. K. 1993b. "Integrative Education for Productivity and Quality Management: The Role of Business and Engineering Schools." In D. J. Sumanth, J. A. Edosomwan, R. Poupart and D. S. Sink, eds., *Productivity and Quality Management Frontiers-IV*. Norcross, Georgia: Industrial Engineering and Management Press.

Adjibolosoo, S. B-S. K. 1993c. "Maximizing the Magnitude of Productivity Enhancing Human Factor for Output Growth and Economic Development." *Unpublished discussion paper*. Trinity Western University, Langley, British Columbia, Canada.

Adjibolosoo, S.B-S.K. 1994a. "The Human Factor and the Failure of Development Planning and Economic Policy in Africa." In F. Ezeala-Harrison and S. B-S. K. Adjibolosoo, eds., *Perspectives on Economic Development in Africa*. New York: Praeger.

Adjibolosoo, S. B-S. K. 1994b. "The Impacts of Bribery and Corruption on Development: A Comparative Analysis of Developed and Developing Economies." In F. Ezeala-Harrison and S. B-S. K. Adjibolosoo, eds., *Perspectives on Economic Development in Africa*. New York: Praeger.

Adjibolosoo, S. B-S. K. 1994c. "The Political Economy of Development in Africa: Reflections on Orthodox Thinking and Policy." In F. Ezeala-Harrison and S. B-S. K. Adjibolosoo, eds., *Perspectives on Economic Development in Africa.* New York: Praeger.

Adjibolosoo, S. B-S. K. 1994d. "A Human Factor Perspective on Failing Social, Economic and Political Institutions and Systems." *Unpublished discussion paper.* Trinity Western University, Langley, British Columbia, Canada.

Adjibolosoo, S. B-S. K. 1994e. "Promoting Technology Transfer for African Development." In T. M. Khalil and B. A. Bayracktar, eds., *Management of Technology IV: The Creation of Wealth.* Vol. 2. Norcross, Georgia: Industrial Engineering and Management Press.

Adjibolosoo, S. B-S. K. 1994f. "Achieving a Cooperative Integration in Sub-Saharan Africa: A Voluntary Piecemal Harmonization Process." *Unpublished discussion paper.* The IIHFD Society, Vancouver, British Columbia, Canada.

Adjibolosoo, S. B-S. K. 1995. "The Significance of the Human Factor in African Economic Development." In S. B-S. K. Adjibolosoo, ed. *The Significance of The Human Factor in African Economic Development.* New York: Praeger.

Adjibolosoo, B-S. S. K. and Mestre, M. 1992. "Wisdom Is Wisdom: The Myth of Culture Shock." In J. Selmer, ed., *Proceedings of the First International Conference on Expatriate Management.* Hong Kong: The Hong Kong Baptist College.

Adjibolosoo, B-S. S. K. and de Wolf, J. 1994. "Industrializing Sub-Saharan Africa: A Co-operative Rather than a Competitive Effort." In F. Ezeala-Harrison and S. B-S. K. Adjibolosoo, eds., *Perspectives on Economic Development in Africa.* New York: Praeger.

Adler, N. J. 1991. *International Dimensions of Organizational Behavior.* Boston: P. W. S. Kent.

Adu-Febiri, F. 1995. "Culture as the Epitome of the Human Factor in Development: The Case of Ghana's Collectivistic Ethic." In S. B-S. K. Adjibolosoo, ed. *The Significance of the Human Factor in African Economic Development.* New York: Praeger.

Akeredolu-Ale, E. O. 1991. "The Human Situation in Africa Today: A Review." In A. Adedeji et. al., eds., *The Human Dimension of Africa's Persistent Economic Crisis.* London: Hans Zell Publishers.

Amin, S. 1991. "The Interlinkage Between Agricultural Revolution and Industrialization: Alternative Strategies for African Development." In A. Adedeji, O. Teriba and P. Bugembe, eds., *The Challenge of Economic Recovery and Development.* Portland, Ore.: Frank Cass.

Anderson, P. 1974. *Passages from Antiquity to Feudalism.* London: Verso (New Left Books).

Apter, D. 1965. *The Politics of Modernization.* Chicago: The University of Chicago Press.

Argote, L. and Epple, D. 1990. "Learning Curves in Manufacturing." *Science,* February 13.

Arrow, K. 1962. "The Economic Implications of Learning by Doing." *Review of*

Economic Studies, 29 (June).

Asante, S. K. B. 1986. *The Political Economy of Regionalism in Africa: A Decade of the Economic Community of West African States*. New York: Praeger.

Asante, S. K. B. 1991. *African Development Strategies: Adebayo Adedeji's Alternative Strategies*. New York: Hans Zell Publishers.

Awoonor, K. 1976. *The Breast of the Earth: A Survey of the History, Culture, and Literature of Africa South of the Sahara*. New York: Anchor Press.

Baran, P. 1957. *The Political Economy of Growth*. New York: Monthly Review.

Baranson, J. and Roark, R. 1985. "Trends in North-South Transfer of High Technology." In N. Rosenberg and C. Frischtak, eds., *International Technology Transfer: Concepts, Measures, and Comparisons*. New York: Praeger.

Barnett, T. 1989. *Social and Economic Development*. New York: The Guilford Press.

Bartley, W. W. and S. Kresge, eds. 1991. *The Trend of Economic Thinking: Essays on Political Economists and Economic History (The Collected Works of A. A. Hayek)*, Vol. III, London: Routledge.

Bauer, P. T. 1984. *Reality and Rhetoric*. Cambridge, Mass.: Harvard University Press.

Bauer, P. T. and Yamey, B. S. 1968. *Markets, Market Control and Marketing Reform*. London: Weidenfeld.

Beach, L. R. 1993. *Making the Right Decision: Organizational Culture, Vision, and Planning*. Englewood Cliffs, N. J.: Prentice Hall.

Bell, D. 1973. *The Comming of Post-Industrial Society: A Venture in Social Forecasting*. New York: Basic Books.

Bellante, D. 1979. "North-South Differential and the Migration of Heterogeneous Labour." *American Economic Review*, 69 (March): 166-175.

Berg, E. J. 1965. "Education and Manpower in Senegal, Guinea, and the Ivory Coast." In F. Harbison and C. A. Myers, eds., *Manpower and Education: Country Studies in Economic Development*. New York: McGraw-Hill.

Berger, P. L. 1974. *Pyramids of Sacrifice: Political Ethics and Social Change*. New York: Basic Books.

Berstein, H., ed. 1973. Underdevelopment and Development. New York: Penguin.

Black, C. E. 1966. *The Dynamics of Modernization: A Study in Comparative History*. New York: Harper and Row.

Boeke, J. H. 1953. *Economics and Economic Policy of Dual Societies as Exemplified by Indonesia*. New York: Institute of Pacific Relations.

Bond, N. A., Jr. 1981. "A Letter to the Editor." *Wall Street Journal*, March 10: 23.

Boulding, K. E. 1966. "The Economics of Knowledge and the Knowledge of Economics." *American Economic Review*, 16 (2): 1-13.

Breckenridge, M. E. and Lee, E. V. 1955. "What are Some of the Laws which Govern Growth?" In M. L. Hamowitz and N. R. Hamowitz, eds., *Human Development: Selected Readings*. New York: Thomas Y. Crowell Company,

1955.

Brokensha, D. 1966. *Social Change at Larteh, Ghana*. Oxford: Clarendon Press.

Brokensha, D. 1974. "Africa, Whither Now?" *Journal of African Studies*, 1 (1): 101-112.

Brown, J.H.U. and Comola, 1991. *Educating for Excellence: Improving Quality and Productivity in the 90's*. New York: Auburn House.

Cairncross, A. K. 1955. "The Place of Capital in Economic Progress." In L. H. Dupriez, ed., *Economic Progress: Papers and Proceedings of a Round Table Conference Held by the International Economic Association*, pp. 235-248. Louvain, France: Institut de Recherches Economique et Sociales.

Cairncross, A. K. 1962. *Factors in Economic Development*. New York: Praeger.

Cameron, R. 1993. *A Concise Economic History of the World: From Paleolithic Times to the Present*. New York: Oxford University Press.

Caputo, R. 1991. "Lifeline for a Nation: Zaire River." *National Geographic*, 180 (5): 5-35.

Carleton University. 1992. *From Basements to Towers (1942-1992): Looking Back and Moving Forward*. Ottawa: Carleton University.

Carlsson, J. 1984. *Recession in Africa*. Uppsala: Scandinavian Institute of African Studies.

Cervenka, Z. 1977. *The Unfinished Quest for Unity: Africa and the OAU*. London: Friedmann.

Chamberlain, N. W. 1963. "The Institutional Economics of J. R. Commons." In *Institutional Economics: Veblen, Commons and Mitchell Reconsidered*. Berkeley: University of California Press.

Chenery, H. B. and Bruno, M. 1962. "Development Alternatives in an Open Economy: The Case of Israel." *Economic Journal*, 72.

Chenery, H. B. and Strout, A. M. 1966. "Foreign Assistance and Economic Development." *American Economic Review*, September.

Chenery, H. B. 1975. "The Structuralist Approach to Development Policy." *American Economic Review, Papers and Proceedings*, May.

Cheru, F. 1990. *The Silent Revolution in Africa: Debt, Development and Democracy*. London: Anvil Press.

Chilcote, R. and Johnson, D. 1983. *Theories of Development*. New York: Sage Publications.

Chisiza, D. K. 1963. "The Outlook for Contemporary Africa." *The Journal of Modern African Studies*, 1 (1): 25-38.

Clark, J. M. 1952. "J. M. Clark on J. B. Clark." In H. W. Spiegel, ed., *The Development of Economic Thought*. New York: Wiley.

Clements, John. 1975. *Chronology of the United States*. New York: McGraw Hill.

Cockcroft, L. 1990. *Africa's Way: A Journey from the past*. London: I. B. Tauris and Company Ltd.

Collier, P. and Lal, D. 1986. *Labor and Poverty in Kenya, 1900-1980*. Oxford: Clarendon Press.

Commons, J. R. 1990. *Institutional Economics: Its Place in Political Economy*. Volumes I & II. New Brunswick, N.J.: Transaction Publishers.

Cornia, G. A. and de Jong, J. 1992. "Policies for the Revitalization of Human Resource Development." In G. A. Cornia, R. van der Hoeven and R. Mkandawire, eds., *Africa's Recovery in the 1990's: From Stagnation and Adjustment to Human Development*. New York: St. Martin's Press.

Covey, S. R. 1989. *The Seven Habits of Highly Effective People: Powerful Lessons in Personal Change*. New York: Simon and Schuster.

Cracknell, B. 1991. "Project Rehabilitation: Lessons from Evaluation Findings." In C. Kirpatrick, ed., *Project Rehabilitation in Developing Countries*. New York: Routledge.

Culpeper, R. 1988. *The Debt Crisis and the World Bank: Adjustment, Workout and Growth*. Washington, D.C.: World Bank.

Dale, T., Carter, V. and Norman, O. K. 1955. *Topsoil and Civilization*. Oklahoma City: University of Oklahoma Press.

David, W. 1986. *Conflicting Paradigms in the Economics of Developing Natioons*. New York: Praeger.

Davidson, B. 1982. "Ideology and Identity: An Approach from History." In H. Alavi and T. Shanin, eds., *Introduction to Sociology of Developing Countries*. London: Macmillan Press Ltd.

Davies, J. C. 1962. "Toward a Theory of Revolution." *American Sociological Review*, 27: 5-19.

Davis, R. H., Jr. 1972. *Bantu Education and the Education of Africans in South Africa* (Papers in International Studies: Africa Series, No. 14). Athens, Ohio: Centre for International Studies.

Dedijer, S. and Jequier, N. 1987. *Intelligence for Economic Development: An Inquiry into the Role of the Knowledge Industry*. New York: St. Martin's Press.

Denison, E. F. 1967. *Why Growth Rates Differ: Post War Experience in Nine Western Countries*. Washington, D.C.: Brookings Institution.

Denison, E. F. 1972. "Some Major Issues in Productivity Analysis: An Examination of Estimates by Jorgenson and Grilliches." *Survey of Current Business*, 52 (May): 65-94.

Denison, E. F. 1974. *Accounting for United States Economic Growth, 1950-1969*. Washington, D.C.: Brookings Institution.

Deutsch, K. 1961. "Social Mobilization and Political Development." *American Political Review*, 14: 493-514.

de Vries, J. 1976. *The Economy of Europe in and Age of Crisis, 1600-1750*. Cambridge: Cambridge University Press.

Dewey, D. 1965. *Modern Capital Theory*. New York: Columbia University Press.

Dollard, J. 1939. *Frustration and Aggression*. New Haven, Conn.: Yale University Press.

Domar, E. 1946. "Capital Expansion, Rate of Growth and Employment." *Econometrica*, 14 (April): 137-147.

Domar, E. 1947. "Expansion and Employment." *American Economic Review*,

37 (1): 34-55.

Dumont, R. 1969. *False Start in Africa*. New York: Praeger.

Durkheim, E. 1975. *Texts*. Paris: Minuit.

Edwards, D. T. 1991. "Improving Agricultural Project Design." In C. Kirkpatrick, ed., *Project Rehabilitation in Developing Countries*. New York: Routledge.

Ehrenberg, R. 1973. "Heterogeneous Labour, Minimum Hiring Standards, and Job Vacancies in Public Employment." *Journal of Political Economy*, 81 (November/December): 1442-1450.

Ely, R. T. 1889. *An Introduction to Political Economy*. New York: Eaton and Mains.

Emmanuel, A. 1972. *Unequal Exchange*. New York: New Left Books.

Encyclopedia Canadiana. 1975. Toronto: Grolier of Canada.

Esman, M. J. 1991. *Management Dimensions of Development: Perspectives and Strategies*. West Hartford, Conn.: Kumarian Press, Inc.

Farber, S. and Newman, R. 1989. "Regional Wage Differentials with Spatial Convergence of Worker Characteristic Prices." *Review of Economics and Statistics*, 71 (May): 224-231.

Fei, G. and Ranis, G. 1961. "A Theory of Economic Development." American Economic Review, Vol. L1, No. 4, September.

Ferre, F. and Mataragnon, R. H., eds. 1985. *God and Global Justice: Religion and Poverty in Unequal World*. New York: Paragon House.

Finley, M. I. 1973. *The Ancient Economy*. Berkeley: University of California Press.

Fisher, S. 1993. "Economic Development: Rostow, Marx and Durkheim." *Journal of Developing Societies*, IX: 53-66.

Forster-Carter, A. 1976. "From Rostow to Gunder Frank: Conflicting Paradigms in the Analysis of Underdevelopment." *World Development*, 4 (3):

Frank, A. G. 1983. "Some Limitations of NIC Export-Led Growth from a World Perspective." *IFDA-Dossier*, 33: 82-85.

Galbraith, J. K. 1964. *Economic Development*. Cambridge, Mass.: Harvard University Press.

Galenson, W. and Leibenstein, H. 1955. "Investment Criteria, Productivity and Economic Development." *Quarterly Journal of Economics*, August.

Gandhi, M. K. 1968. *An Autobiography: The Story of my Experiments with Truth*. Boston: Beacon Press.

Garen, J. 1985. "Worker Heterogeneity, Job Screening, and Firm Size." *Journal of Political Economy*, 93 (August): 715-739.

Ghanaian Times. Various issues (1982-1989).

Ghai, D. Godfrey, M. and Lisk, F. 1979. *Planning for basic needs in kenya: Performance, Policies and Prospects*. Geneva: International Labor Office.

Ghosh, P. K. 1984. *Developing Africa: A Modernization Perspective*. London: Greenwood Press.

Gillis, M., Perkins, D. H., Roemer, M. and Snodgrass, D. R. 1992. *Economics of Development*. New York: W. W. Norton and Company.

Gordon, W. 1980. *Institutional Economics: The Changing System*. Austin:

University of Texas Press.

Goulet, D. 1978. *Looking at Guinea-Bissau: A New Nation's Development Strategy* (Occasional Paper No. 9). London, England: Overseas Development Council (March 1978, p. 52).

Goyder, G. 1951. *The Future of Private Enterprise: A Study in Responsibility.* Oxford, England: Basil Blackwell.

Green, R. H. 1967. "Four African Development Plans: Ghana, Kenya, Nigeria and Tanzania." *Readings in Applied Economics of Africa*, 2: 21-32.

Greenaway, D., ed. 1967. *Economic Development and International Trade.* London: Macmillan.

Gurr, T. J. 1968. "A Causal Model of Civil Strife: A Comparative Analysis Using New Indices." *American Political Science Review*, 42: 1104-1124.

Gutek, T. L. 1993. *American Education in a Global Society: Internationalizing Teacher Education.* New York: Longman.

Haberler, G. 1950. "Some Problems in the Pure Theory of International Trade." *Economic Journal*, LX (238):

Haberler, G. 1959. *International Trade and Economic Development.* Cairo: National Bank of Egypt.

Hailey, L., ed. 1938. *An African Survey.* London: Oxford University Press.

Hamelink, C. J. 1983. *Cultural Autonomy and Global Communication.* New York: Longman.

Hammer, W. C. 1974. "Reinforcement Theory and Contingency Management in Organizational Setting." In H. L. Tosi and W. C. Hammer, eds., *Organizational Behaviour and Management: A Contingency Approach.* Chicago: St. Clair Press.

Hanson, J. W. and C. S. Brembeck, eds. 1966. *Education and the Development of Nations.* New York: Holt, Rinehart and Winston.

Harris, J. and Todaro, M. 1970. "Migration, Unemployment and Development: A Two Sector Analysis." *American Economic Review*, March.

Harrison, R. 1972. "Understanding Your Organization's Character. *Harvard Business Review*, May-June: 119-128.

Harrod, R. F. 1936. *The Trade Cycle: An Essay.* Oxford: Clarendon Press.

Harrod, R. F. 1939. "An Essay in Economic Dynamic." *Economic Journal*, Vol. 193 (April): 14-33.

Harrod, R. F. 1948. *Towards a Dynamic Economics.* London: Macmillan Press.

Harvey, S. and Dodds, V. P. 1963. *How a Region Grows.* Supplementary Paper, No. 17. New York: Committee for Economic Development.

Hayek, F. A. 1937. "Economics and Knowledge." *Econometrica*, 4: 33-54.

Hayek, F. A. 1945a. *Individualism and Economic Order.* Chicago: The University of Chicago Press.

Hayek, F. A. 1945b. "The Use of Knowledge in Society." *American Economic Review*, 35 (4): 519-530.

Haynes, R. J. and Haykin, S. M. 1991. "The United States Assistance Strategy for Africa." In A. Adedeji, O. Teriba and P. Bugembe, eds., *The Challenge of Economic Recovery and Development.* Portland, Ore.: Frank Cass.

Hayter, T. 1981. *The Creation of World Poverty: An Alternative View to the*

Brandt Report. London: Pluto Press.

Heckscher, E. and Ohlin, B. 1933. *Interregional and International Trade*. Cambridge, Mass.: Harvard University Press.

Heckscher, E. F. 1950. "The Effect of Foreign Trade on the Distribution of Income." In H. S. Ellis and L. M. Metzler, eds., *Readings in the Theory of International Trade*. Homewood, Ill.: Irwin.

Helleiner, G. K. 1992. "Structural Adjustment and Long-Term Development in sub-Saharan Africa." In F. Stewart, S. Lall and S. Wangwe, eds., *Alternative Development Strategies in Sub-Saharan Africa*. London: Macmillan.

Herskovits, M. 1962. *The Human Factor in Changing Africa*. New York: Vintage Books.

Heywood, J. 1986. "Labour Quality and the Concentration: Earnings Hypothesis." *Review of Economics and Statistics*, 68 (May): 342-346.

Hicks, J. R. 1965. *Capital and Growth*. New York: Oxford University Press.

Higgins, B. 1956. "The Dualistic Theory of Underdeveloped Areas." *Economic Development and Cultural Change*, January.

Higgins, B. 1968. *Economic Development: Problems, Principles and Policies*. New York: W. W. Norton and Company.

Hirschman, A. 1958. *The Strategy of Economic Development*. New Haven, Conn.: Yale University Press.

Hirschman, A. O. 1981. *Essays in Trespassing: Economics to Politics and Beyond*. Cambridge: Cambridge University Press.

Holmes, A. F. 1991. *Shaping Character*. Grand Rapids, Mich.: William B. Eerdmans.

Hope, K. R. 1984. *The Dynamics of Development and Development Administration*. Westport, Conn.: Greenwood.

Hunt, D. 1989. *Economic Theories of Development: An Analysis of Competing Paradigms*. New York: Harvester Wheatsheaf.

Ingham, B. and Simmons, C., eds. 1987. *Development Studies and Colonial Policy*. London: Frank Cass.

International Bank for Reconstruction and Development and World Bank. 1994. *Adjustment in Africa: Reforms, Results, and the Road Ahead*. New York: Oxford University Press.

International Institute for Human Factor Development (IIHFD) Society (Its Mission, Goals and Objectives). 1992. Vancouver: The IIHFD Society.

James, J. and James, M. 1991. *Passion for Life: Psychology and the Human Spirit*. New York: A Dutton Book (Penguin Books U. S. A., Inc.).

Jameson, K. P. and Wilber, C. K., eds. 1979. *Directions in Economic Development*. Notre Dame: University of Notre Dame Press.

Jewkes, J. 1958. "The Sources of Invention." Quoted in T. Morgan, G. W. Betz and N. K. Choudhry, eds. 1963. *Readings in Economic Development*. Belmont: Wadsworth Publishing Company, Inc.

Johnson, H. G. 1976. "Development as a Generalized Process of Capital Accumulation." In G. M. Meier, ed. *Leading Issues in Economic Development*. New York: Oxford University Press.

Jorgenson, D. W. and Grilliches, Z. 1967a. "The Explanation of Productivity

Changes." *Review of Economic Studies*, 34 (July): 249-283.

Jorgenson, D. W. and Grilliches, Z. 1967b. "Surplus Agricultural Labour and the Development of the Dual Economy." *Oxford Economic Papers*, 19 (3):

Jorgenson, D. W. and Grilliches, Z. 1972. "Issues in Growth Accounting: A Reply to Edward F. Denison." *Survey of Current Business*, 52 (May): 65-94.

Jorgenson, D. W., Gollop, F. and Fraumeni, B. 1987. *Productivity and U. S. Economic Growth*. Cambridge, Mass.: Harvard University Press.

Kelly, A. C., Williamson, G. and Cheetham, R. J. 1972. *Dualistic Economic Development: Theories and History*. Chicago: University of Chicago Press.

Kenen, P. 1967. *International Economics*. 2nd ed. Englewood Cliffs, N.J.: Prentice Hall.

Kennedy, C. and Thirlwall, A. P. 1972. "Technical Progress: A Survey." *Economic Journal*, 82 (March): 38-39.

Killick, T. 1978. *Development Economics in Action: A Study of Economic Policies in Ghana*. London: Heinemann.

Kimble, G. H. T. 1960. *Tropical Africa*. New York: Panthon Books.

King, F. H. 1986. *Aviation Maintenance Management*. Carbondale: Southern Illinois University Press.

Kiros, T. 1992. *Moral Philosophy and Development: The Human Condition in Africa*. Athens: Ohio University Press.

Kitamura, H. 1968. "Capital Accumulation and the Theory of International Trade." *Malayan Economic Review*, 3 (March).

Kitching, G. 1982. *Development and Underdevelopment in Historical Perspective: Populism, Nationalism and Industrialization*. New York: Methuen.

Knauft, E. B., Berger, R. A. and Gray, S. T. 1991. *Profiles of Excellence: Achieving Success in the Nonprofit Sector*. San Francisco: Jossey-Bass Publishers.

Koury, A. J. 1982. "Maintenance Technology Concept." In T. R. Strives and W. A. Williard, eds., *Innovation for Maintenance Technology Improvements*.

Kraar, L. 1989. "Asia's Rising Export Powers." *Fortune* (Fall): 43-50.

Kravis, I. B. 1970. "Trade as a Handmaiden of Growth: Similarities Between the Nineteenth and Twentieth Centuries." *Economic Journal*, Vol. 80 (December): 850-873.

Kumar, P. and Coates, M. 1982. "Occupational Earnings, Compensating Differentials and Human Capital: An Empirical Study." *Canadian Journal of Economics*, 15 (August): 442-457.

Kuznets, S. 1955. "Economic Growth and Income Inequality." *American Economic Review*, 45 (March), 1955.

Kuznets, S. 1959. *Six Lectures on Economic Growth*. Glencoe, Ill.: The Free Press.

Kuznets, S. 1965. *Economic Growth and Structure: Selected Essays*. New York: W. W. Norton and Company.

Lal, D. 1983. *The Poverty of Development Economics*. London: The Institute of Economic Affairs.

Lall, S. 1985. "Trade in Technology by a Slowly Industrializing Country:

India." In N. Rosenberg and C. Frischtak, eds., *International Technology Transfer: Concepts, Measures, and Comparisons*. New York: Praeger.

Lane, E. R. 1966. "The Decline of Politics and Ideology in a Knowledgeable Society." *American Sociological Review*, 21 (5): 650.

Lane, H. W. and Distefano, J. J. 1992. *International Management Behavior*. Boston: P. W. S. Kent.

Langlois, R. N. 1986. "The New Institutional Economics: An Introductory Essay." In R. N. Langlois, ed., *Economics as a Process: Essays in the New Institutional Economics*. Cambridge: Cambridge University Press.

Leeson, P. 1988. "Development Economics and its Comparisons." In P. Leeson and M. Minlogue, eds., *Perspectives on Development*. Manchester: Manchester University Press.

Leibenstein, H. 1966. "Allocative Efficiency." *American Economic Review*, 56 (June): 392-415.

Leonard, H. J. 1989. *Environment and the Poor: Development Strategies for a Common Agenda*. Washington, D.C.: Overseas Development Council.

Letiche, J. M. 1960. "Adam Smith and David Ricardo in Economic Growth." In B. F. Hoselitz, et. al., eds. *Theories of Economic Growth*. Glencoe, Ill.: The Free Press.

Lewis, W. A. 1954. "Economic Development with Unlimited Supply of Labour." *Manchester School of Economic and Social Studies*, Vol. 22.

Lewis, W. A. 1955. *The Theory of Economic Growth*. Homewood, Ill.: Richard D. Irwin, Inc.

Lewis, W. A. 1984. "The State of Development Theory." *American Economic Review*, 74 (1): 1-10.

Lisk, F. 1978. *Basic Needs Activities and Poverty Alleviation in Kenya*. Geneva: International Labor Office.

Little, I. 1982. *Economic Development: Theory, Policy and International Relations*. New York: Basic Books.

Little, I.M.D., Scitovsky, T. and Scott, M.F.G. 1970. *Industry and Trade in some Developing Countries*. London: Oxford University Press for the OECD Development Centre.

Lloyd, P. C. 1971. *Classes, Crises and Groups: Themes in the Sociology of Developing Countries*. London: MacGibbon and Kee.

Lorsch, J. W. 1989. "Managing Culture: The Invisible Barrier to Strategic Change." In A. A. Thompson, Jr., and A. J. Strikeland III, eds., *Strategic Formation and Implementation: Tasks of General Manager*. Boston: Irwin.

Love, J. 1980. "Raoul Prebisch and the Origins of the Doctrine of Unequal Exchange." *Latin American Economic Review*.

Luthans, F. 1973. *Organizational Behaviour*. New York: McGraw-Hill.

Mabogunje, A. L. 1989. *The Development Process: A Spatial Perspective*. London: Unwin Hyman.

Machlup, F. 1962. *The Production and Distribution of Knowledge in the United States*. Princeton, N.J.: Princeton University Press.

MacNeill, J. 1989. "Strategies for Sustainable Development." *Scientific American*, September.

Mansfield, E. 1993. *Managerial Economics*, pp. 268-271. New York: W. W. Norton and Company.

Marshall, A. 1930. *Principles of Economics: An Introductory Volume*. London: Macmillan and Co., Ltd.

Mazrui, A. A. 1978. *Political Values and the Educated Class in Africa*. London: Heinemann.

McCord, W. and McCord, A. 1986. *Paths to Progress: Bread and Freedom in Developing Societies*. New York: W. W. Norton and Company.

McGregor, D. 1960. *The Human Side of Enterprise*. New York: McGraw-Hill.

McKinley, J. L. and Bert, R. D. 1967. *Maintenance and Repair of Aerospace Vehicles*. New York: McGraw-Hill.

McPhail, E. 1987. *Electronic Colonialism: The Future of International Broadcasting and Communication*. Beverly Hills, Calif.: Sage.

Meier, G. 1963. *International Trade and Development*. New York: Harper and Row.

Meier, G. 1968. *International Economics of Development: Theory and Policy*. New York: Harper and Row.

Meier, G. 1984. "The Formative Period." In G. Meier and D. Seers, eds., *Pioneers in Development*. New York: Oxford University Press.

Mitchell, W. C. 1937. "Quantitative Analysis of Economic Theory." In *The Backward Art of Spending Money*. New York: Augustus Kelley.

Mitchell, W. C. 1969. "The German Historical School: Gustav von Schmoller." In *Types of Economic Theory, II*. New York: Augustus Kelley.

Moore, W. E. 1964. *Social Change*. Englewood Cliffs, N.J.: Prentice Hall.

Morris, M. D. 1979. *Measuring the Condition of the World's Poor: The Physical Quality of Life Index*. New York: Pergamon.

Mosley, P. 1987a. *Conditionality as Bargaining Process: Structural-Adjustment Lending*. Princeton, N.J.: International Finance Section, Department of Economics, Princeton University.

Mosley, P. 1987b. *Overseas Aid: Its Defence and Reform*. Brighton: Wheatsheaf.

Mosley, P. and Smith, L. 1989. "Structural Adjustment and Agricultural Performance in sub-Saharan Africa: 1980-1987." *Journal of International Development*, 1 (3).

Myint, H. 1959. "The Classical Theory of International Trade and the Underdeveloped Countries." *Economic Journal*, 68 (1959): 317-337.

Myint, H. 1964. *The Economics of the Developing Countries*. London: Hutchinson.

Myint, H. 1969. "International Trade and the Developing Countries." In P. A. Samuelson, ed., *International Economic Relations*. London: Macmillan.

Myint, H. 1970. "Economic Theory and Development Policy." In T. Morgan and G. W. Betz, eds., *Economic Development: Readings in Theory and Practice*. Belmont: Wadsworth Publishing Company.

Myrdal, G. 1963. *The Asian Drama*. London: Allen Lane.

Myrdal, G. 1970. *The Challenge of World Poverty*. London: Penguin.

National Commission for Democracy. *Evolving a True Democracy: Summary of*

NCD's Work Towards the Establishment of a New Democratic Order. Report presented to the PNDC, March 25, 1991.

Newcomb, S. 1885. *Principles of Political Economy.* New York: Harper and Brothers.

Nurkse, R. 1952. "Some International Aspects of the Problem of Economic Development." *American Economic Review,* May.

Nurkse, R. 1958. *Problems of Capital Formation in Underdeveloped Countries.* Oxford: Basil Blackwell.

Nzula, A. T., Potekhin, I. I. and Zusmanovich, A. Z. 1979. *Forced Labour in Colonial Africa.* London: Zed Press.

Ofori-Amoah, B. 1995. "The Saturation Hypothesis and Africa's Development Problems: On the Nature of Development Theory and Its Implications for the Human Factor in Africa's Development." In S. B-S. K. Adjibolosoo, ed. *The Significance of the Human Factor in African Economic Development.* New York: Praeger.

Ohlin, B. 1933. *Interregional and International Trade.* Cambridge, Mass.: Harvard University Press.

Oi, W. 1983. "Heterogeneous Firms and the Organization of Production." *Economic Inquiry,* 21 (April): 147-171.

Oman, C. P. and Wignaraja, G. 1991. *The Postwar Evolution of Development Thinking.* London: Macmillan Academic and Professional Ltd.

Onimode, B. 1982. *A Political Economy of the African Crisis.* London: Zed Press.

Onitiri, H.M.A. 1991. "Measures and Mechanisms for a New Momentum for African Economic Recovery and Development." In A. Adedeji, O. Teriba and P. Bugembe, eds., *The Challenge of Economic Recovery and Development.* Portland, Ore.: Frank Cass.

Orde Browne, G. St. J. 1967. *The African Labour.* London: Cass and Company Limited.

Peoples' Daily Graphic. Various issues (1982-1989).

Perroux, F. 1955.   "Note on the Concept of Growth Poles." *Economie Appliquee,* 8.

Peter, L.J. 1977. *Peter's Quotations: Ideas for Our Time.* New York: Bantam Books.

Prebisch, R. 1959.   "Commercial Policy in Underdeveloped Countries." *American Economic Review, Papers and Proceedings,* May.

Prebisch, R. 1971. *Change and Development-Latin American's Great Task.* A report submitted to the Inter-American Development Bank. New York: Praeger.

Preston, P. 1982. *Theories of Development.* New York: Routledge.

Ranis, G. and Fei, J. 1961. "A Theory of Economic Development." *American Economic Review,* September.

Rest, J. 1986. *Moral Development: Advances in Research and Theory.* New York: Praeger.

Richta, R. and a Research Team. 1969. *Civilization at the Crossroads: Social and Human Implications of the Scientific and Technological Revolution.* White

Plains, N. Y.: International Arts and Sciences Press.

Rideken, G. 1962. "Discontent and Economic Growth." *Economic Development and Cultural Change*, 2: 1-15.

Robbins, L. 1968. *The Theory of Economic Development in the History of Economic Thought*. New York: St. Martin's Press.

Robinson, R. K. 1985. *A Handbook of Training Management*. London: Kogan Page.

Rogow, A. A. and Lasswell, H. D. 1963. *Power, Corruption, and Rectitude*. Englewood Cliffs, N.J.: Prentice-Hall.

Rolka, H. 1982. "Innovation for Maintenance Technology Improvements." In T. R. Strives and W. A. Williard, eds. *Innovation for Maintenance Technology Improvements*.

Rosenberg, N. and Frischtak, C. 1985. *International Technology Transfer: Concepts, Measures and Comparisons*. New York: Praeger.

Rosenstein-Rodan, P. N. 1943. "Industrialisation of Eastern and South Eastern Europe." *Economic Journal*, 53.

Rosenstein-Rodan, P. N. 1957. *Notes on the Theory of the "Big Push."* Cambridge, Mass.: Massachusetts Institute of technology, Center for International Studies.

Rostow, W. W. 1960. *The Stages of Economic Growth: Non-Communist Manifesto*. Cambridge: Cambridge University Press.

Rostow, W. W. 1971. *Politics and the Stages of Growth*. Cambridge: Cambridge University Press.

Rostow, W. W. 1978. *The World Economy: History and Retrospect*. London: University of Texas Press.

Rudner, M. 1987. "Colonial Education Policy and Manpower Underdevelopment in British Malaysia." In B. Ingham and C. Simmons, eds., *Development Studies and Colonial Policy*. London: Frank Cass.

Rushton, J. P. 1988a. "Race Differences in Behaviour: A Review and Evolutionary Analysis." *Personality & Individual Differences*, 9 (6): 1009-1029.

Rushton, J. P. 1988b. "The Reality of Racial Differences: A Rejoinder with New Evidence." *Personality & Individual Differences*, 9 (6): 1035-1040.

Sagasti, F. R. 1987. "Techno-Economic Intelligence for Development." In S. Dedejir and N. Jequier, eds., *Intelligence for Economic Development: An Enquiry into the Role of the Knowledge Industry*. New York: St. Martin's Press.

Saint, W. S. 1992. *Universities in Africa: Strategies for Stabilization and Revitalization*. Washington, D.C.: The World Bank.

Schmidheiny, S. 1992. *Changing Course: A Global Business Perspective on Development and the Environment*. Cambridge, Mass.: The MIT Press.

Schuler, R. S. and Jackson, S. E. 1989. "Linking Competitive Strategies with Human Resource Management Practices." In F. K. Foulkes, ed., *Human Resources Management: Readings*. Englewood Cliffs, N.J.: Prentice Hall.

Schultz, T. W. 1961. "Connections Between Natural Resources and Economic Growth." In J. J. Spengler, ed., *Natural Resources and Economic Growth*.

Washington, DC.: Resources for the Future.

Schumacher, E. F. 1973. *Small is Beautiful: Economics as if People Mattered.* New York: Harper and Row.

Schumpeter, J. A. 1942. *Capitalism, Socialism and Democracy.* New York: Harper and Row.

Schumpeter, J. A. 1961. *The Theory of Economic Development: An Inquiry into Profits, Capital, Credit, Interest, and the Business Cycle.* New York: Oxford University Press.

Scitovsky, T. 1954. "Two Concepts of External Economies." *Journal of Political Economy*, Vol. LXII (2): 143-151.

Seers, D. 1969. "The Meaning of Development." *International Development Review*, 11 (4): 6.

Seers, D. 1972. "What Are We Trying to Measure?" In N. Baster, ed., *Measuring Development.* London: Frank Cass.

Seers, D. 1979. "The Birth, Life and Death of Development Economics: Revisitng a Manchester Conference." *Development and Change*, 10 (4): 707-719.

Sells, S. B. 1962. *Psychology.* New York: Ronald Press.

Sesay, A. 1980. "Conflict and Collaboration: Sierra Leone and Her West African Neighbours, 1961-1980." *African Spectrum*, 2: 163-180.

Shaw, T. M. ed. 1982. *Alternative Futures for Africa*, pp. 279-304. Boulder, Colo.: Westview Press.

Shives, T. R. and Willard, W. A., eds. 1982. *Innovation for Maintenance Technology Improvements.* Washington, D. C.: U. S. Department of Commerce.

Siegel, A. W., Kirasic, K. C. and Kail, R. W. 1978. "Stalking the Elusive Cognitive Map." In I. Altman and J. F. Wohlwill, eds., *Children and the Environment.* New York: Plenum.

Sills, D. L., ed. 1968. *International Encyclopedia of the Social Sciences.* New York: Macmillan

Sims, H. P., Jr. and Lorenzi, P. 1992. *The New Leadership Paradigm: Social Learning and Cognition in Organizations.* London: Sage Publications.

Smith, A. 1976. *An Enquiry into the Nature and Causes of the Wealth of Nations.* Oxford: Clarendon Press.

Solow, R. M. 1956. "A Contribution to the Theory of Economic Growth." *The Quarterly Journal of Economics*, 70: 65-94.

Spencer, E. 1967. *The Evolution of Society.* Chicago: University of Chicago Press.

Spengler, J. J. 1960. "John Stuart Mill and Economic Development." In B. F. Hoselitz, et al., eds., *Theories of Economic Development.* Glencoe, Ill.: The Free Press.

Spooner, N. J. and Smith, L. D. 1991. *Structural Adjustment Policy Sequencing in sub-Saharan Africa.* Rome: Publications Division, FAO of the United Nations.

Steele, L. W. 1979. "Transnational Enterprises and Technology Flows: A Business Viewpoint." In J. Ramesh and C. Weiss, eds., *Mobilizing*

Technology for World Development. New York: Praeger.

Stone, R. D. 1992. *The Nature of Development: A Report from the Rural Tropics on the Quest for Sustainable Economic Growth.* New York: Alfred A. Knopf.

Streeten, P. 1981. *Development Perspectives.* London: Macmillan.

Streeten, P. 1984. "Development Ideas in Historical Perspective." In G. Meier and D. Seers, eds., *Pioneers in Economic Development.* New York: Oxford University Press.

Stewart, F. 1992. "Short-Term Policies for Long-Term Development." In G. A. Cornia, R. van der Hoeven and T. Mkandawire, eds., *Africa's Recovery in the 1990's: From Stagnation and Adjustments to Human Development.* New York: St. Martin's Press.

Swanda, J. 1979. *Organizational Behaviour: Systems and Applications.* Sherman Oaks, Calif.: Alfred Publishing Company, Inc.

Swindoll, C. R. 1987. *Living Above the Level of Mediocrity: A Commitment to Excellence.* Waco, Texas: Word Books Publisher.

Thompson, V. and Adloff, R. 1958. *French West Africa.* Stanford, Calif.: Stanford University Press.

Thompson, V. B. 1969. *Africa and African Unity.* London: Longman

Tinbergen, J. 1965a. *Econometric Models of Education: Some Applications.* Paris: OECD.

Tinbergen, J. 1965b. *International Economic Integration.* Amsterdam: Elsevier.

Todaro, M. P. 1989. *Economic Development in the Third World.* New York: Longman.

Toffler, A. 1980. *The Third Wave.* New York: William Morrow & Company.

Tolman, E. C., Richie, B. F. and Kalish, D. 1946. "Studies in Spatial Learning. Part II: Place Learning versus Response Learning." *Journal of Experimental Psychology,* 36: 221-229.

Trebilcock, C. 1990. *The Industrialization of the continental Powers: 1780-1914.* London: Longman.

Ulrich, D. 1991. "Using Human Resources for Competitive Advantage." In R. H. Kilmann, I. Kilmann and Associates, eds., *Making Organizations Competitive: Enhancing Networks and Relationships Across Traditional Boundaries.* San Francisco: Jossey-Bass Publishers.

United Nations General Assembly Resolution 2626 (XXV), October 24, 1970.

United Nations Statistical Yearbook. Various issues.

Vaizey, J. and Debeauvais, M. 1961. "Economic Aspects of Educational Development." In A. H. Halsy, J. Floud and C. A. Anderson, eds., *Education, Economy and Society: A Reader in Sociology of Education.* Glencoe, Ill.: The Free Press.

Vaizey, L. 1981. "Economic Growth as an Endogenous Process: Human Resources and Motivation." In H. Giersch, ed., *Toward an Explanation of Economic Growth.* Kiel: Institut fur Weltwirtschaft an der Universitat Kiel, pp. 71-87.

Veblen, T. 1921. *The Engineers of the Price System.* New York: Viking Press.

Veblen, T. 1934. *The Theory of the Leisure Class.* New York: Modern Library.

Viner, J. 1952. *International Trade and Economic Development*. New York: The Free Press.

Viner, J. 1953. *International Trade and Economic Development*. Oxford: Clarendon Press.

Von Mises, L. 1949. *Human Action: A Treatise on Economics*. New Haven, Conn.: Yale University Press.

Wallerstein, I. 1967. *Africa: The Politics of Unity*. New York: Vintage Press.

Waterston, A. 1965. *Development Planning: Lessons of Experience*. Baltimore: Johns Hopkins Press.

Weber, M. 1968. *The Protestant Ethic and the Spirit of Capitalism*. New York: Scriber.

Welch, G. 1965. *Africa: Before They Came: The Continent, North, South, East and West, Preceding the Colonial Powers*. New York: William Morrow and Company.

Wiesner, E. 1985. "Domestic and External Causes of the Latin American Debt Crisis." *Finance and Development: A Quarterly Publication of the IMF and the World Bank*, 22 (1): 24-26.

Williamson, J. 1987. "Discussion on Session 1: Bank-Fund Papers." In Corbo, V., Goldstein, M. and Khan, M. eds., *Growth-Oriented Adjustment Programs*. Washington, D.C.: IMF and World Bank.

Yagci, F., Kamin, S. and Rosenbaum, V. 1985. "Structural Adjustment Lending: An Evaluation of Program Design." *World Bank Staff Working Papers*, No. 735. Washington, D.C.: World Bank.

Zahlan, A. B. 1981. "The Problematic of the Arab Brain Drain." In A. B. Zahlan, ed., *The Arab Brain Drain*. London: Ithaca.

Index

About the Author

SENYO B-S. K. ADJIBOLOSOO is currently Associate Professor of Business and Economics at Trinity Western University in Canada and Director of the International Institute for Human Factor Development (IIHFD) Society. His research interests include heteroskedasiticity pretesting in regression analysis, human factor development, history of economic thought, and international business and trade. He is coeditor of *Perspectives on Economic Development in Africa* (Praeger, 1994), and editor of *The Significance of the Human Factor in African Economic Development* (Praeger, 1995).